Daniel Lyons

Christianity and Infallibility - Both or neither

Daniel Lyons

Christianity and Infallibility - Both or neither

ISBN/EAN: 9783337023942

Printed in Europe, USA, Canada, Australia, Japan

Cover: Foto ©Lupo / pixelio.de

More available books at **www.hansebooks.com**

CHRISTIANITY AND INFALLIBILITY—

BOTH OR NEITHER

Nihil obstat:

> D. PANTANELLA, S. J,
>
> *Censor Deputatus.*

Imprimatur:

> ✠ NICOLAUS CHRYSOSTOMUS MATZ,
>
> *Episcopus Denverensis.*

DENVERENSIS, *die* 16 *Octobris*, 1891.

CHRISTIANITY

AND

INFALLIBILITY--

BOTH OR NEITHER

BY THE REV.

DANIEL LYONS

SECOND EDITION.

NEW YORK
LONGMANS, GREEN & CO.
15 East Sixteenth Street
1892

The Caxton Press
171, 173 Macdougal Street, New York

PREFACE.

This little volume was written under the influence of a strong conviction that the subject of which it treats is to-day, of all others, the most worthy of the attention of the thoughtful, religious mind. The incontrovertible logic of facts is daily bringing into clearer light the truth which the Catholic Church has ever insisted on, viz: that Christianity, to maintain its rightful hold on the reason and conscience of men, needs a living, infallible Witness to its truths and principles; a living, infallible Guardian of its purity and integrity, and a living, infallible Interpreter of its meaning. The most superficial observer of the course of religious thought cannot fail to see that, among those who reject the living, infallible Witness, Guardian, and Interpreter of Christianity, there is a growing tendency to reject Christianity itself as a body of positive truths. Nor can it be otherwise with those who examine the grounds of their belief. When they reflect on the subject, they see—and the more they reflect on it the clearer they see—that to believe in a revelation which confessedly contains truths for the most part wholly incomprehensible to reason, and at the same time to refuse to believe in a living, infallible Witness, Guardian, and Interpreter of its contents and meaning is to occupy a position which no one can successfully defend at the bar of reason. To believe in a supernatural revelation, and in a living, infallible Witness, Guardian, and Interpreter of the same, is most reasonable; but to believe in the one and to reject the other is logically indefensible. For what reasonable grounds can such a man have for his belief in the specific truths of said revelation? How can he determine, with the certainty which divine faith presupposes and demands, what those truths are in detail, and what is their genuine meaning? To the truth-seeker, therefore, as well as to the Christian believer, who wishes to have an adequate reason for his faith, the question of Infallibility is of the first and most pressing importance. Indeed, it may be said to be the only question; for the doctrine of Infallibility goes to the very root of the Christian controversy, and supplies the only complete and thoroughly satisfactory solution of the many and grave difficulties which it involves. Comprehensive and complex as the controversy may appear, after all, when analyzed, it presents but this single issue, viz: Did God appoint for all time a living, infallible Witness, Guardian, and Interpreter of the Apostolic Revelation? This is really the only question to be decided. If He appointed such an authority, at once there is an end to all controversy, difficulty, doubt, and uncertainty in religious matters. An infallible authority cannot teach error; it cannot mistake the teaching of Revelation or its genuine meaning. Whatever it teaches must be true; and whatever it condemns must be false, for it can neither deceive nor be deceived. Difficulties to its creed there may be, but they can be only apparent; they must have a solution agreeable to its teaching. To know the truth, then, I have only to listen to the voice of the infallible Teacher. On the other hand, if God did not appoint such an authority, then the history of non-Catholic Christianity for the past three centuries, with its confusion of tongues, no less than right reason, unmistakably points to the conclusion that the Christian controversy is simply insoluble. The state of the case, then, is this: Grant the doctrine of Infallibility, and in that you have a ready, easy, and at the same time a perfectly satisfactory solution of the religious controversy with all its difficulties. Reject the doctrine of Infallibility, and your path, as a believer in Christianity, is beset with insuperable difficulties. In short, the doctrine of Infallibility is the key to the whole Christian controversy; and hence to the logical mind the question is simply—*Christianity and Infallibility: Both or Neither.*

To explain, establish, and defend this thesis is the object of the following Chapters.

By Christianity I mean that body of sacred truths which the Almighty revealed through the ministry of Christ and His Apostles. What I mean by Infallibility is fully explained in Chapter I. To the exposition there given it may be objected that it is too scientific, and will, in its many and sometimes perhaps subtle distinctions, appear unreal to the ordinary reader. But how otherwise explain fully and accurately, and in a manner to preclude misconception, the Catholic dogma. Any one at all acquainted with non-Catholic views of the subject knows that the majority of objections to the dogma arise from a misunderstanding of its true scope and meaning. For this reason it seemed to me that the end I had in view demanded such an exposition as I have given. To assure the reader that this exposition is trustworthy, I have given frequent references to standard writers on the subject, and where available I have given their very words in preference to my own.

Some readers may object to the Title on the ground that it implies that the doctrine of Infallibility is not a part of Christianty, but something superadded to it. But, notwithstanding this objection, I have deliberately chosen it because it expresses, in a more striking manner than any other I could find, the central idea which I proposed to emphasize and enforce.

PREFACE. ix

With few exceptions, texts of Scripture are quoted from the authorized Protestant Version. The exceptions are: II. Cor. x. 5; Job xvi. 19; Ps. iv. 9, 10; Is. lix. 21; John i. 42; Luke xxii. 32.

There is nothing new in the following pages but the treatment of the subject; the exposition of the dogma, the arguments in proof of it, and the objections and answers are all old. The setting and wording alone are new. Whether, as here presented, they will do any good it is for the reader to say.

In conclusion, I beg to thank the Ordinary of this Diocese, the Right Rev. Nicholas Matz, for his *Imprimatur;* and the Rev. D. Pantanella, S. J., for his kindness and trouble in reading the proof-sheets. A few years since, the Professor of Dogmatic Theology in Woodstock College, Md., his *Nihil obstat* is a guarantee that the work contains nothing unsound or dangerous in doctrine.

DENVER, COLORADO.
Feast of the Maternity of the B. V. M., 1891.

AUTHOR'S NOTE.

When *Christianity and Infallibility—Both or Neither* was given to the public somewhat more than seven months since, the Author little thought that a Second Edition would be called for so soon. This unexpected success was due, in a great measure, to the very favorable reception accorded to it by the Press—both Catholic and Secular. For so valuable a service the Author tenders to all concerned his grateful acknowledgment.

In this Edition the text has been revised where necessary, and an index has been added.

July, 1892.

CONTENTS.

	PAGE
PREFACE	v

CHAPTER I.
The Dogma of Infallibility, What does it Really Mean?... 1

CHAPTER II.
Why do Catholics Believe in the Dogma of Infallibility? 31

CHAPTER III.
Why do Catholics Believe in the Dogma of Infallibility? 84

CHAPTER IV.
How do Catholics Meet the Objections to Infallibility?... 155

CHAPTER V.
How do Catholics Meet the Objections to Infallibility?... 208

APPENDIX A.
The Happiness of Converts... 251

APPENDIX B.
Some Facts relating to the Vatican Council... 264

APPENDIX C.
Pontifical Decrees and the Obedience due to Them... 282

CHRISTIANITY AND INFALLIBILITY.

CHAPTER I.

THE DOGMA OF INFALLIBILITY.—WHAT DOES IT REALLY MEAN?

"THE doctrine of Papal Infallibility," wrote the late distinguished scientist, R. A. Proctor,[1] "as commonly understood, is of course preposterous on the face of it. *But the common mistakes about the doctrine are themselves preposterous.*" To prove that this candid non-Catholic writer did not overstate the case, and—what is more to my purpose—to emphasize the true meaning of the Catholic doctrine of Infallibility, I will instance a few of these "mistakes." The writers, it will be seen, are men of no mean reputation and influence in the world of letters. "Infallibility," says Dr. Draper,[2] "means omniscience." "It is," says Prof. Schulte,[3] "omnipotence." The Pope in claiming Infallibility, says Prof. Geffken,[4] arrogates to himself "a divine nature"; Infallibility, says Prof. Schulte,[5] "has invested the Pope with divinity." An "accurate writer," says Dr. Pusey,[6] "recently returned from Rome, had the impression that 'some of the extreme' Ultramontanes, if they do not say so in so many words, imply a quasi-hypostatic union of the Holy Ghost with each successive Pope." In claiming Infallibility, gravely writes a contributor to Macmillan's Magazine,⁷ the Pope claims to be "the Incarnate and Visible Word of God." The dogma of Infallibility, says Mr. Kingsley,⁸ means "that the Pope of Rome had the power of creating right and wrong; that not only truth and falsehood, but morality and immorality depended on his setting his seal to a bit of parchment." Infallibility enables the Pope, says Dr. Draper,⁹ "to accomplish all things by miracle, if need be." Infallibility, says a host of writers,¹⁰ means Inspiration, and an infallible Pope an inspired Pope—one empowered to make new revelations, create¹¹ new doctrines, and impose them, at will, on the belief of Catholics. By reason of Infallibility, "all the decisions of the Pope on faith and morals," says Dr. Littledale,¹² "are divinely inspired"; and, "being divinely inspired... they become so much more Holy Scripture. It does not mean less than this." Infallibility, says the multitude, means that the Pope can do no wrong, can commit no sin,—that he is impeccable. Infallibility, according to Dr. Littledale, enables the Pope "at any time to modify or alter the old belief, just as a Parliament of Queen Victoria may repeal any statute of an earlier reign"; and "so the faith of Roman Catholics depends now on the weakness or caprice of a single man." By virtue of his Infallibility "the Pope might in one day," says Prof. Shulte,¹⁴ "abolish all the established dogmas of the Church." Janus' represents the power of Infallibility as utterly unbounded, as extending to all departments of life and of science; while, to Mr. Gladstone,"⁶ its "reach" is absolutely "as wide as it may please the Pope or those who may prompt the Pope to make it." Dr. Draper¹⁷ has it simply, "Infallibility embraces all things."

With such views of Papal Infallibility quite common among non-Catholics, is it a matter for wonder that we daily hear the Dogma denounced as "preposterous," "irrational," "revolting to common sense," "blasphemous," "antagonistic to the liberty and welfare of the State," "incompatible with the duties of the citizen," etc., etc.? But, as in so many other cases¹⁸ of Catholic doctrine, it is not the doctrine itself that is at fault, but the views of those who condemn it. They are mistaken, distorted, entirely false,—in the forcible language already quoted, of one who, though not a believer in the Dogma of Infallibility, yet took pains to inform himself on its meaning, they are in most cases simply "preposterous." A clear, full, and accurate exposition of the Catholic dogma will make this evident. What, then, does Papal Infallibility really mean?

The word infallibility means freedom or exemption from the liability to err. It does not mean merely freedom from actual error—that would be simple inerrency—it means more, freedom from the possibility of erring,—freedom from the very *liability* to err. Infallibility is not impeccability, nor is it to be confounded with it; the former excludes the possibility of error in the *interpretation* of the law, the latter the possibility of sin in the *observance* of the law. The two gifts, therefore, are altogether different; and that not only in meaning but in purpose also; for the one is granted primarily for the benefit of the Church, while the primary purpose of the other is the personal benefit of the recipient: or, to use the language of the schools, infallibility is a *gratia gratis data;* impeccability a *gratia gratum faciens.* Furthermore, between the two gifts there is neither necessary connection nor dependence; and hence it is that the Pope may be infallible though not impeccable.

The Catholic dogma of Infallibility means that the Pope, by virtue of a special supernatural assistance of the Holy Spirit of Truth promised to him, in and through St. Peter, is exempt from all liability to err when, in the discharge of his Apostolic Office of Supreme Teacher of the Universal Church, he defines or declares, in matters of or appertaining to Christian faith or morals, what is to be believed and held, or what is to be rejected and condemned by the faithful throughout the world. This definition substantially embodies the whole Catholic teaching on the subject of Infallibility.

With a view to develop to some extent this teaching, I propose to answer the following questions: First, What is the origin and cause of Infallibility? Secondly, What is the purpose or object of Infallibility? And thirdly (*a*) In what capacity is the Pope infallible? (*b*) in what matters? (*c*) and under what conditions?

1. Infallibility has its origin in the express promises[19] of Christ to his Church, and to its visible Head, the Pope; they constitute the source whence the doctrine is derived. And the sole efficient cause of Infallibility is the presence and assistance of the Holy Spirit of Truth pledged through these *to abide with them forever; to guide them unto all truth.*[20]

Three things, therefore, are clear: First, That Papal Infallibility did not originate in the Vatican Council (July 18, 1870). The Pope was infallible since the day of Pentecost; and all the Vatican Council did was merely to authenticate that fact by a formal definition;" second, That Infallibility is not a natural, but a supernatural endowment,—that it belongs to the order of grace rather than of nature; and third, That it does not consist in the learning or wisdom of man, but *in the power of God.*" The Pope is infallible, not because he is prudent or wise, not because he is aided by the learning and prudence and wisdom of the entire Church, but *simply* and *solely* because he is supernaturally assisted" by the Holy Spirit of Truth, according to Divine promise. The learning or the ignorance, the wisdom or the unwisdom, the virtues or the vices of the Pope in no way affect his Infallibility. Infallibility is altogether independent of the one and the other.

Again, though infallible, the Pope is not inspired; far from it. "No Pope," writes Cardinal Hergenröther," "has ever attributed to himself *inspiration*; but Divine assistance only." "Never have Catholics," says Perrone," "taught that the gift of infallibility is given by God to the Church, *after the manner of inspiration.*" "The inspiration of the Pope or of the Church," says Cardinal Newman," "in the sense in which the Apostles were inspired, is *contrary to our received teaching.*"

In Catholic theology," the gift of inspiration implies four things: (1) *A divine illumination* of the mind of the teacher, in which the truth to be taught is directly and immediately communicated, or, if previously known, suggested to him; (2) a *divine impulse* to his will which directly and efficaciously (without, however, destroying his liberty) determines him to write or speak; (3) a *divine direction* to insure that the inspired agent faithfully teaches *all* that, and *only* that, which God wishes him to teach, by writing or word of mouth; and (4) a *divine assistance* to the end, that the truths supernaturally conceived are, without fail, correctly expressed. Infallibility, on the other hand, merely implies a divine *assistance* or guardianship, which guarantees to the Pope immunity from all liability to err when officially teaching the Universal Church. Infallibility, then, agrees with inspiration in the fourth point; in the other three it differs from it. Hence it is that, though there can be no inspiration without infallibility, there can be infallibility without inspiration. "The infallible teacher as such," writes Father Knox,[18] "receives no interior revelations or suggestions from God. The Holy Ghost does not dictate to him what to say. It is only his external utterances which are overruled, so that he cannot in his official character teach the faithful anything at variance with the truth."

"The assistance [of Infallibility]," writes Cardinal Hergenröther,[19] " is not a direct communication from the Holy Spirit, in other words, an inspiration; but by it the Pope is preserved from error in declaring and defining the truths of Revelation." "Some have thought," says Cardinal Manning,[20] "that by the privilege of Infallibility was intended a quality inherent in the person, whereby, as an inspired man, he could at any time, and on any subject, declare the truth. Infallibility is not a quality inherent in any person, but an *assistance* attached to an office; and its operation.... is not the discovery of new truths, but the guardianship of old ones. It is simply an assistance of the Spirit of Truth, by whom Christianity was revealed, whereby the head of the Church is enabled to guard the original deposit of Revelation, and faithfully declare it to all ages." And Cardinal Newman," describing in what the assistance * of infallibility really consists, tells us that it is "simply an external guardianship, keeping them [the Pope and the Church] from error (as a man's good angel, without at all enabling him to walk, might on a night's journey keep him from pitfalls on his way); a guardianship saving them, as far as their ultimate decisions are concerned, from the effects of their inherent infirmities, from any chance of extravagance, of confusion of thought, of collision with former decisions, or with Scripture, which in seasons of excitement might reasonably be feared."

From all of which we gather the following important points of difference: In the case of inspiration the Holy Spirit informs the mind, excites and moves the will, and directs and guards the tongue and pen of the teacher; in the case of infallibility he does not act at all, except by his ordinary grace," on the will and mind. He merely guards the tongue and pen of the teacher, so as to secure him against the possibility

---

* The word used by the Church, and by her theologians, more accurately expresses the doctrine. It is *assistentia* from *ad-sistere*, to stand by. The English word "assistance" implies positive coöperation or help; this, neither the Latin word, nor the doctrine which it is intended to express, does. The doctrine calls for nothing more than the divine guarantee of inerrancy which is implied in the very presence (the standing by) of the Spirit of truth.

of error, when officially witnessing, proposing, defining, and defending the Christian Revelation. In the case of inspiration the action of the Holy Spirit is chiefly *positive;* in the case of infallibility it is wholly *negative;* in the case of inspiration the Holy Spirit directly *reveals* or *suggests* the truth; in the case of infallibility, He directly *prevents* error; in the case of inspiration there is question of an *inherent* quality; in the case of infallibility there is question of an *external* relationship; finally, in the case of inspiration, the work is, in the strictest sense, the work of the Holy Spirit; God is literally its Author; while in the case of infallibility the work is strictly the work of man after examination and inquiry, *with God for its Sponsor.* These points of difference are sufficient, surely, to show that, in the belief of Catholics at least, infallibility is not inspiration. Not "being divinely inspired," it follows at once that the "decisions of the Pope on faith and morals" do not "become, when committed to writing, so much more Holy Scripture." "No man (Catholic) living," writes Bishop Fessler," "would utter such a *downright untheological absurdity* as to compare a Papal utterance with the Gospel." I have dwelt at some length on this point, because non-Catholic writers and speakers commonly and persistently assert that infallibility means or implies inspiration.

Again, infallibility does not imply the gift of miracles; neither does it mean that the Pope is protected from error by "a miracle." " He is protected from error by a divine assistance, which is supernatural indeed, but not miraculous,—the result not of an extraordinary, but of an ordinary Providence.

Now, seeing what Infallibility really means, what an utter perversion of the truth! to call it "divinity," or "omnipotence," or "omniscience," or to say that the Pope, by reason of it, arrogates to himself "a divine nature" or claims to be "the Incarnate Visible Word of God," or that, in the belief of Catholics, it implies or demands "a quasi-hypostatic union of the Holy Ghost with each successive Pope." All such notions are simply blasphemous.

2. The purpose of Infallibility is to guarantee for all time the safe keeping and preaching, in its unity, purity, and integrity, of "*the faith which was once delivered unto the saints*";[38] to enable the Church in all ages to fulfil effectively the great mission intrusted to her by her Divine Founder of "*teaching* [all nations] *all things whatsoever I have commanded you;*"[38] to "*guide*" her "*into all truth,*"[39] that we may "*all come into the unity of faith,*"[33] and "*be no more children tossed to and fro and carried about by every wind of doctrine,*"[36] "*ever learning and never able to come to the knowledge of the truth.*"[40] In one word, the purpose of Infallibility was to make the Church "*the pillar and ground of the truth,*"[41] and thereby assure all men that they can, with the utmost confidence, intrust to her direction the great interests of their souls.

Infallibility, then, does not raise the Pope above the Divine Law, or above the Ten Commandments; it does not enable him "to make evil good;" it does not give him, nor does he, by reason of it, claim "the power of creating right and wrong;" nor, again, does it make "truth and falsehood," "morality and immorality," in any way depend upon his will or act.

It does not enable him to make new revelations, or to create new doctrines, to be believed by Catholics. In Catholic teaching there is no power on earth authorized to add to, or to take from, or to alter in one jot or tittle the *Deposit* or Revelation completed in the Apostles;" nor can any doctrine not contained, formally or virtually, in that sacred *Deposit*, ever be made a dogma of Catholic faith." "The Holy Spirit," says the Vatican Council," "was not promised to the successors of Peter that by His revelation *they might make known new doctrine*, but that by His assistance, *they might inviolably keep and faithfully expound the revelation or deposit of faith delivered by the Apostles.*" "The office of the Church, therefore," observes Cardinal Manning," "is to declare what was contained in the original revelation, and Infallibility is the result of a divine assistance, whereby what was divinely revealed in the beginning is divinely preserved to the end."

Infallibility does not enable the Pope, nor does he claim, by virtue of it, the power to "abolish all the established dogmas of the Church," nor "at any time to modify or alter the old belief, just as a Parliament of Queen Victoria may repeal any statute of an earlier reign." A doctrine once proposed or defined by the infallible authority of the Pope or of the Church remains forever absolutely unalterable. "The Pope," writes Cardinal Newman," "cannot by virtue of his Infallibility reverse what has always been held." "Never," wrote Bossuet," on one occasion to Leibnitz, "will an example be found of a definition once made being deprived of its power by posterity." " A definition once made," says Cardinal

Hergenröther,[48] "*remains unchanged and unchangeable for all times.*" Only ignorance or malice could lead to any such statement as that, since the Vatican Council, "the faith of Roman Catholics depends on the weakness or caprice of a single man."

Infallibility does not empower the Pope to depose sovereigns or absolve peoples from their obligations to the State. "There are," said Pius IX.,[49] "many errors regarding Infallibility; but the most *malicious* of all is that which includes in that dogma the right of deposing sovereigns, and declaring the people no longer bound by the obligation of fidelity." "The Vatican decrees," says Cardinal Manning,[50] "have in no jot or tittle changed either the obligations or conditions of civil allegiance."

Again, Infallibility does not mean that the Pope is incapable of committing sin or of doing wrong. As far as Infallibility is concerned, he is as liable to commit sin or do wrong as any other man; and if he should do either, the conditions of grace and pardon are the same for him as for the humblest of his children.

Once more, Infallibility is not a *personal*, but an *official* prerogative; it is attached not to the person, but to the office of the Pope. But, because the office of the Primacy to which it is attached, is held by the Pope alone, and not in partnership with or dependently on others, it is sometimes called personal.[51] Moreover, it may be called personal inasmuch as the Pope cannot communicate or delegate his Infallibility to another."[52]

3. (*a*) Clearly two characters are distinguishable in the Pope, as in all persons in authority, viz.—his

private or personal character, and his public or official character." With the Pope in his private character —as an individual believer, private teacher, or author; as a theologian, canonist, philosopher, historian, jurist, scientist, or scholar—we have nothing to do here. As such he does not claim to be, and is not infallible. As far as the dogma of Infallibility is concerned, the Pope's personal views in philosophy, theology, or even in matters of faith, may be altogether false and untenable, nay more, positively heretical." For Infallibility has to do, not with what he himself thinks or believes; but with what he teaches for the belief of the Church.

Then for his public or official capacity: The Pope may be considered as a simple Priest, or as the (local) Bishop of Rome, or as the Archbishop and Metropolitan of the Roman Province, or as the Primate of Italy, or as the Patriarch of the West, or, finally, as the Supreme Head of the Church,—Christ's Vicar on earth; for all these titles, as well as the several offices they represent, belong to him." But, again, with the Pope as Priest, Bishop, Archbishop or Metropolitan, Primate, or Patriarch, we are not concerned here; for in none of these characters does he claim Infallibility. The question here solely regards the Pope as *Supreme Visible Head* of the Universal Church.

Again, the Pope, as Supreme Head of the Church, combines in his person four distinct offices, namely: first, the office of Teacher and Guardian of the Christian Revelation; secondly, the office of Legislator in Ecclesiastical matters; thirdly, the office of Judge in Ecclesiastical causes; fourthly, the office of Governor and Ruler of God's spiritual kingdom on earth. In this fourfold character the Pope is Supreme, and has the plenitude of authority over the entire Church, and over every branch of it throughout the world. But, *and mark this well*, he is infallible only in the discharge of the office of Teacher and Guardian of Revelation. He is not infallible as Supreme Legislator, or as Supreme Judge, or as Supreme Ruler; he is infallible *only* as Supreme Teacher; for to the teaching office alone has Infallibility been promised, and to that office it is expressly restricted by the Vatican Council." Consequently, objections based on the acts of the Popes in their capacity of Legislator, Judge, or Executive, have no force against the dogma of Infallibility. The only act of a Pope that can be justly made the ground of objection to his Infallibility is an act of his teaching office, and that, as we shall see later on, not any act, but one attended by certain well-defined conditions.

(*b*) According to the Vatican Council" four classes of matters come under the supreme authority of the Pope, as Visible Head of the Church; namely: first, *matters of faith*, or what the Gospel commands us to believe; secondly, *matters of morals*, or the principles of right and wrong prescribed by the same Divine Code for our observance; thirdly, *matters of discipline*, or what relates to public worship, to the liturgy, sacred rites, the administration of the sacraments, psalmody, the election, ordination, appointment, and manner of life of the clergy, ecclesiastical processes, prohibitions, censures and other penalties, ecclesiastical privileges, vows, fasts, feasts, division of dioceses, administrations of Church property and such like;"⁰ and fourthly, *matters of government*, that is, what relates to the form and course of Church government and to the administration of the laws regulating it."⁰

Now, in Catholic belief and teaching, the Pope is not infallible in matters of discipline,"⁰ or of government; he is infallible *only* in matters of faith and morals; that is, *exclusively* in the doctrines that are to be believed and the duties that are to be fulfilled under the Christian Dispensation. All objections to Infallibility, therefore, founded on Bulls, Briefs, Constitutions, or Letters of Popes, or Decrees of Councils dealing with any of the many points of discipline and government just mentioned are at once disposed of. They do not touch the doctrine; they are simply irrelevant."¹

Here I observe, (1) That the Office of infallible Teacher of faith and morals, clearly and of necessity, implies the right to define, with infallible authority, not only all matters directly of faith and morals, but also all other matters which, though not directly matters of faith or morals, are yet so connected with, or so bear upon them, that the latter cannot be fully and infallibly expounded without an infallible discernment of the former; (2) That the office of infallible Guardian of faith and morals also clearly and necessarily implies the right to proscribe and condemn all propositions and principles that are in any measure at variance with the truths and principles of faith and morals, or are in any way prejudicial to their unity, purity, or integrity. Otherwise, as is obvious, the deposit of faith and morals could not be inviolably guarded;"² but (3), *and be this noted,* in those matters which, though not directly matters of faith and morals, yet fall under the jurisdiction of Infallibility, the Pope or Church is infallible only *because*, and, consequently, only *in so far as*" an infallible discernment of them is necessary to the complete exposition and defence of faith and morals; and (4) that the infallibility of the teaching office of the Church (or Pope)" "extends itself not only to the truths themselves, but also to the expressions, the formulas, the words in which the revealed truth is expressed,"" or the error is condemned. For, "if a Council and the Pope were not infallible so far in their judgment of language, neither Pope nor Council could draw up a dogmatic definition at all, for the right exercise of words is involved in the right exercise of thought."" What matters, specifically and in detail, appertain to the domain of Infallibility, it belongs to the Pope (or to the Church including the Pope) alone to determine finally; for he alone has from God the right to define authoritatively and infallibly the subject-matter of his jurisdiction, its extent, contents, and limits." Nor is there anything dangerous, or startling, or new in this claim; it is (the infallibility of the decision apart) the claim of the Court of final appeal in the State as well as in the Church.

(c) According to what has been said so far, the infallibility of the Pope is circumscribed by his teaching office, and has to do solely with matters of faith and morals. The question now arises,—"Is every utterance of the Pope, as Supreme Teacher of the Church, on faith and morals, a dogmatic or infallible utterance? And the answer is decidedly—*No*." Theologians[69] distinguish the utterances of the Pope on faith and morals into two classes. The first class comprises what are technically called *ex cathedra* (sometimes also called *dogmatic*) utterances; utterances of the second class are called simply *doctrinal*. This is a most important distinction, and has to be kept in mind to avoid confusion and error.[72]

Now *ex cathedra* utterances *alone*[71] are infallible. No other utterance of the Pope, no matter how important and authoritative it may appear—not even though it should be expressly promulgated by virtue of his Supreme Apostolic authority, and formally addressed to the whole Church[72]—is or claims to be infallible. The Pope then speaks infallibly *when* and *only when* he speaks *ex cathedra;*[73] and the Vatican Council[74] tells us in precise and authoritative terms, that he speaks *ex cathedra* "when in the discharge of the office of Pastor and Doctor of all Christians, by virtue of the Supreme Apostolic authority, he defines a doctrine concerning faith or morals to be held by the Universal Church." That is, in other words, the Pope speaks *ex cathedra* when he speaks under the following four conditions;[75] first as Supreme Teacher of the Universal Church, by virtue of the authority conferred by Christ on St. Peter, the first Pope; secondly, defining a doctrine; thirdly, concerning faith or morals; fourthly, with the intention of binding the whole Church to accept and interiorly assent to his decision. A fifth condition, scil—that he must be perfectly free in his action is of course essential, but this is necessarily implied in the fourth."[76] When these four conditions are present, unquestionably, the Pope speaks *ex cathedra* or infallibly; when any one of them is absent, then, *no matter in what form and with what solemnity* he may speak, his utterance does not claim to be and is not infallible. Such is the dogma of Papal Infallibility as defined by the Vatican Council and incorporated in the Catholic Creed. To mark more definitely the force of the above conditions, a few observations on each are necessary.

First: The Pope speaks infallibly, or *ex cathedra* (the two phrases mean exactly the same thing), "*when he speaks as Supreme Teacher of the Universal Church.*" We have here precisely determined the capacity in which the Pope is Infallible. "By this condition," writes Cardinal Manning," "all the acts of the Pontiff, as a private person, or a private doctor, or as a local Bishop, or as a Sovereign of a State, are excluded. In all these acts the Pontiff may be subject to error; *in one, and only one, capacity* he is exempt from error; that is, *as teacher of the whole Church.*"

Secondly: "*defining a doctrine.*" This condition points out the precise acts of the Pope, which alone have the guarantee of Infallibility; namely, acts in which he *defines* a *doctrine*. All the dogmatic acts or judgments of the Pope, whether definitions of truths, or declarations of facts, or condemnations of errors,"⁶ are here included. All other acts are excluded.

Again, this condition, as is manifest, demands a *positive* act on the part of the Pope; for with *omissions*, whether culpable or not, Infallibility is in no way concerned. "It is plain," says Father Knox," "that the simple omission to define a dogma or condemn an error, even though the neglect were culpable and hurtful to the Church, is in no way inconsistent with the prerogative of Infallibility. For the Pope is infallible only when he teaches; and to *teach* is one thing, and to *omit* to teach another."

In considering the effect of this condition special attention has to be paid to the exact meaning of the terms employed. The word "define" (*definire*), as used in the definition of the Vatican Council, means to settle definitively, to determine finally. Hence, in order to exercise his Infallibility, the Pope must intend to pronounce an irrevocable, irreformable, absolutely final decision;[30] if the decision is not absolutely final and unalterable, there is undoubtedly no exercise of Infallibility.

The word "doctrine" also is noteworthy especially in reference to the domain of morals. In *morals* we must carefully distinguish between *doctrine* and *conduct*—between *principles* and *practice*—between the truth in the *abstract* and its *application* to particular cases. Now the Pope is infallible in defining the doctrine—the general principle—the truth or law in the abstract; but he is not infallible in applying it to the various individual cases that may arise. In other words, the Pope is infallible in his judgments upon *moral principles*, but not in his judgments upon *moral actions*. "Infallibility," writes Cardinal Hergenröther,[31] "only relates to *moral precepts*, to the *general principles* which the Pope prescribes to all Christians as a rule of conduct, not to the *application* of these principles to individual cases, and thus by no means excludes the possibility of the Pope making mistakes in his government by too great severity or otherwise. His Infallibility, which is his only as teacher, preserves him indeed from falsifying the doctrines of the Church as to faith and morals, but is no security that he will always *rightly apply* these doctrines and never personally commit an offence against them." And again, "Innocent III. (whom by the way non-Catholics regard as the most imperious and autocratic of all the Popes) clearly states that judgments about persons, in individual cases, *must not be supposed to be infallible.*"²

What has just been said also suggests the reason why, as Cardinal Newman observes," Infallibility and Conscience can never come into direct conflict. The subject-matter of both is different. Infallibility presides over the domain of thought; Conscience over the domain of action. The office of Infallibility is to define the doctrine, the general principle, the abstract truth,—to direct aright the thought; the office of Conscience is to apply the doctrine, principle, or truth so defined, in the individual concrete case,—to direct aright the action. To point out and define the rule of conduct belongs to Infallibility; to apply that rule to each particular act of conduct belongs to Conscience. That is, in other words, Infallibility has to do with the truth and falsehood of doctrine and principles; Conscience, with the lawfulness and unlawfulness of actions; Infallibility answers the question, "Is such or such a doctrine or principle true or false in the abstract?" Conscience: "Is such a course of conduct right or wrong, justifiable or otherwise in the present case and circumstances?"

Thirdly—"*concerning faith or morals.*" This condition determines the subject-matter of Infallibility. "It limits," says Cardinal Manning," "the range, or, to speak exactly, the object of Infallibility, to the doctrine of faith and morals. *It excludes, therefore, all other matter whatsoever.*" From which it clearly follows that "the reach of infallibility" is not quite "as wide as it may please the Pope, or those who prompt the Pope, to make it;" nor does it "embrace all things"; nor extend to all departments of life and science.

Fourthly, "*with the intention of binding the whole Church to accept, and interiorily assent to his decision.*" This condition, as interpreted by theologians, implies two things: (*a*) The Pope must have the *intention* of binding the intellectual assent of the whole Church; and (*b*) this intention must be *clearly* manifested. The Pope can exercise his prerogative of Infallibility only when he addresses the entire Church with the intention of binding every member of it throughout the world to yield an absolute inteiror assent. The obligation of an infallible judgment, therefore, must extend to the Universal Church,—the Church everywhere or nowhere, in all countries, or in none at all. "Accordingly," writes Cardinal Newman,[86] "orders which issue from him [Pope] for the observance of particular countries or political or religious classes, have *no claim* to be utterances of his Infallibility." Secondly, the intention of the Pope to pronounce an infallible judgment must be made clear beyond all reasonable doubt. Theologians are emphatic on the necessity of this condition. "The intention of binding all the faithful," says Cardinal Hergenröther,[89] "*must be expressly stated*"; it "*ought be manifested and knowable by clear signs or tokens,*" say Cardinals Franzelin" and Mazzella.⁸⁸ What the Pope, therefore, might think, or intend to say, but did not actually and clearly *express*, is not to be considered as included in his infallible utterance.⁸⁹ Although there are certain forms or phrases which are never used except in *ex cathedra* judgments;⁹⁰ yet the Pope is not bound to any set formula when exercising his Infallibility.⁹¹ The Pope may, moreover, when speaking *ex cathedra*, directly address the Bishops of a certain nation, or even a single Bishop.⁹²

The conditions, then, essential to an infallible judgment are: 1, on the part of the Pope, that he should speak as Supreme Teacher of the Church; 2, on the part of the subject-matter, that it should appertain to the domain of faith or morals; 3, on the part of the form, that the judgment should be pronounced with the clearly manifested intention of commanding absolute intellectual assent; and, 4, on the part of the subject, that it should be binding on the entire Church. Beyond these four conditions none other is required. The Pope, to be sure, is bound,⁹³ before pronouncing an *ex cathedra* judgment on any question, to have recourse to human means to discover the truth. He should carefully examine the subject in the light of Scripture and tradition, consult with the Cardinals, and pray for light and direction from above; for, as we have already seen, he is merely *assisted*, not *inspired*, by the Holy Spirit in his infallible utterances. But this condition is necessary only for the *licit*,⁹⁴ not for the *valid*, exercise of the prerogative of Infallibility.

One observation more, and we have determined the

one special and definite act in which alone the Pope is infallible. In the case of an actual *ex cathedra* utterance, there may, obviously, be question of the investigation that precedes it, of the preface or introduction to it, of what is mentioned in it incidentally, or only indirectly, of the explanations, quotations and references made, of the reasons or arguments adduced in proof of the truth to be defined, or in disproof of the error to be condemned. In all this, however, there is no exercise of Infallibility; only the actual definition of the truth, or the actual condemnation of the error in question is *ex cathedra*, and, therefore, the work of Infallibility. This is the common teaching of Catholic theologians. "In the dogmatic (*i.e.*, infallible) decrees of Popes as well as of Councils," writes Cardinal Hergenröther,["] "it is necessary to distinguish between the definition of a dogma, and the reasons, explanations, etc., added to it. *Infallibility can only belong to the actual definition.*" "What Providence has guaranteed," says Cardinal Newman,["] "is only this, that there should be no error in the *final step, in the resulting definition or dogma.* Accordingly all that a Council, and all that the Pope, is infallible in, is in the *direct answer* to the special question which he happens to be considering; his prerogative does not extend beyond a power, when in his *Cathedra*, of giving *that very answer truly.*" Exactly the same distinction is made and acknowledged in the authoritative judgments of our Civil Courts. What is recognized as law and binding, is not the preliminary remarks of the judge, or his explanations, or quotations, or even arguments however weighty and worthy of respect they may be, but only his actual decision in the case. I have emphasized this limitation because ignorance or forgetfulness of it has led to many irrelevant objections. From what has been said so far, it is clear: 1, that Papal utterances are not *always*[97] infallible utterances; 2, that *a fortiori* the decrees and decisions of the Roman Congregations as *such*, are not infallible; 3, that to be infallible, it is not enough that the Pope confirms them by his Apostolic authority, and orders them to be published;[98] he must, moreover, make them his own by an act *invested with the conditions* of an *ex cathedra* utterance above stated;[99] and 4, that, as only an *ex cathedra* act is an act of infallibility, so *only* an *ex cathedra* act, as is manifest, can justly be made the ground of objection to Infallibility.[100]

By this time, it must be abundantly evident that Infallibility is not without limits. For, as we have seen, it is limited, 1, to the teaching office of the Pope and Church; 2, to the domain of Christian faith and morals and what bears upon them; 3, to *ex cathedra* judgments; and, 4, by all preceding *ex cathedra* judgments whether of Pope or of the Church. "It in no way," says a document[101] of high authority and already quoted, "*depends upon the caprice of the Pope, or upon his good pleasure*, to make such and such a doctrine the object of a dogmatic definition: he is tied up and limited to the divine revelation, and to the truths which that revelation contains; he is tied up and limited by the Creeds already in existence, and by the preceding definitions of the Church; he is tied up and limited by the divine law, and by the constitution of the Church. Lastly, he is tied up and limited by that doctrine, divinely revealed, which affirms that alongside religious society there is civil society; that alongside the Ecclesiastical Hierarchy there is a power of temporal Magistrates, invested in their own domain with a full sovereignty, and to whom we owe in conscience obedience and respect in all things morally permitted, and belonging to the domain of civil society."

With the true exposition of Papal Infallibility now before us, what, I ask, is there "preposterous," or "monstrous," or "irrational," or "blasphemous," or "dangerous" about it? What does it teach, or demand incompatible with the rights of the State or with the duties of the Citizen, or with the development of true Science? What is there in it, or about it, that would justify any one, who believes in the Christian Revelation, and in the institution and mission of the Church of Christ, in calling the doctrine unreasonable, or unlikely, or unworthy of God? Only consider the subject calmly and intelligently; consider true not false Infallibility, the Infallibility of Catholic teaching,[102] not the Infallibility of non-Catholic ignorance, prejudice and misrepresentation; and instead of joining in an unreasonable condemnation of the dogma you will, on the contrary, *"be disposed to think that it well becomes a religion revealed by God, a Church founded by God, to have an organ by means of which, according to the will of God, and through God's special assistance, the divine doctrine may ever be preserved unfalsified without admixture of any human error."*[103]

NOTES TO CHAPTER I.

1 "Knowledge," vol. ix., p. 273.
2 "History of the Conflict between Religion and Science," p. 225.
3 Cf. Fessler, "True and False Infallibility," p. 133.
4 "Church and State," vol. ii., p. 334, quoted by Cardinal Manning in "The Story of the Vatican Council," p. 200.
5 Cf. Cardinal Hergenröther, "Catholic Church and Christian State, vol. i., p. 79.
6 "Eirenicon," pp. 326-327.
7 December, 1874.
8 Quoted in Cardinal Newman's "Apologia," pp. 3-4.
9 "History of the Conflict between Religion and Science," p. 284.
10 Cf. "The Pope and the Council," by Janus, p. 40; "The Infallibility of the Church," by George Salmon, D. D., Provost of Trinity College, Dublin, preface, p. 42; Mr. Gladstone, "Vaticanism," p. 47; Dr Littledale, "Plain Reasons for Not Joining the Church of Rome," p. 178: Dr. Draper, "History of Conflict," etc., p. 359; Hallam, "Literature of Europe," vol. ii., p. 401.
11 Janus, p. 30.
12 "Plain Reasons," etc., p. 184; Dr. Salmon, *loc. cit.* Janus, *loc. cit.*
13 "Plain Reasons," etc., p. 15.
14 Cf. Cardinal Hergenröther, "Catholic Church and Christian State," vol. i., p. 201.
15 P. 40.
16 "Vatican Decrees," p. 17.
17 "History of Conflict," etc., p. 361.
18 Mr. W. H. Mallock concludes a chapter of "Is Life Worth Living?" in which he gives several instances of the mistaken views of the Catholic Church and of her doctrines entertained by non-Catholics, with the following remarkable passage;
"To sum up then; if we would obtain a *true* view of the general character of Catholicism *we must begin by making a clean sweep of all the views that, as outsiders, we have been taught to entertain about her.* . . Let honest inquirers do this to the best of their power, and *their views will undergo an unlooked-for change.*" Chapter xi. pp. 301,302 (Caxton Edition). Cf. also Gother's "A Papist Misrepresented and Represented" (price 20c).
19 Math. xvi. 18; xxviii. 18-20 Luke x. 16; xxii. 31-32. John xiv. 16; xvi. 13; xxi. 15-17.
20 John, *ibid.*
21 Cf. Hittinger, "The Supremacy of the Apostolic See," chapters xix.-xxi.
22 I. Cor. chap. ii. 4, 5, 13.
23 Cf. "Vatican Council Const. De Ecclesia," cap. iv. ; Cardinal Franzelin, "De Traditione" (ed. 3), pp. 92, 115-116; Cardinal Hergenröther, "Catholic Church and Christian State," vol. i., p 84; Cardinal Manning, "Petri Privilegium," part iii., p. 79. In a *Pastoral Instruction* to their flocks (June, 1871) the Swiss Bishops, after stating that, hereafter as be-

fore the Vatican Council, the Pope will be bound to use every means in his power to obtain a full understanding of the subject on which he is to speak infallibly, go on to say: "*Yet it is not this purely human knowledge however complete it may be, but it is the assistance of the Holy Spirit—that is to say, it is a special grace of his state peculiar to himself—which gives the Pope the indubitable assistance of Infallibility; and which guarantees to all the faithful with an absolute certainty that the definitions of faith of the supreme teaching office of the Pope are exempt from error.*" Cf. Fessler, "True and False Infallibility," pp. 62-63.

[24] "Anti-Janus," p. 73.
[25] "De Locis Theologicis," part i., n. 366.
[26] "Letter to the Duke of Norfolk," postscript, p. 172.
[27] Cf. Cardinal Franzelin, "De Traditione," p. 342, *et seq.;* Cardinal Mazzella, "De Virtutibus Infusis," n. 946.
[28] "When Does the Church Speak Infallibly?" p. 8.
[29] "Catholic Church and Christian State," vol. i., p. 83.
[30] "Story of the Vatican Council," p. 183.
[31] Letter to the Duke of Norfolk," p. 132. Cf. also, "Via Media," vol. i., p. 310, note; Cardinal Manning, "The Temporal Mission of the Holy Ghost," chap. iii.
[32] Cf. Cardinal Newman, "Letter," etc., pp. 131-132.
[33] "True and False Infallibility," p. 81. Cf. also *ibid.*, p. 80.
[34] Dr. Littledale, "Plain Reasons," etc., p. 17.
[35] Jude, chap. i. 3. [36] Math. xxviii. 20.
[37] John xvi. 13. [38] Ephes. iv. 13.
[39] *Ibid.*, 14; Hebrs. xiii. 8, 9.
[40] I. Tim. iii. 7. [41] I. Tim. iii. 15.
[42] Cf. Cardinal Franzelin, "De Traditione," p. 272; Cardinal Newman, "Letter, etc.," p. 131; Cardinal Manning, "The Grounds of Faith," lecture iii., p. 45.
[43] Cf. Cardinal Franzelin, *op. cit.*, p. 274. Perrone, "De Fide," nn. 113, 117; Cardinal Newman, "Letter," etc., pp. 133, 134; Cardinal Manning, "Petri Privilegium," part ii., p. 62; "The Faith of Catholics," vol. i. p. 1.
[44] Vatican Council, "Const. Dogmat. De Ecclesia Christi," cap. iv.
[45] "Story of the Vatican Council," p. 184. Cf. also Cardinal Franzelin, *op. cit.*, p. 273; Cardinal Mazzella, "De Virtutibus Infusis," n. 513; "The Faith of Catholics," vol. i., introducton, viii.-ix., xxxv.-xxxvi.
[46] "Letter," etc., p. 172.
[47] Cf. Cardinal Hergenröther, "Catholic Church and Christian State," vol. i., p. 159.
[48] Ibid., p. 200.
[49] Address to the "Roman Academia," July 20, 1871.
[50] Letter to *The Times*, Nov. 7, 1874.
[51] Cf. Cardinal Manning, "Petri Priviligium," part iii., pp 103-105, 113-115.
[52] Cf. Cardinal Franzelin, "De Traditione," p. 128; Cardinal Mazzella, "Virtutibus Infusis," n. 450; Hurter, "Theologia Generalis," vol. i., n. 680.
[53] It has been asserted that this is a new distinction specially invented to meet difficulties and quiet consciences. Cardinal Hergenröther, in reply, shows that it is an old and well-recognized distinction among theolo-

gians.—"Anti-Janus," p. 55, and "Catholic Church and Christian State," vol. i., p. 85. Cf. also Cardinal Franzelin, "De Traditione," p. 144; Cardinal Mazzella, "De Ecclesia," n. 1048; Bishop Fessler, "True and False Infallibility," pp. 76, 113, 115.

[54] "Canon Law" (cap. "Si Papa," dist. 40), says Dr. Hettinger, "seems to admit the possibility of the Pope, as a *private individual*, falling into heresy."—"The Supremacy of the Apostolic See," p. 73. Gregory XI. actually inserted in his will a clause retracting whatever he might have said, in speech, conversation, or writing, *contrary to the Catholic faith.*—Cf. Cardinal Hergenröther, "Catholic Church and Christian State," vol. i., pp. 80-81. "According to the more probable opinion," says Dr. Smith, "the Pope may fall into heresy and err in matters of faith as a *private person*." At the same time this writer adds: "Yet it is *universally admitted* that no Pope ever did fall into heresy *even as a private doctor*."—"Elements of Ecclesiastical Law," vol. i., p. 210. Cf. also Cardinal Mazzella, "De Ecclesia," nn. 1045-1047; Hurter, "Theologia Generalis," vol. i., p. 424; Cardinal Newman, "Letter," etc., postscript, pp. 158, 172; Fessler, "True and False Infallibility," p. 75.

[55] Benedict XIV., "De Synodo," lib. li., cap. i., pp. 29, 30.

[56] Cf. Constit. "De Ecclesia," cap. iv. It is worthy of note that the original title of this chapter read, "On the Infallible Authority of the Roman Pontiff," and that it was changed into the present one, "On the Infallible Teaching Office of the Roman Pontiff," "*with the express intention* of marking that the infallible authority was limited to *teaching*."—Archbishop Ullathorne, "Mr. Gladstone's Expostulation Unravelled," p. 54; cf. also Bishop Fessler, the Secretary-General of the Vatican Council, in "True and False Infallibility," p. 38; Cardinal Manning, "Story of the Vatican Council," p. 173.

[57] Vatican Council, "Const. Dogmat. De Ecclesia Christi," cap iii.

[58] Cf. Perrone, "De Locis Theologicis," part i., n. 411.

[59] Cf. Cardinal Newman, "Letter," etc., p. 52.

[60] It may happen, in some rare cases, that discipline is so closely bound up with matters of faith and morals, or is so necessary to the conservation of their integrity and purity, as to be inseparable from them. In such cases the Pope is infallible in the matter of discipline; but then, in such cases, discipline comes under the head of faith and morals, and strictly appertains to the office of teaching and guarding them. See what follows in next paragraph of Text. Cf. also Cardinal Hergenröther, "Catholic Church and Christian State," vol i., p 228; Cardinal Manning, "Petri Priviligium," part iii., p. 89 Denzinger, "Enchiridion," nn. 1441, 1547. Knox, "When Does the Church Speak Infallibly?" pp. 65-66

[61] The great majority of the objections advanced by Professor Schulte, and not a few of those urged by Janus, belong to this class.—Cf. Fessler, "True and False Infallibility," p. 65 *et seq.*; Hergenröther, "Anti-Janus," pp. 203, 256, 257, and "Catholic Church and Christian State," vol. i., p. 35, *et seq.* To the same class belong the objections based on the disciplinary decrees of the "Index" in the case of Galileo (cf. Ryder, "Catholic Controversy," pp. 33-36; Newman, "Letter," etc., p 70; Proctor, "Knowledge," vol. ix., p. 273), and of Lasserre's version of the Gospels. A writer in the

Contemporary Review (June, 1888) considers this (latter) case to be fatal to the Pope's claim to infallibility The reader will find the case fully treated in reference to the article in question in an excellent pamphlet entitled "The Pope and the Bible," by Rev. Richard F Clarke, S. J.

⁶² Cf. Franzelin, "De Traditione," pp. 121-127, 176, 209, note; Mazzella, "De Ecclesia," nn. 805-826; Hurter, "Theologia Generalis," vol. i., pp. 275-283; Hettinger, "The Supremacy of the Apostolic See," pp. 120-123; Manning, "Petri Priviligium," part iii., pp. 60-78, 88-89, 173; Knox, "When Does the Church Speak Infallibly?" pp. 49-81. Cardinal Newman's illustration of this and the preceding point is both forcible and happy. Infallibility, writes his Eminence, "has the prerogative of an indirect jurisdiction on subject-matters which lie beyond its own proper limits, *and it most reasonably has such a jurisdiction;* it could not act in its own province unless it had a right to act out of it It could not properly defend religious truth without claiming for that truth what may be called its *pomœria;* or, to take another illustration, without acting as we act as a nation in claiming as our own not only the land on which we live, but what are called British waters."—"Apologia," p. 281 (2d ed. 257). Cf. also pp. 274-275 (2d ed. 249-250).

⁶³ Cf. Franzelin, "De Traditione," pp. 125-126, 710-726; Hergenröther, "Catholic Church and Christian State," vol. i., p 81; Manning, "Petri Privilegium," part iii., pp. 77-78; Vatican Council "Const. Dogmat. De Fide Catholica," cap. iv.

⁶⁴ The Vatican Council defined that the Pope "is possessed of that infallibility with which the Divine Redeemer willed that His Church should be endowed for defining doctrine regarding faith and morals."—Vatican Council "Const. Dogmat. De Ecclesia Christi," cap. iv. The infallibility of the Pope, therefore, exactly coincides in extent with the infallibility of the Church.

⁶⁵ Hettinger, "The Supremacy of the Apostolic See," p. 120.

⁶⁶ Newman, "Letter," etc., p. 134.

⁶⁷ Cf. pp. 209-213.

⁶⁸ Cf. Perrone, "De Locis Theologicis," part i., n. 726; Hettinger, "The Supremacy of the Apostolic See," p. 75.

⁶⁹ Cf. Franzelin, "De Trad.," pp. 129, 144-146.

⁷⁰ The necessity for this remark is notably illustrated in the case of Professor Schulte. Cf. Franzelin, *ibid.;* pp. 145-147.

⁷¹ Cf. Franzelin, *op. cit.*, p. 117. note; Newman, "Letter," etc., p. 121

⁷² Hergenröther, "Catholic Church and Christian State," vol. i., p. 44; Fessler, "True and False Infallibility," pp. 65, 74, (note), 122.

⁷³ "*Ex cathedra* is equivalent to *ex cathedra Petri* (from the Chair of Peter), and distinguishes those acts of the Successor of Peter which are done as Supreme Teacher of the whole Church." "The value of this phrase," continues the eminent authority from whom I am quoting. "is great, inasmuch as it excludes all *cavil* and *equivocation* as to the acts of the Pontiff in any other capacity than that of Supreme Doctor of all Christians, and in any other subject-matter than the matters of faith and morals."—Cardinal Manning, "Petri Privilegium," part iii., p. 59; cf. also Cardinal Newman, "Letter," etc., p. 129; Hettinger, *op. cit.*, p. 74.

⁷⁴ Vatican Council, "Const. Dogmat. De Ecclesia Christi," cap. iv. "No

NOTES TO CHAPTER I. 29

sooner does the Church in Council introduce the term *ex cathedra*," writes Archbishop Ullathorne, "than she gives its authentic definition."—"Mr. Gladstone's Expostulation Unravelled," p. 47. And yet, strange to say, Mr. Gladstone tells his readers "*there is no established or accepted definition of the phrase 'ex cathedra.'*"—"Vatican Decrees," p. 18; cf. also Dr. Littledale, "Plain Reasons," etc., p. 17.

[75] Cf. Newman, "Letter," etc. p 129, Manning "The Vatican Decrees," p. 34; Hergenröther. "Catholic Church and Christian State," vol. i., pp. 85, 86, Mazzella, "De Ecclesia," nn. 1048-1051.

[76] Cf. Hergenröther, "Catholic Church and Christian State," vol. i., pp. 83, 86, (note); Hettinger, "The Supremacy of the Apostolic See," pp. 76, 161.

[77] "Petri Privilegium," part iii., p. 59; cf. also Bellarmine, "De Summo Pontifice," cap. iv., 2; *Pastoral Instruction* of Swiss Bishops in Fessler's "True and False Infallibility," p. 145.

[78] "The Infallibility whether of the Church or of the Pope," writes Cardinal Newman, "acts principally or solely in two channels—in direct statements of truth and in condemnation of error. The former takes the shape of doctrinal definitions; the latter stigmatizes propositions as heretical, next to heresy, erroneous, and the like."—"Letter," etc., p. 136.

[79] "When Does the Church Speak Infallibly?" p. 92; cf. also Fessler, "True and False Infallibility," p. 43 (note); Perrone, "De Locis Theologicis," part i., n. 726, (note); Mazzella, "De Ecclesia," n. 1049.

[80] Cf. Franzelin, "De Traditione," p. 129; Hurter, "Theologia Generalis," vol. i., n. 563; Newman, "Letter," etc., p. 133; Fessler, *op. cit.*, p. 42.

[81] "Catholic Church and Christian State," vol. i., pp. 42-43.

[82] *Ibid.* p. 85. Cf. also pp. 21-22; "Anti-Janus," p. 75; Newman, "Via Media," vol. i., p. 48 (note); Hettinger, *op. cit.*, p. 123; Fessler, *op cit.*, pp. 43, (note), 54; Perrone, "De Locis Theologicis," part i., n. 726 (note). There is here, of course, no question of what theologians call "*dogmatic facts*," i. e., facts which are so intimately connected with or related to revealed truth or law (dogma) as necessarily to belong to the province of the infallible Teacher and Guardian of faith and morals. For instance: Does such a book, letter, or proposition contain false or dangerous doctrine? Are the canonized really saints? Does the rule of such a religious community? does the constitution of such a society? does such a system of education harmonize with the principles of the Gospel? Is such a version of the Scriptures substantially accurate? Was Pius IX. a rightful Pope? Did the Vatican Council possess all the essentials of an Œcumenical Council? It is plain that the infallible Teacher and Guardian of Revelation, to be able to fully expound its doctrines and precepts and effectively safeguard them in their purity and integrity, must have the right to take cognizance of such facts, and the authority, if need be, to pronounce an infallible judgment on them. See above, p. 14. In the Text there is question solely of personal and particular facts, acts of conduct, cases of conscience.

[83] "Letter," etc., pp. 69, 70, 143.

[84] "Petri Privilegium," part iii., p. 50; see also p. 86.

[85] "Letter," etc., p. 135; cf. also Mazzella, "De Ecclesia," n. 385; Man-

NOTES TO CHAPTER I.

ning, "Petri Privilegium," part lii., p. 87; Hergenröther, "Anti-Janus," p. 57.

[86] "Catholic Church and Christian State," vol. i., p. 86; see also p. 41.
[87] Cf. "De Traditione," p. 119.
[88] "De Ecclesia," n. 1050.
[89] Cf. Fessler, "True and False Infallibility," pp. 57, 58, 69.
[90] Cf. Franzelin, op. cit., p 119; Mazzella "De Ecclesia," n. 1050.
[91] Cf. Franzelin, ibid.; Mazzella, ibid.; Hettinger, op. cit., p. 75.
[92] Cf. Mazzella, op. cit., n.1052.
[93] Cf. Hergenröther, "Catholic Church and Christian State," vol.i., p.84, and "Anti-Janus," p.56; Swiss *Pastoral Instruction*,above,foot note 23,p.25.
[94] Cf. Mazzella, op. cit., n. 792; "Smith's Elements of Ecclesiastical Law," vol.i., 214."
[95] "Catholic Church and Christian State," vol. i., p. 81; see also p. 37 (note), and vol. ii., p. 100.
[96] "Letter," etc., p. 132; see also ibid., pp. 130, 131, 133; Hettinger, "The Supremacy of the Apostolic See," pp. 76, 102; Mazzella, "De Ecclesia," nn. 385, 386, 794, 1049; Fessler, "True and False Infallibility," pp. 46, 55.
[97] As a matter of fact, *ex cathedra* utterances form but a very small percentage of Papal utterances. Cf. Newman, "Letter," etc., p. 140; Fessler, op. cit., p. 53.
[98] Cf. Franzelin, "De Traditione," p. 141; Hurter, "Theologia Generalis," vol. i., n. 680.
[99] Cf. Franzelin, ibid., pp. 128-130; Hurter, ibid.
[100] Of the many Papal documents quoted by Prof. Schulte against the dogma only *two* are *ex cathedra*; and even these are not *ex cathedra* to the extent claimed. This remark equally applies to Janus. Cf. Fessler, "True and False Infallibility," pp. 54-59, 101-102, 132; Hergenröther, "Anti-Janus," pp. 256-267, and "Catholic Church and Christian State," vol. i., p. 35 *et seq.* The cases of Popes Liberius and Honorius, and of Galileo, will be treated in Chapter V.
[101] *Pastoral Instruction* of the Swiss Bishops, June, 1871, quoted in Fessler's "True and False Infallibility," p. 63. This Pastoral called forth a Brief of approbation from Pius IX.
[102] There have been even Catholics who misconceived the doctrine, and on that account, opposed the definition of it. Such was the case with the well-known Père Gratry, whose words are often quoted by those who assail the dogma of Papal Infallibility. But he, in time, discovered his mistake, and publicly acknowledged it. In a letter to the *Correspondant*, February 25, 1872, he wrote: "I combated an *inspired* Infallibility; the Council *rejects* inspired Infallibility. I combated a *personal* Infallibility; the decree gives but an *official*. Writers of a school I thought excessive were undesirous of a limitation to Infallibility *ex cathedra* as being too narrow; and the decree but gives Infallibility *ex cathedra*. I almost feared a *scientific* Infallibility, a *political* and *governmental* Infallibility, and the decree gives but *doctrinal* Infallibility in matters of faith and morals."—Quoted by Archbishop Ullathorne in "Mr. Gladstone's Expostulation Unravelled," pp. 56-57.
[103] Fessler, "True and False Infallibility," p. 130.

CHAPTER II.

WHY DO CATHOLICS BELIEVE IN THE DOGMA OF INFALLIBILITY?

To give directness and the force of personal conviction to my argument I will answer the above question by stating the reasons why I, a Catholic, believe in Infallibility.

I believe in Infallibility, then, for the following, to me, very good reasons:'

I. Because I believe in the importance and necessity of my soul's salvation; and both call for the guidance and security of Infallibility.

II. Because I believe in the Goodness of God and in His Love for man; and this belief justly leads me to expect from Him the concession of Infallibility.

III. Because I believe that God made a supernatural Revelation of His will for the benefit of man to the end of time; and from this fact I conclude that the Wisdom of God must have provided a living Infallible Witness, Guardian and Interpreter to authenticate, protect, and teach in all ages this Revelation in its purity and integrity.

IV. Because I believe, moreover, that God imposed this Revelation on the belief and practice of man as a law of faith and conduct; and from the existence of this divine obligation I conclude that God, in His Justice, must have appointed an Infallible Witness to its contents, and an Infallible Interpreter of its meaning.

V. Because I believe that God made divine faith in the teaching of this Revelation a condition of my salvation; and such faith in its plenitude is impossible without the aid of Infallibility.

VI. Because assuming a divine faith in the contents of Revelation to be necessary, nothing short of the certainty and security of Infallibility can satisfy the legitimate demands of my reason and conscience.

VII. Because a living Infallible Authority is at once the source of the greatest blessings, and a safeguard against the greatest evils.

VIII. Because only a living Infallible Authority can satisfactorily settle the Christian controversy, and be equal to the many and grave difficulties connected with it. Only a living Infallible Authority can adjust and harmonize the respective claims of Reason and Revelation, Science and Faith, Liberty and Authority, Nature and Grace; in one word, of the Natural and Supernatural.

IX. Because the doctrine is a teaching of Revelation, and is and ever has been the belief of the great majority of Christians.

X. Because the history of the dogmatic teaching of the Church for eighteeen hundred years points to Infallibility in *fact*.

XI. Because without Infallibility, logically speaking, I would have no valid reason,—no sufficient grounds for the profession, I will not say of Catholicism, but of Christianity. In short, to me the only consistent and tenable position is Christianity and Infallibility,—both or neither. The reasons here briefly summarized will be developed in the following pages.

FIRST ARGUMENT: THE IMPORTANCE OF SALVATION.

When I enter into contemplation and turn my thoughts in upon myself, and seriously consider that I possess a soul of ineffable value, a soul purchased by the Blood of the Cross; that the salvation of that soul is to me the *one thing necessary;* that the loss of that soul means the loss of all that constitutes the true happiness, the *summum bonum*, of man; and that to lose it once is to lose it, beyond all hope or possibility of recovery, for all eternity,—when I seriously reflect on these awful truths, questions the most momentous and urgent at once present themselves to my thoughts and weigh upon my mind: 'Am I surely in the way of salvation?' 'Do I know, beyond all prudent doubt or danger of deception, the conditions of salvation?' 'Am I quite clear and certain as to what God wishes me to believe and to do to attain my destiny?' Confronted by questions of such vital importance, and realizing the magnitude of the interests at stake, and, consequently, the great necessity there is for absolute certainty and security* in the matter, will it not immediately occur to me that nothing could be more desirable, or better adapted, or indeed more necessary, to the needs and welfare of my soul than a Guide* to whose direction I could, with entire confidence, intrust its everlasting interests, and to which I could turn for a satisfactory answer to all questions affecting them? And will it not also occur to me that such a Guide, to be equal to the necessities of the case—to be able to guarantee the certainty, the intellectual security,

---

* *No security,"* says a holy man, *"can be too great where eternity is at stake."*

which interests so great demand, and to remove all fear of conscience and anxiety of heart—ought to be beyond the reach of error or deception,—in other words, ought to be Infallible? Man cannot afford to run any risk when there is question of the salvation of his soul. I conclude, therefore, that the surpassing value of the soul and the vital importance of securing its salvation suggest and call for the aid of Infallibility.

SECOND ARGUMENT: THE GOODNESS AND LOVE OF GOD.

And what the wants and interests of my soul suggest and call for, my belief in the infinite Goodness and Love of God justifies me in looking for as granted. For how can I believe in the riches of the Goodness and Love of God, and in the immense blessings which through them He has bestowed on man, and not find in such belief ample reason for concluding that the blessing of Infallibility is among the number? God in His Omnipotence can bestow it, and God in His Goodness and Love has bestowed on us what is infinitely greater. And when we take into consideration what has just been observed,—how well adapted to the wants of the soul Infallibility is, and how desirable for the proper safeguarding of its everlasting interests its unerring guidance would be, does not the belief that an infinitely good and loving God, our Father in heaven, has actually granted the boon of Infallibility, become most natural, reasonable, and just? To put the argument in another form, Did the God who gave up to the torments of Calvary His own divine and only begotten Son for our souls' redemption and salvation,—the God who expressly assures us that, *He wills all men to be saved and to come to the knowledge of the truth,*' Did He, after all, leave us, without a living unerring Guide to the truth, to grope our way amidst the darkness of a hundred conflicting creeds, and liable at any moment to be ensnared by error and its apostles?* The teaching of St. Paul certainly does not point to such a conclusion. " He who spared not even His own Son, but delivered Him up for us all, *how hath He not also with Him given us all things?* "*

THIRD ARGUMENT: THE WISDOM OF GOD.

To my mind, it is clear that if God made a supernatural Revelation of His will, and intended the same for the benefit of man to the end of time, He must have provided a living Infallible Witness to its authenticity and genuineness, a living Infallible Guardian of its purity and integrity, and a living Infallible Interpreter of its contents and meaning. For, firstly, without a living Infallible Witness, how is this Revelation to be certainly identified? How is man to distinguish with certainty what is Revelation from what is not Revelation?—true from false? genuine from spurious Revelation? In case of doubt or controversy, and there have been many such cases of the greatest importance, what adequate means has he of ascertaining the truth? In other words, if there is no living Infallible Witness to this Revelation and to its contents, what sufficient guarantee have I that what is proposed for my assent is, beyond all reasonable doubt or prudent fear of error, the identical Message delivered by God nearly two thousand years ago?

Secondly, without a living Infallible Guardian, how is Revelation to be properly safeguarded? How preserve it in its divine purity and integrity? Revelation is a body or system of truths expressed in human language; how effectively protect this sacred deposit from the assaults and encroachment of error? Expressed as it is in changeable, corruptible, perishable language, how secure it against innovation, perversion, corruption and decay? How keep and transmit it whole and unsullied from one generation to another amidst the falsifying influences of men and time? Don't tell me the Bible can do this. The Bible, indeed, contains the divine Message in part; but, in no true sense, can it be called an adequate Guardian, a sufficient guarantee for its purity and integrity. Besides the Bible itself, as we shall see, no less than Revelation, needs a living Infallible Witness, Guardian and Interpreter. The argument is as strong in the one case as in the other.

Thirdly, without a living Infallible Interpreter of Revelation, how can I be certain that I understand aright its teaching? Admittedly, Revelation is open to more than one interpretation. As a matter of fact many and, not infrequently, the most opposite meanings have been put upon some of its most important parts. How in such cases determine with certainty its true meaning,—the meaning intended by its Divine Author, if there be no living Infallible Interpreter of it? And if its true meaning cannot be certainly ascertained, of what practical value, I ask, would such a Revelation be to man? And what would be the wisdom or the object of making it?

Assuming, then, that God made a supernatural

Revelation of a body of truths for man's benefit for all time, the Wisdom of God, I repeat, must have provided it with a living Infallible Witness to identify and authenticate it, a living Infallible Guardian to protect it intact and defend it against the assaults of error, and a living Infallible Interpreter to determine and declare unerringly its genuine meaning.'

Deny this and what follows? Why, the absurd conclusion, that an infinitely wise God sent from heaven no less a person than His own Son to make for man's guidance a Revelation of His will, and that at the same time He made no adequate provision for its proper identification, preservation, or usefulness in after ages; that He delivered a most important Message, and appointed no one to bear witness to it before future generations,—no one to safeguard it against the encroachments of heresy,— no one to define its contents or to declare its meaning, or to decide the many grave controversies that were sure to arise in the course of time concerning it; that He left His sacred truth to be the sport of the theories, fancies, follies, disputes, contentions and contradictions of men, not caring whether they received it or not, or in what sense they received it, whether true or false, or whether they received it in different or even contradictory senses; in a word, that God was perfectly indifferent both as to the custody of the Revelation itself and as to the success of its mission. Is this view of the case more acceptable to reason and to common sense? At least it does not seem very flattering to that Wisdom that orders all things wisely and well.

An illustration will help us to realize the full force

of this argument. What would be thought of the government that would make and promulgate laws and leave them, without court or judge, to the private interpretation of its subjects? What, think you, would be the natural result of such a course of action? Chaos and anarchy in the State, precisely the counterpart (I say it without intending to offend) of what we have before our eyes in the religious dissensions, divisions and contradictions of those who accept a supernatural Revelation, and at the same time reject a living Infallible Witness, Guardian, and Interpreter of the same.

To conclude, then, one of two things is to me perfectly certain; either God made no Revelation at all, or he provided it with a living Infallible Witness, Guardian, and Interpreter. To make a Revelation, and not make such provision for its preservation and propagation would be as absurd as to make a law and leave it without a judge to declare and apply it. Many Protestant writers of eminence admit the force of this argument. "When we start from a supernatural principle in religion we must necessarily admit that the Divinity who has deigned to make this Revelation to man *must have taken care that it should not be abandoned to the arbitrary judgment of men. Not to admit this principle is to argue inconsistently.*"* "What the doctrine of Divine Providence is with regard to Creation," says another Protestant, "such is the doctrine of the Infallibility of the Church with regard to Divine Revelation; *they must stand or fall together.*" "Any supernatural religion," writes Mr. Mallock,° "that renounces its claim to this [Infallibility], it is clear can profess to be a semi-revelation only. It is a hybrid thing, partly natural and partly supernatural, and it thus practically has all the qualities of a religion that is wholly natural. In so far as it professes to be revealed, it of course professes to be infallible; but if the revealed part be in the first place *hard to distinguish*, and in the second place *hard to understand*—if it may mean many things, and many of those things contradictory—it might just as well have never been made at all. To make it in any sense an Infallible Revelation, or in other words a Revelation at all, *to us*, we need a power to interpret the Testament that shall have equal authority with that Testament itself."[10]

Rationalists see and acknowledge the force of this argument; and hence it is that because they either cannot or will not accept the living Infallible Witness, Guardian, and Interpreter of Revelation, they reject altogether the doctrine of a supernatural Revelation. This conclusion is one which every Christian must deplore; but, all the same, it is logical.

FOURTH ARGUMENT: THE JUSTICE OF GOD.

God did not leave it optional with man to accept or reject His Revelation. He made it obligatory on his belief and practice; He ordained it to be his rule of faith and conduct, and that under the penalty of eternal damnation. For the believer in Revelation this is beyond all controversy or doubt. Our divine Lord's words are explicit and emphatic: "*Preach the Gospel to every creature . . . he that believeth not shall be damned.*"[11] Now, I ask, would or could a God of infinite Justice make faith in Revelation obligatory on man under so extreme a penalty, without furnishing him with the means of knowing beyond all danger of error what the specific truths of this Revelation were, and what their genuine meaning was? If you answer in the affirmative, then I say you impugn the Justice of God, and at once write yourself down a blasphemer; and if you answer in the negative, then, I contend, you have no alternative but to profess yourself at once a believer in Infallibility.. For, seeing that God does not vouchsafe to speak to us Himself, what other means, besides an Infallible Witness and Teacher, are there of determining with certainty what Revelation teaches on each point of necessary faith? None; and therefore I conclude that if God made faith in a body of supernaturally revealed truths a condition of my salvation, He, most certainly, has appointed and commissioned some one to tell me with unerring authority what these truths are, and the precise sense in which He wishes me to receive them. Otherwise I am forced to believe that God laid upon me a most grievous obligation, and at the same time did not furnish me with the necessary means of fulfilling it.

In what I have said so far, as well as in what follows, I must not be understood as arguing for the *absolute* necessity of Infallibility, or that Infallibility is necessary in any and every order of things. I insist on its necessity merely in the present order of Divine Providence. Almighty God, of course, could speak directly and immediately to man; but here we are dealing with an order of things in which He does not speak personally to us, but in which He spoke through a special body of men in one generation the law for all future generations.

FIFTH ARGUMENT: THE CHARACTERISTICS OF FAITH.

God demands of man faith in the teaching of Revelation.[12] Faith, considered as an act of reason, is defined to be an act by which we firmly and without condition or reserve believe a truth of Revelation. The assent of faith must be undoubting, unconditional, absolute; and the truth to which this assent is given must be one supernaturally revealed by God. In order, then, that an act of faith be a reasonable act, it is plain that the mind that makes it should know for certain that the doctrine proposed for its belief is really a truth of Revelation; or, in other words, an act of faith presupposes and demands certainty not only as to the fact that God has spoken, but also that the truth or doctrine in question is part of what He said. Probability, even the highest, will not do;[13] absolute certainty is required; for faith and doubt are wholly incompatible, and certainty alone can remove all doubt. Now, I ask, how is the average man to attain to such certainty without the aid of an Infallible Teacher of God's word? Without the testimony of an Infallible Witness to the fact, how is it possible for any man to have such certainty in the case of each and every one of the truths to which the divine command to believe extends? And without the authority of an Infallible Interpreter of those truths, how can any one be sure that he understands aright their divine meaning? As, then, no man can believe by divine faith doctrines of whose revelation and genuine meaning he is not absolutely certain, it follows at once, that to have divine, saving faith, at least in its *plenitude*, I must have an Infallible

Witness to the specific truths of faith, and an Infallible Interpreter of their true meaning.*

God willed that His Revelation should be believed everywhere, and by all men, and believed everywhere and by all men in its integrity and unity. He willed that it should be believed (1) *everywhere;* for our Divine Lord expressly said to His Apostles, "Go ye into *all the world,*"[14] and again: "Ye shall be witnesses unto Me . . . *unto the uttermost part of the earth*"[15] (2) *by all men;* for He ordered it to be taught to "*all nations,*"[16] to be preached to "*every creature,*"[17] (3) *in its integrity;* that is, God willed that all men should believe all that His Revelation contains. "Go," He says, "into the whole world, and preach *the Gospel* to every creature." He does not say, "Go and preach a *part* of the Gospel, or *selections* from the Gospel; but go and preach *the Gospel,*—the Gospel whole and entire. And, as if to leave no room for doubt about His meaning, He expressly says, in the parallel passage in St. Mathew, "Go ye, therefore, and teach all nations . . . teaching them to observe *all* things, whatsoever I have commanded you."[18] There is not a word here about essentials and non-essentials, about fundamentals and non-fundamentals,—not a shadow of authority for any such distinction."[19] There is no option left to the believer to pick and choose according to his judgment, good pleasure, or taste. The command of God is to preach *the Gospel* in its integrity to every creature, to teach all nations "*all* (not

---

* "Nothing, says Cardinal Newman, "is clearer than this, that if faith in God's word is required of us for salvation, the Catholic Church is the *only* medium by which we can exercise it."—Discourses to Mixed Congregations," p. 231.

some) *things whatsoever I have commanded you"*; and faith in "the Gospel," in "all things whatsoever I have commanded you," is demanded under the penalty of *eternal damnation*. "And He said unto them, Go ye into all the world, and preach the Gospel to every creature. He that believeth and is baptized shall be saved, *but he that believeth not shall be damned.*"[20] Saving faith, then, must include the whole revealed word of God. So much is clear from the words of Scripture.

That Reason teaches the same truth, will appear from the following considerations: (*a*) If God spoke and made a Revelation of His will to man, assuredly this was with the intention that man should believe whatever He said. To make a Revelation, and leave man free to accept or reject it wholly or in part would be absurd. To Reason, the fact of a Revelation implies a precept to believe all it contains. (*b*) The moment man comes to know for certain that God has spoken to him, Reason tells him that it is his duty to believe whatever God has said. For, what would the denial or the refusal on his part to believe a single point of such a Revelation mean? Clearly one or other of four things.[21] It would be to offend against (1) the Knowledge of God, by virtually accusing Him of error, or (2) against His Veracity, by virtually charging Him with deceit, or (3) against His Wisdom, by virtually accusing Him of having spoken without purpose, or (4) against His Authority, by refusing to submit to it. Man cannot, therefore, deny or refuse to believe a single truth of revelation without sin. (*c*) Because to deny or refuse to believe a single truth of Revelation would mean the loss of faith altogether, inasmuch as it would involve a denial of the very principle—the formal motive or reason—of faith. The sole motive or reason why we believe any truth by divine faith is the authority of God who revealed it; no other motive is sufficient for divine faith. But all the truths of Revelation alike rest on the same Divine Authority. Therefore, to reject any one of them would be to reject the Authority of Him who revealed it,—the very principle of faith. Hence St. Augustine" well remarks that the man who believes what he likes of the Gospel and rejects what he likes, believes himself rather than God or the Gospel." Sacred Scripture furnishes a similar argument: " Whosoever," says St. James ii. 10, " shall keep the whole law, and yet offend in *one* point, *he is guilty of all.*" Now, if the man who transgresses one precept of the law is considered guilty of transgressing the whole law because he contemns the Law-Giver, *a pari* the man who denies or refuses to believe a single truth of Revelation is guilty of denying all Revelation, because he contemns the Divine Revealer.

God willed His Revelation to be believed everywhere, and by all men, in its *unity*. He willed that all men should always and everywhere have *one and the same* faith. The evidence of Scripture on this head is abundant. St. John tells us that so much did our Divine Lord desire unity among His followers teachers and taught, that the last prayer He uttered before His Sacred Passion was that they may be *one* "These words spake Jesus, and lifted up His eyes to heaven and said . . . Holy Father, keep through thine own Name those whom thou hast given me, *that they may be one* . . . Neither pray I for these [the Apostles] alone; but for them also which shall *believe* on me through their word: *that they all may be one.*"[24] Moreover, it is recorded in the same place that He intended this unity among all believers to be a proof to the world of His Divine Mission. "That they all [believers] may be one . . . that the world may know *that thou hast sent me.*"[25] And the unity He prays for is one modelled after the most perfect pattern, namely, the unity that exists between Himself and the Father. Therefore a unity not merely of heart and will, but also of mind and of thought; a unity not merely of charity, but also of faith. "For them also [I pray] *which shall believe* on me through their word: that they all may be one . . . *even as we are one.*"[26] On this point St. Paul, who so often and so forcibly inculcates the necessity of unity in faith, leaves no room for doubt. In his Epistle to the Ephesians,[27] he reminds his readers that as there is but "one body," "one spirit," "one Lord," and "one baptism," so there is but "*one* faith;" and, therefore, they are to be careful not merely "to keep the unity of the spirit," but also to possess the "one faith." And, a little farther on, he expressly tells them that the object of our Divine Lord in appointing the Pastors of His Church, was to insure "*unity of the faith*," and to guard the faithful from being deceived by false teachers and carried about with every wind of doctrine. "And He gave some Apostles; and some, Prophets . . . and some Pastors, and teachers . . . for the work of the ministry . . . *till we all come in the unity of the faith* . . . that we henceforth be no more children, *tossed to and fro, and carried about with every wind of doctrine,* by the sleight of men, and cunning craftiness, whereby they lie in wait to deceive."[28]

But perhaps the Apostle is clearer in his First Epistle to the Corinthians, where, treating of the necessity of unity in faith, he imploringly writes, "Now I beseech you, brethren, by the name of our Lord Jesus Christ, that ye all speak the *same thing;* and that there be no *divisions* among you; but that ye be *perfectly joined together in the same mind and in the same judgment.*"[29] In conformity with this teaching we find the Apostle instructing Titus as to how he is to deal with heretics,[30] solemnly admonishing the faithful "*to avoid*" those who "*cause divisions and offences contrary to the doctrine they had learned,*"[31] and reckoning the sins of heresy and schism, of sects and divisions among those that exclude from heaven."[32] Finally, we have those terrible words which cannot fail to impress any reader, that, in the mind of St. Paul at least, unity of faith among Christians was necessary; and that heresy, or the violation of that unity, was a most grievous sin: "As we said before, so say I now again, if any man preach *any other* Gospel unto you than *that you have received* let him be *accursed.*"[33] The teaching of SS. Peter and John is to the same effect.[34]

But, why multiply references to Scripture for proof of the truth in question? Does not reason itself clearly teach that unity is essential to truth, and, therefore, that faith, to be true, must be one? Is it not evident to reason and common sense that God cannot be the Author of many conflicting religions; that infinite truth cannot teach doctrines in any measure at variance one with another, or sanction different and contradictory creeds? This obvious teaching of reason and common sense ever insisted upon by the Catholic Church has come to be fully and widely realized; and hence to-day among all true believers in Revelation there is a loud and earnest cry for *unity*. A long and sad experience has convinced those outside the Church that variation in faith necessarily implies error, that division logically means weakness, dissolution and decay, and that the multiplication of sects is an unanswerable argument in the mouth of the enemy of Christianity, as well as a great obstacle to the conversion of the heathen." And so, sick and tired of the multitude of sects, and of the widespread doubt, uncertainty, scepticism, and unbelief they have led to, they are craving for unity, certainty, and peace.

And now to come to the point of our argument. How is it possible to attain and perpetuate this worldwide, all-embracing integrity and unity of faith without an Infallible Authority? How is it possible to *join together perfectly*, as St. Paul would have it, all men everywhere "*in the same mind and in the same judgment*," and get them to "*speak the same thing*"? How is it possible to get all men everywhere to agree in believing by divine faith the same creed, and in believing it in exactly the same sense, without an Infallible Teacher to determine unerringly both the articles of the creed and their genuine meaning? In case a difference of opinion should arise on any vital point, how then maintain the integrity and unity of faith without an Infallible Judge to declare the truth and put an end to controversy? The thing is impossible, and that it is so the history of Protestant Christianity furnishes a conclusive proof.

Some three hundred and fifty years ago or more, all Western Christendom was one in faith, because it acknowledged a living Infallible Teacher of Revelation. All of a sudden large numbers rejected the Infallible Teacher, and what was and is to this day the manifest result? Simply that non-Catholic Christendom is split up into hundreds of sects, all differing in faith; some contradicting and some even condemning and denouncing what others hold to be most sacred.* And as time goes by, every day witnesses a worse state of things,—sects constantly subdividing, creeds ever changing, one point of Christian doctrine after another called in question, doubted and denied; and men, weary of strife and bewildered by controversy, and hopeless of attaining certainty and repose in Christian belief, taking refuge in indifferentism, skepticism, and infidelity. Is this picture

---

* In a letter to Melancthon, towards the end of the year 1552, Calvin writes: "*It is more than absurd that we, who have been compelled to separate from the whole world, should in the very beginning fly apart from one another.*"—Op.,tom. ix.,p. 66, in Allnatt's "Which is the True Church?" p. 50.

Melancthon himself writes: "*The Elbe with all its waters could not furnish tears enough to weep over the miseries of the distracted Reformation.*"—Epist., lib. ii., ep. 202.

Theodore Beza, the principal adherent and successor of Calvin, writes: "*On what point of religion do the churches which have declared war against the Roman Pontiff agree among themselves? If you run through them all, from head to foot, you will hardly find anything affirmed by one which the other does not immediately exclaim against as impious.*"—Th. Beza, "Epist. ad Audream Dudit," in Murphy's "The Chair of Peter," p. 288.

"*The suppression of the authority of the Pope has sowed endless germs of discord in the world: as there is no longer any sovereign authority to terminate the disputes which arise on all sides, we have seen the Protestants split among themselves, and tear their bowels with their own hands.*—Puffendorf, "De Monarch. Pont. Rom.," in Balmes' "Protestantism and Catholicity Compared, etc.," p. 424.

overdrawn? Does not the state of religious belief which it represents prove beyond a doubt that unity and integrity of faith is an utter impossibility without the authority of Infallibility?" To create and maintain unity or oneness of faith in its fulness demands an Authority which is able to produce universal and undoubting conviction of the absolutely unerring truth of its teaching; and only an Authority endowed with the supernatural prerogative of Infallibility can do this.

Again, sacred Scripture, as we have seen, tells us that *heresy* is one of the greatest of sins. But how condem any man's belief or teaching as heresy except on the principle of an Infallible Teacher of divine truth? Heresy is dissent from the word, not of a human and fallible, but of a Divine and Infallible Teacher." What right, then, can any Teacher or body of Teachers, or Council or Church, that claims not Infallibility, have to condemn and denounce as heretical the creed or opinions of those who may differ with them, seeing that the one has the same authority for his belief and the same right to hold that it is the genuine teaching of Revelation as the other? The charge of heresy, or a trial for heresy by a Body that claims not the unerring divine judgment of Infallibility, is an absurdity,—a solemn farce. To provide effectively, then, against heresy and schism, against divisions and sects in the Christian body; to create and perpetuate everywhere, and in all minds, divine and saving faith in its integrity and unity, there must necessarily be a Teacher whose authority is, beyond question, divine, and whose judgment is, beyond suspicion, infallible.

And the necessity of the case being so manifest, Can we for a moment believe that our Divine Lord, who willed and fervently prayed for unity of faith among His followers, failed to provide the only adequate means of guaranteeing it?

SIXTH ARGUMENT: THE RIGHTS OF REASON AND CONSCIENCE.

My sixth argument is based on the rights of Reason and Conscience; and briefly stated it is this: Assuming a divine faith in the teaching of Revelation to be necessary to salvation, then I hold that nothing short of the certainty and security of Infallibility can satisfy the legitimate demands of Reason and Conscience. To understand fully the force of this argument it is necessary to have a clear conception of the nature of faith and of what it requires of reason; and for this purpose a few words of explanation will be in order. No one who believes the Bible to be the Word of God can for a moment doubt that divine faith is necessary to salvation. St. Paul lays down this necessity in the plainest terms: "*Without faith it is impossible to please him* (God);"[18] and our Lord Himself, in words that cannot be mistaken, emphatically declares, "*He that believeth not shall be damned.*"[19]

What, then, is faith, and what does it demand of reason? Fundamentally, faith is a belief in or an acceptance of information solely on the word or authority of the person who gives it. When the informant is man our faith in what he says is *human;* but when the informant is God, then our faith is *divine.* Theologically defined, an act of divine faith, with which alone we are here concerned, is a free act of the intellect illumined by grace, by which, under the command of the will inspired by grace, it fully and unhesitatingly assents to divinely revealed truths because God has revealed them. The point of this definition to which I wish to direct attention is this: It is of the very essence of faith that the assent of the intellect should be absolutely undoubting, unconditional, unhesitating, unreserved; otherwise there is and can be no supernatural, no divine faith. There may be opinion, or private judgment, or a tendency, or willingness to believe; but real faith there cannot be, for that absolutely excludes all doubt or distrust of any kind."[10] The reason of this is clear. The sole motive or reason of divine faith is the authority of God. When we make an act of divine faith in any doctrine, the mind assents to the doctrine, not because reason convinces us of its truth, not because the senses and their experience supply us with evidence of its truth, not because, as it may happen, it is the unanimous teaching of the most learned among men; not because it is the teaching of any Church"— no, but *simply* and *solely* because God revealed it. No other authority is sufficient for an act of divine faith."[*] Now God's authority excludes even the possibility of error in all that He reveals, for His Knowledge and Veracity being infinite, or as the theologians put it, being truth itself *in essendo, cognoscendo, et dicendo,* He can neither deceive nor be deceived. Consequently there can be no room for doubt or distrust, no justification for hesitation or reserve, or for ever revoking or wavering in an assent once given.

And now for the argument. Faith has its rights, and so has Reason; and the rights of the latter as well as of the former have to be respected and its just demands fully satisfied. Reason then argues as follows: 'Faith demands of me a firm, unhesitating, an absolutely unwavering and irrevocable assent. It demands a complete and abiding submission of the intellect; for faith, as St. Paul tells us," is a *captivity* of the understanding. Now, before I submit to this demand of faith and yield the assent it calls for, I have a right to exact and must have absolute certainty (1) on the truths of faith,—what they are; and (2) on their genuine meaning. I am not and cannot be bound to the obedience of faith before I am satisfied beyond all reasonable doubt or prudent fear of error on these two points." And as nothing less than an Infallible Teacher of Revelation can give or guarantee such certainty, I therefore demand the security of such a Teacher before I give the assent of faith to any body of teaching.

'Understand me clearly,'. continues Reason, 'I believe in the existence of God, and if God has certainly made a Revelation (which I doubt not), I believe that faith in the contents of that Revelation is most reasonable; for nothing can be more reasonable than to believe the word of God. Moreover, I readily admit that the assent of faith ought to be perfectly undoubting, absolutely unreserved. What I contend for as my strict right is that, before I am bound to give this assent, I must be thoroughly satisfied that what is proposed for my acceptance is, beyond doubt, the teaching of Revelation, the word, not of man, but of God, and that the meaning proposed is the true meaning intended by God. So much security I certainly have a right to exact—so much, in fact, it is my duty to exact—to safeguard myself against error or deception in a question of such vital importance to me."

'No man, therefore, no organization, no Church can justly claim, or have any right to ask for my obedience to its teaching unless it can completely satisfy me on these two heads; and if it is not infallible, how can it succeed in doing this? For if I know that it may be mistaken about the contents of Revelation, or about the genuine meaning of its contents, how can I be sure that it is not actually so; and, therefore, that it is not asking me to accept as the word of God the erroneous word of man?'

To put this argument in a concrete form, let us suppose the following case: A Missionary from one of the Protestant bodies undertakes the work of converting an unbeliever. He begins by telling him about the Divine Founder of Christianity, who He was, and about His Mission on earth, what its object was. He tells him of the Gospel He preached for the salvation of man, of its sublime teaching, of the hope it inspired, and of the great reward it promised here and especially hereafter to all who would faithfully observe its precepts. He next passes on to the evidences of Christianity, and puts before the unbeliever the proofs of our Lord's Divine Mission and of the fact of His having preached the Gospel of Christianity, and having made it the rule of faith and conduct for all men to the end of time. Having fully and forcibly stated the evidences, he turns at once to the work of convincing his hearer that the particular creed professed by his Church, be it Episcopalianism, Presbyterianism, Congregationalism, Methodism, or Baptist, as the case may be, is the true Christianity which Christ Himself preached. At the conclusion of his discourse on this head, Can we not easily imagine the intelligent unbeliever taking up the argument and continuing somewhat after this fashion? Friend, I have been charmed with your account of Christianity and its Founder; its doctrines are beautiful and consoling, and your arguments in proof of the fact that the Founder of Christianity was no other than the Son of the Eternal One made man, and, therefore, that Christianity is a Divine Religion, the teaching of God Himself—these are strong and convincing. But when we have got as far as this your argument begins to lose force and fails to satisfy me. Let me tell you why. I have been to America and have lived there for some time. It is a professedly Christian country, believing in God and in the Gospel of Christ. Now what did I find in this Christian America of yours? I found that its Christians were divided into a hundred and more different bodies, forming as many distinct and different sects, each with its own place of worship. All differ one from the other, and differ on points of admitted importance; some even on the very first principles of Christianity. Now, my friend, I would like to be a Christian, but here I am confronted with a hundred and one different forms of it; and at once the question arises, Which is the true one? All cannot be true; that is certain. It is equally certain that only one form can be true; for God is a God of truth, and truth is essentially one indivisible and immutable like God Himself—*the same yesterday, and to-day, and forever.*" God cannot be the Author of contradictions. He could not teach one body one thing, and teach another the very opposite of that. He could not teach one Church for sacred saving truth what He teaches another Church to be error, aye, worse, blasphemy and idolatry. I could far more easily and, in my opinion, more reasonably believe that there was no God at all than believe in a God of variations, divisions, and contradictions.

Now this Church tells me that Christ the Son of God was the Author of its creed; and that other tells me that the same Christ, God and man, was the Author of its creed, though the latter differs essentially from the former; nay more, perhaps denounces and anathematizes it. A third Church, differing from both, makes precisely the same claim for its creed; and so for dozens and scores of others,—all claim to have the divine and immutable teaching of Christ; and yet no two of them agree. Well, you speak to me in the name of one of these Churches, and you tell me that the particular Church, whose Missionary you are, claims my allegiance; and you would have me believe that I am bound to accept by divine faith its teaching as the pure and unadulterated word of God. Now, friend, how do you justify this claim, on the part of your Church, on my belief and conscience? You ask for the complete submission of my intellect, will, and conscience to your teaching as the Gospel of Christ. Are you able to guarantee me against error or deception if I yield to your demands, accept your creed, and say *credo*, I believe? Can you assure me, beyond all reasonable doubt or prudent fear of error, that yours is the only true form of Christianity, and that in embracing it, I, certainly and surely, believe what Christ commissioned His apostles to preach to "*every creature,*" and in reference to which, He said, "*He that believeth not shall be damned*"? If you cannot give me this assurance, I cannot prudently, I cannot reasonably or conscientiously give to your Church and its creed the obedience you ask for. Remember the all-important interests that are at stake. You tell me that my soul is of inestimable value; that its salvation is the one thing necessary,—the crown of all blessings; that it involves the consideration of eternity, and where there is question of salvation and eternity you say I cannot be too cautious or too secure. Moreover, you tell me that salvation under the Gospel depends on knowing, believing, and practising what it teaches. Well, what if you should be wrong in your view of the Gospel? What if the teaching you put forward as God's saving truth should turn out to be error? You are not infallible, your Church is not infallible,—neither of you claim to be. You are, therefore, liable to err; and how, I ask, can I be sure that you do not actually err in what you believe and would have me accept as the true teaching of Christianity? You have no more certainty, no more security for the truth of your position, than the hundred other Christian bodies around you which differ with and contradict you, and which in your opinion are wrong. They are a hundred to one against you, and they are composed of believers as sincere, as learned, as good and as pious as any in your body. They are, too, as dogmatic as you in asserting that their forms of Christianity are severally the true and pure Christianity of Christ. Perhaps one or other of these is right;

if so, you must be wrong, so far at least as you differ. How, then, can you justly claim for your creed, and how could I reasonably yield to it, the obedience of faith? How could I as a reasonable man, and fully alive to the importance of my act, bow down before your teaching, and, accepting it as the supernaturally revealed word of God, make an act of divine faith in it? No, friend, I cannot do it. My Reason and Conscience both demand, in a matter of such surpassing interest to my soul, the security of an Authority that cannot deceive me, of an Authority that can, beyond the possibility of a mistake, tell me what true Christianity is, solve my difficulties, and clear up my doubts on all religious questions.

I conclude, then, that Reason has a strict right to demand, and ought to have, the guarantee of Infallibility in matters of religion in order to be certain that nothing shall be proposed for its belief but the pure and unadulterated teaching of God, and that nothing shall be required of it in morals save what the law of God prescribes. Without this Reason would not have that certainty to which it has a right, nor would Conscience have that security which is essential to its peace and happiness.

Here the reader may interpose in his thoughts and say: 'But have we not the Bible? Is not that an Infallible Teacher and Guide? Have we not there God's own inspired Word, pure and unadulterated; and what more do we need?' Decidedly we need more. Dear friend, if to-morrow you resolved on studying for any profession, on acquiring a thorough knowledge of any branch of science or art, would you think it enough to buy the best book on the subject, and apply yourself to the study of it without any aid from Tutor or Professor? You have a grown son, and you want him to be a lawyer or a doctor; or a daughter, and you want her to become proficient in music, drawing, or painting. Are you satisfied with providing books and saying to them, 'There, you have the very best treatises on the subject; go, study, and master the science or art'? Do you not, moreover, consider it necessary to place them under competent teachers, who will answer their questions and solve their difficulties as they proceed with their respective studies? Why, then, is it that you think and act differently in the case of religion? How is it that you can there dispense with the competent living, speaking teacher, and be contented with a book to acquire a knowledge of the most important of all sciences,—that which concerns the everlasting interests of your immortal soul? Is it that the Bible, with its impenetrable mysteries, profound doctrines, and strange idioms, phraseology, figures, and style, is more easily interpreted, and its contents more readily mastered? Don't you see anything unreasonable or strange in your position? Besides, what about the hundreds of thousands who cannot read? How is the Bible to be an Infallible Teacher and Guide to them?

Again, how, without a living Infallible Witness to the fact, can you know that the Bible is the inspired Word of God pure and simple? There is no other book on which scholarship, the most critical and profound, has labored so long and so industriously; and what is the result? Why, that at this moment nearly every question connected with it is involved in bitter controversy. Its authenticity,—was it written

THE DOGMA OF INFALLIBILITY?

by those whose names it bears, and at the times stated? Its veracity,—is it a trustworthy record of the history it narrates, and is its teaching true throughout? Its integrity,—is it a faithful copy of the original work in all its parts? Its divinity,—is it a revelation from God? Its inspiration,—does it not only contain the teaching of Divine Revelation, but is it moreover an inspired record of that Revelation? All these are vital questions, and there is not one of them that is not involved in endless controversy. Now how are these controversies to be satisfactorily settled? Private judgment, with all the aids of human learning, has failed to decide them. And the Bible, your Infallible Teacher and Guide, cannot settle them, for it is deaf and dumb. It cannot speak, and therefore cannot decide any controversy. Besides, its own authority being the subject of the controversies, to appeal to it as judge would not be allowable.[15] How, then, I ask again, is controversy to be put to rest, and the fact to be finally established that the Bible, in all its parts, is beyond all doubt the inspired Word of God? Clearly, only by means of a living Infallible Witness. Without such an authority its divine inspiration cannot be established. This Rationalists have proved to demonstration against those who reject the doctrine of Infalliblity; and eminent Protestant writers have admitted it.[17] Fourteen hundred years ago the great St. Augustine saw this when he gave utterance to the celebrated saying: "*I should not have believed the Gospel if the authority of the Catholic Church had not moved me thereto.*"[46]

But, passing over the difficulties mentioned, and assuming the Bible to be, beyond all controversy, the inspired Word of God, you still need a living Infallible Interpreter of its contents. For what good is it to you to know that you have in the Bible the pure Word of God unless you are certain that you understand aright its genuine meaning? Bear in mind that the Bible is the Word of God only in the sense in which God inspired it. Now can you, without the aid of an Infallible Interpreter, determine beyond question what the divine meaning is in every necessary instance? The text of the Bible is open to different interpretations, and it is a notorious fact that men of great ability and vast learning, men of unquestionable honesty of purpose and eager to attain the truth, have put different, sometimes contradictory, interpretations upon some of its most important passages. Do not, as a matter of fact, a hundred different sects confidently appeal to its text in support of as many different creeds?"[49] In such a conflict of interpretations what value is your Infallible Teacher and Guide to you in determining the truth? The Bible cannot interpret itself; it cannot say who is right and who is wrong; it cannot tell you the meaning God intended it to bear. How then, I ask, can you look upon it as a safe guide in religion,—such a guide as we have seen to be necessary to properly safeguard the all-important interests of your soul, and fully satisfy the demands of Faith, Reason, and Conscience? The celebrated Bossuet long ago put to himself your objection:— "Have I not God's Word in the Bible?" and answered, "Yes, undoubtedly you have a Word holy and adorable, but a Word nevertheless leaving itself to be explained and treated as *every one pleases*, making no objection to those who explain it badly."[50]

THE DOGMA OF INFALLIBILITY? 61

The Bible itself, then, to be of any value to us, needs not only a living Infallible Witness to its inspiration, but a living Infallible Interpreter of its meaning,—a living, speaking, and Infallible Expounder of its teaching. Otherwise we can never be certain that the meaning we give to it is the genuine meaning. The words in which Cardinal Newman argues for the necessity of an authorized Infallible Interpreter of the Bible will conclude my remarks on this head: "Surely, then," writes His Eminence," "if the revelations and lessons in Scripture are addressed to us personally and practically, the presence among us of a formal judge and standing expositor of its words is imperative. *It is antecedently unreasonable to suppose that a book so complex, so unsystematic, in parts so obscure, the outcome of many minds, times, and places, should be given us from above without the safeguard of some authority; as if it could possibly, from the nature of the case, interpret itself.* Its inspiration does but guarantee its truth, not its interpretation. How are private readers satisfactorily to distinguish what is didactic and what is historical, what is fact and what is vision, what is allegorical and what is literal, what is idiomatic and what is grammatical, what is enunciated formally and what occurs *obiter*, what is only of temporary and what is of lasting obligation? Such is our natural anticipation, and it is only too exactly justified in the events of the last three centuries in the many countries where private judgment on the text of Scripture has prevailed. *The gift of inspiration requires as its complement the gift of Infallibility.*" "

SEVENTH ARGUMENT: WITH AND WITHOUT INFALLIBILITY.

A summary contrasting the advantages of accepting the doctrine with the disadvantages of rejecting it will bring to a close the argument for the necessity of Infallibility.

I. With Infallibility Christianity is not something uncertain, indefinite, or vague. We know precisely and for certain what it is, what it teaches, what it commands and what it condemns. It is a great objective reality,—certain in its divine origin and authority, definite in its teaching, and consistent and harmonious in its various parts. Its dogmas are irreversible and unchangeable,—the same everywhere, at all times, and for all men.

II. With Infallibility an unerring knowledge of the truths and means of salvation is within the reach of all, and is easily attained by the unlearned as well as the learned. There is no need of great or of labored study, or of lengthened examination. All the believer has to do is to listen to the Infallible Teacher, and he learns at once the truth as God revealed it.

III. With Infallibility all the difficulties of the religious controversy disappear. In it you have the means of determining, beyond the possibility of mistake, the truths of faith, and of deciding unerringly all points of controversy, answering satisfactorily all objections, and dispelling effectually all doubts in reference thereto. In it you have a principle that triumphantly vindicates the truth of whatever it teaches, and completely justifies the most absolute faith in it.*
"*The Catholic faith,*" says the Protestant Gfrorer,"

* See page 77.

"*if we concede its first axiom*, which neither the Lutherans nor the Reformed, nor even the followers of Socinus denied, *is as consistent and consecutive as the books of Euclid*. The entire Romish religion is founded on the fact of a supernatural revelation, designed for the whole human race, which, as it embraces all generations, future as present, can never be interrupted; otherwise the sublime work, accomplished by a God-man, and sealed by his blood, would be exposed, which is contrary to the hypothesis, to suffer and eventually to perish by the weakness and errors of men. *These consequences of the first principles are indisputable, and there is not a single article of Catholic belief which is not justifiable, by the closest deduction, from this principle.*"

Guizot, the celebrated Protestant historian, in comparing the Catholic religion with the Protestant, which "did not fully comprehend and accept its own principles or effects," says, "*Catholics could point to their first principles and boldly admit all the consequences that might result from them.*"[14]

A celebrated Scotch metaphysician gave the substance of this in reply to some ministers who visited him in his last sickness: "Gentlemen," said he, when they pressed the subject of religion on his attention, "were I a Christian it is not to you I should address myself, but to the priests of the Catholic Church; *for with them I find premises and conclusion, and this I know you cannot offer.*"[15]

IV. With Infallibility there is perfect unity of faith among believers. It unites men of all races, countries, and nationalities in one and the same faith. However men may differ in other respects,—in customs, manners, habits, languages, and interests—yet under Infallibility all believe the same doctrines, profess the same creed, worship at the same altar, receive the same sacraments and render obedience to the same supreme ruling authority. Under Infallibility there is no room for dissension or division, schism or sect, contradiction or confusion of any kind. All is unity, harmony and peace. "If there is one thing," says Mathew Arnold, "specially alien to religion it is divisions; if there is one thing specially native to religion it is peace and union. Hence the original attraction towards unity in Rome, and hence the great charm for men's minds of that unity when once attained. *I persist in thinking that Catholicism has, from this superiority, a great future before it; that it will endure while all the Protestant sects dissolve and perish.*"

V. With Infallibility my faith is fixed and permanent. It does not vary from day to day, or from year to year, to meet the requirements of ever-changing public opinion, or the fickle judgment of men. What it was yesterday, it is to-day and will be to-morrow. What it was in the beginning, it is and will be to the end,—*semper eadem*, as unalterable and immutable as truth. The least variation, contradiction or inconsistency is impossible.

VI. With Infallibility Christianity is perfectly secure against the assaults of its enemies. All the efforts of scepticism and unbelief to destroy its influence over the minds and hearts of men, and to undermine their faith in its teaching, are vain. Expounded and safeguarded by Infallibility it is completely unassailable. The New York *Sun*, a short time ago, in a leading article on the dissolving effect of scepticism on the various creeds of Protestantism, significantly remarked that " *the only Christian communion on which modern scepticism seems to make no impression is the Roman Catholic.*"⁶⁶ And why? Because Infallibility stands in the way, and to its shafts opposes an invulnerable front. This is the source of the Church's vigorous life and unfailing strength and stability, of her majestic unity and world-wide Catholicity. "*Behold my witness is in heaven, and my champion is on high.*" ⁶⁶* This is what enables her to maintain intact the *faith once delivered unto the saints*. This is why she commands the respect, and extorts the admiration even of her enemies. "We Protestants as we are," says one of this number, in speaking of the Catholic Religion, "when we take in view this wondrous edifice, from its base to its summit, must acknowledge that we never beheld a system which, the foundations once laid, is laid upon such certain, secure principles; whose structure displays in its minutest details so much art, penetration, and consistency, and whose plan is so proof against *the severest criticism of the most profound science.*"⁶⁷ "Four times," writes Lord Macaulay,¹⁸ "since the authority of the Church of Rome was established in Western Christendom, has the human intellect risen up against her yoke. Twice that Church remained completely victorious. Twice she came forth from the conflict bearing the marks of cruel wounds, but with the *principle* of life still strong within her. When we reflect on the tremendous assaults she has survived, we find it difficult to conceive in what way she is to perish."

This is why her missionary labors are so fruitful in results, while those of other denominations are so barren. "The Catholic Church," says Mr. Mallock,[59] "represents success, where the others (the Protestant Churches) represent failure," and this though "*of monetary means at her disposal, she had not so much as any one of our Protestant societies.*"[60] Finally, Infallibility is the grand secret of the wonderful influence the Church wields over the minds and consciences and hearts of 230,000,000 of Catholics.

VII. Under Infallibility there is no conflict, no antagonism between Reason and Revelation, Science and Faith, the Natural and Supernatural. Both are in perfect accord; not enemies, but mutual friends and helpers.[61] Between them Infallibility holds the scales of justice, and with unerring judgment determines, adjusts, and harmonizes their respective rights and claims.

VIII. Infallibility protects us from the aberrations of reason, and from the waywardness of the will. It is, as Cardinal Newman observes,[62] "a provision adapted by the mercy of the Creator to preserve religion in the world, and to restrain that freedom of thought, which of course in itself is one of the greatest of our natural gifts, and to rescue it from its own suicidal excesses."

IX. Under Infallibility all is certainty, security, calm, and repose.[63] You are completely protected from the strife and confusion of tongues. Infallibility gives to the intellect a divine certainty, to the conscience a heavenly security, and to the soul a blessed peace based on a firm faith and an unfailing hope. The believer in Infallibility is never troubled with a doubt about the truth of his faith, or the means of salvation. The question 'What must I do to save my soul?' causes him no anxiety; the question 'Perhaps I may be wrong,' never occurs to him as it does to others. On these momentous questions he has absolute certainty and is wholly at peace. Safe in the bosom of the Church he can sing with the Psalmist, "*In peace in the self-same I will sleep, and I will rest, for Thou, O Lord, singularly hast settled me in hope.*"[4] What a blessing Infallibility is! What a source of certainty, security, happiness and peace[5] through life, but especially at the dread hour of death, when the terrors of judgment are in view, and the question of salvation or damnation for all eternity comes up for decision! It is then indeed, that the great benefit of Infallibility is fully realized.

I. Without Infallibility Christianity becomes vague, indefinite, and uncertain in its teaching. What the specific truths it embodies are, and what their genuine meaning is, cannot be determined with certainty. To one mind it will teach one set of doctrines; to another a different and perhaps a contradictory set. To-day its creed is different from what it was yesterday; and what is divine truth to-day will be error to-morrow. That is, in other words, Christianity, without Infallibility, will be whatever the bias of the individual mind, or the public opinion of the time or place calls for. This is not an exaggerated picture; it is literally verified in the history of the variations of Protestant Christianity.[6] What Protestant body can at this moment say that it believes all the fundamental doctrines of the Reformation? believes all the doctrines that were then preached as infallibly true and divinely revealed? "Were Luther," writes a stanch follower of his, "to rise up from his grave he could not possibly realize as his own, or as members of the Society he founded, those teachers who in our Church would fain, nowadays, be considered as his successors."[67]

To convince yourself of the absolute necessity of Infallibility you have only to ask yourself the simple question, 'What is Protestant Christianity?' "Simple as this truth seems (that a supernatural Revelation to be of use to us needs an Infallible Interpreter), mankind have been a long time learning it. Indeed, it is only in the present day that its practical meaning has come generally to be recognized. *But now at this moment, upon all sides of us, history is teaching it to us by an example, so clearly that we can no longer mistake it.*" What is the example referred to? "*That example*," continues Mr. Mallock, from whom I am quoting, "*is Protestant Christianity*, and the condition to which, after three centuries, it is now visibly bringing itself. It is at last beginning to exhibit to us *the true result of the denial of Infallibility to a religion that professes to be supernatural.* We are at last beginning to see in it neither the purifier of a corrupted revelation, nor the corrupter of a pure revelation, but the practical denier of all revelation whatsoever. It is fast evaporating into a mere natural theism, and is thus showing us what, as a governing power, natural theism is. Let us look at England, Europe, and America, and consider the condition of the entire Protestant world. Religion, it is true, we shall still find in it; *but it is religion from which not only the supernatural element is disappearing, but in which the natural element is fast becoming nebulous.* It is indeed growing, as Mr. Leslie Stephen says it is, *into a religion of dreams. All its doctrines are growing vague as dreams, and like dreams their outlines are forever changing.*"[68]

II. Without Infallibility, a certain knowledge of the necessary truths of faith, and of the means of salvation, would be impossible, if not to all, at least to the great majority of men. For in any other theory every point of faith has to be proved, and all the difficulties surrounding it have to be answered; and, supposing this possible, life would not be long enough for the work. Nor would the knowledge of the truths to which God assures us He wishes *all men to attain*[69] be accessible to all. Then, as some one has happily observed, "*Salvation would be by scholarship alone.*" In the theory of Infallibility only one point has to be established, viz., the doctrine of Infallibility itself. This question once settled will satisfactorily settle all other questions. For when I have once fully satisfied myself that there exists, by God's appointment, a living Infallible Teacher of the truth, then all I have to do is to interrogate this Divine Teacher on the point of doctrine, or on the subject of my doubt, difficulty, or ignorance, and without further trouble I have the truth beyond the possibility of error.

III. Without Infallibility every article of Christian belief would be involved in inextricable difficulties; controversy would be endless, and eventually nothing would be certain. Men would be "*tossed to and fro and carried about with every wind of doctrine,*"[70] "*always learning and never coming to the knowledge of the truth.*"¹ Without Infallibility the Christian believer is like a man at sea without pilot, rudder, or compass; he is the sport of the winds and waves of controversy, doubt, and uncertainty."² He can have no certainty about the truths of faith, for he has no principle of certainty to appeal to, no standard of truth to consult, no unerring guide to the contents and meaning of Revelation.

IV. Without Infallibility there can be no unity in matters of faith. Without an acknowledged Infallible Teacher men will disagree as to what is, and what is not, of necessary faith. There will be dissensions and contradictions, divisions, schisms and sects—a perfect babel of tongues—until no man knows what to believe. "What, then, do we see in this land?" asks Cardinal Manning.³ "Sects without number perpetually subdividing; each equally confident, all contradictory; and that dominant communion which claims to be authoritative in teaching, itself confounded by internal contradictions of its own. *How has this come to pass? It is because the Rule of Faith is lost, and the principle of certainty is destroyed.*" Lord Macaulay has described the Church of England as "*a hundred sects battling within one Church.*"⁴ And a living witness, no other than one of its own bishops, represents it as being at present "*in a state of chaotic anarchy and lawlessness.*" "Things," continues this authority, "had come to such a pass *that it did not appear to matter a jot what a clergyman held and believed.*"⁵

The bishop's testimony is corroborated by a recent distinguished convert. "In the last place in which I ministered as an Anglican clergyman," writes Rev. Luke Rivington,"⁶ "I was in full communion with the following religious teachers: One good and really learned man thanked God that the Church of England had never taught the doctrine of eternal punishment, in which he sincerely disbelieved; another delighted in teaching the poor Italians to read their Bible instead of going to Mass; a third agreed with him; a fourth considered this a grievous sin, and felt it advisable to interpolate the Anglican Communion Service with prayer from the Roman, or (which is the same thing) the Sarum Missal; a fifth, good as gold, and with all the charm of innocence, was vague as Maurice and Kingsley; a sixth would take the greatest trouble to get a (Roman) Catholic priest to attend a dying Catholic; a seventh had left the Church of England, or at least given up his ministry, on the ground that she had committed herself to a position of indifference on the subject of everlasting punishment. We were presided over by a Bishop, an amiable man, whose opinions on our points of disagreement we were never able to discover. Now I am not retailing scandals. These men were, I have every reason to suppose, men of blameless moral character. *But here was the Church of England in miniature*—failing in the one point without which a Church is no longer what the Church was when she came forth from the Upper Chamber in Jerusalem—*an authoritative teacher of one faith.*"

V. Without Infallibility there was no guarantee for permanency or stability in matters of faith, no security for a single dogma of Christianity. What is of faith will be ever subject to change and changing; mutability and variation will mark its daily history. What was believed yesterday is called into question and doubted to-day, and will be denied to-morrow. Dogma after dogma will meet the same fate until there will be left no fixed, invariable truths, no necessary articles of belief, no objective historical faith. God might as well have never spoken. Mr. Leslie Stephen cites the doctrine of eternal punishment in illustration of the point here, and Mr. Mallock, after observing that "Mr. Stephen has pitched on a very happy illustration," goes on to observe, "The critic, in the foregoing passages, draws his conclusion from the condition of but one Protestant doctrine. *But he might draw the same conclusion from all; for the condition of all of them is the same.* The divinity of Christ, the nature of His atonement, the constitution of the Trinity, the efficacy of the sacraments, the inspiration of the Bible—there is not one of these points on which the doctrines, once so fiercely fought for, are not now, among Protestants, getting *as vague and varying, as weak and as compliant to the caprice of each individual thinker*, as the doctrine of eternal punishment. And Mr. Stephen and his school exaggerate nothing in the way in which they represent the spectacle. Protestantism, in fact, is at last becoming explicitly what it always was implicitly, not a supernatural religion which fulfils the natural, but a natural religion which denies the supernatural."[77]

VI. Without Infallibility no Church, no Creed, could successfully resist the encroachments of scepticism and infidelity, or withstand their dissolving influence. Again the case of Protestantism is our proof, and Protestants themselves are our witnesses

to the fact. Emerson, speaking for America, writes:
"The creed of the Puritans is passing away, and
worse arise in its room. I think no one can go with
his thoughts about him, into one of our churches, *without feeling that what hold the public worship had on men is gone, or going*. It has lost its grasp on the
affections of the good and the fears of the bad. In the
country neighborhoods *half the parishes are signing
off*—to use the local term; for the motive that holds
the last there, is now only a hope and a waiting."[78]

Mr. Wilbur Larremore, who also is speaking of
American Protestantism, says: "The Churches are
daily becoming greater theoretical anomalies. The
avowed basis of organization is always a set of allegations about supernatural matters, in which the communicants are supposed unanimously to believe. *In
point of fact, scarcely anybody believes everything,
and many believe scarcely anything.*"[79]

The Protestant Bishop of Liverpool will speak
for England. In his last charge[80] to his clergy, Dr.
Ryle made use of these words: "I beseech you to realize the painful fact *that the Protestantism of this
country is gradually ebbing away.*" And Mr. W.
J. Canybeare, also speaking of England, says:[81] "It is
a melancholy fact that the men who make our steam-engines and railway carriages, our presses and telegraphs, the furniture of our houses and the clothing of
our persons, *have now in a fearful proportion renounced all faith in Christianity.*" "However
the sections of the working class," said Canon Money
at the Plymouth Church Congress in 1876, "might
differ in intelligence, in sobriety, in honesty, they
nearly all agreed in this—*they were alienated from*

Christianity. Barely five per cent. attended public worship."

Speaking of Germany, Mr. Samuel Lang, a Scotch Presbyterian, writes: "*The Lutheran and Calvinistic Churches in Germany and Switzerland are in reality extinct; the sense of religion, its influence on the habits, observances, and life of the people, is alive only in the Roman Catholic population.*"[82] "Prussia," writes Mr. Vizetelly in 1879, "presents the singular spectacle of the most pious sovereign in Europe, the *rex fidelissimus* among living monarchs, ruling over subjects *the most unbelieving in all Christendom.* . . . *Prussian Protestantism* . . . . *has been gradually sliding into pure Pantheism and even Atheism.*" . . . . "In the sphere of religion," laments one Berlin journal, "*liberal Protestantism has long since destroyed all respect for the commandments of God, and Christianity seems absolutely dead in our midst.* . . . If, as Menzel says, Berlin in the eighteenth century was the elysium of Free-thinkers, in the nineteenth it is unquestionably the limbo of Atheism, and Atheism, moreover, which proclaims itself from the house-tops."[83] "The majority of educated men in Germany," writes the author of *Religious Thought in Germany*, p. 15, "*are estranged from the dogmatic teaching of the Christian creed.*" "The land which was the cradle of the Reformation," says the *Edinburgh Review*,"[84] "has become the grave of the Reformed faith. . . . All comparatively recent works on Germany, as well as all personal observation, tell the same tale. *Denial of every tenet of Protestant faith among the thinking classes, and indifference in the masses, are the posi-*

tive and negative agencies beneath which the Church of Luther and Melancthon has succumbed. . . . In contiguous parishes of Catholic and Protestant populations, one invariable distinction has long been patent to all eyes and conclusions: *The path to the Catholic Church is trodden bare; that to the Protestant Church is rank with grasses and weeds to the very door.*"

The orthodox de Wette, after confessing that "*the dissolution of Protestantism is inevitable,*" exclaims: " Oh, Protestantism, has it at last come to this with thee, that thy disciples *protest against all religion? Facts, which are before the eyes of the whole world, declare aloud that this signification of thy name is no idle play of words;* though I know that the confession will excite a flame of indignation against myself." [66]

VII. Without Infallibility, Reason and Revelation, Science and Faith, Liberty and Authority—the Natural and the Supernatural—will be irreconcilable. Friction, antagonism, contradiction—a perpetual war —will mark their relations, for there is no means of determining their respective rights and of adjusting and harmonizing their respective claims.

VIII. Without Infallibility there would be nothing to protect religion from the vagaries and extravagances of the "aggressive, capricious, and untrustworthy intellect,"[66] and the waywardness and excesses of the will. "*There is hardly any conceivable aberration of moral license,*" says Mr. Mallock,[67] "*that has not, in some quarter or other, embodied itself into a rule of life, and claimed to be the proper outcome of Protestant Christianity.* Nor is this true only of the wilder and more eccentric sects. It is true of graver and more weighty thinkers also; so much so, that a theological school in Germany has maintained boldly '*that fornication is blameless and is not interdicted by the precepts of the Gospel.*'"

IX. Without Infallibility no Church or organization would have a right to undertake the mission of converting those without it; for being unable to assure them of the truth of its creed, it could not rightfully demand or ask of them the assent of faith.

X. Without Infallibility the Christian believer is ever exposed to the misery of doubt and uncertainty. Any moment the dreadful thought 'Perhaps I may be wrong; perhaps what I hold to be the saving truth of Jesus Christ may after all be error,' may come to disturb his peace, and torment his soul. He sees that others, who adopt the same Rule of Faith, entirely differ with him, and having the very same means of knowing the truth that he has, he cannot justly deny that they may be right. He cannot, consequently, be quite sure that his is the only true and saving faith of Christ. Then the perplexing question arises, 'If I am in error will God hold me excusable in the day of judgment?' And what anxiety reflection upon such a question must bring to the religious mind! "'*What shall we do to be saved?*' *men are again crying, and the lips* [of Protestantism] *that were once oracular now merely seem to murmur back confusedly, 'Alas! what shall you do?*'" "No wonder, as this same writer observes, that "its [Protestantism's] practical power—its

THE DOGMA OF INFALLIBILITY? 77

moral, its teaching, its guiding power—is fast *growing as weak and as uncertain as its theology.*" [89]

XI. Without Infallibility religion, as some one has justly remarked, would be little more than "*a dismal hell of mere speculation.*"

XII. Without Infallibility every day will witness, in increasing numbers, defections from the standard of Christian faith. Men will not, they cannot, believe without an adequate reason; and an adequate reason for a divine faith in the truths of a supernatural Revelation a living Infallible Authority alone can furnish. Here the argument for the necessity of Infallibility closes.

---

* Page 62, last line, immediately before quotation, read the following sentence: "What has been said of the doctrine of a supernatural revelation may, with greater reason, be said of the doctrine of infallibility."

NOTES TO CHAPTER II.

¹ Non-Catholics, too often, take it for granted that Catholics can show no justification for their faith in the dogma of Infallibility. This is not so surprising when we consider that, as a rule, they take their views on the subject from such oracles as *The Quarterly Review.* This unquestionably competent authority has declared *ex cathedra* that the doctrine of Papal Infallibility is one which "every man *competent* to form an *intelligent* opinion on the matter *knows to be absolutely incapable of honest defence.*" —January, 1888, p. 45. Quoted in *Dublin Review,* July, 1888, p. 123. Cf. also Mathew Arnold, "God and the Bible," Preface, xxvi.

² Luke x. 42; Math. xvi. 26; Mark viii. 36, 37.

³ In medical matters, in legal matters, in worldly matters of importance I do not trust my own judgment, I look for guidance to the judgment of others. Now is there not much greater reason for mistrusting my own judgment in matters of religion—in matters that concern my soul and its everlasting happiness? Is there not much greater reason here to look for guidance outside of myself?

⁴ I. Tim. iii. 15.

⁵ "Whoever says that our Master has not left us guides in so dangerous and difficult a way, says that he wishes us to perish."—St. Francis de Sales, "The Catholic Controversy," p. 69.

⁶ Rom. viii. 32. To those who object to the doctrine of Infallibility and say, "It is too good to be true," I commend these words of the Apostle of the Gentiles.

⁷ When God gave His law to the Jews, though much more definite in its provisions and minute in detail, He appointed Moses to interpret and declare it for the people. See Deuteronomy xxxi. 9-11; xvii. 9-12. Malachy ii. 7. ⁸ *Staendlin Magazine,* vol. iii. p. 83.

⁹ "Is Life Worth Living?" chap. xi., p. 274.

¹⁰ The same thought is expressed by Cardinal Manning thus: "A Divine revelation in human custody is soon lost; a Divine revelation expounded by human interpreters, or enunciated by human discernment, puts off its Divine character and becomes human, as St. Jerome says of the Scriptures when perverted by men."—"The Temporal Mission of the Holy Ghost," chap. i., p. 93.

¹¹ Mark xvi. 16.

¹² Mark xvi. 16. Faith is essentially, though not exclusively, an act of reason. Grace and reason coöperate in it. It may be well to note here that the word faith is taken in three different senses: (1) for the virtue or habit which is infused into the soul with the grace of justification; (2) for the truths which we believe; and (3) for the act of belief, or the exer-

cise of the virtue of faith about one of the truths which form its object. The context determines the meaning.

¹³ Cf. Prop. xxi., condemned by Innocent XI. In this faith differs from the moral virtues. A *practically* certain judgment, which may be formed on prudent or probable grounds, suffices for the exercise of the latter; a *speculatively* certain judgment is required in the case of the former. For the reasons of the difference see Hurter, "Theol. Gen.," vol. i., nn. 625, 666.

¹⁴ Mark xvi. 15.
¹⁵ Acts i. 8.
¹⁶ Math. xxviii. 19.
¹⁷ Mark xvi. 15.
¹⁸ Math. xxviii. 19, 20.

¹⁹ And even though such a distinction, in the sense of those who make it, were authorized by Scripture, then the question would arise, "What are essentials and what are not?" "What are fundamentals and what not?" And how decide satisfactorily this question without an infallible Judge?

²⁰ Mark xvi. 15, 16.
²¹ Council of Cologne, tit. i. cap. 4, in Hurter, "Theol. Gen.," vol. i. p. 464 (note).
²² I. 17. Cont. Faustum, c. 2, in Mazzella, "De Virt. Inf.," n. 309.
²³ "The Christian faith," says Dr. Brownson, "is not made up of separate and unrelated articles, dogmas, or propositions, whereof one or more may be denied without lesion to the others. All in it, so to speak, hangs together, and what we call different articles, dogmas, or propositions are really only so many different aspects of one uniform, indissoluble whole, in which the parts, if parts are conceivable, have that mutual dependence on each other, and that relation to the whole, *that the denial of any one part or aspect is, logically considered, the denial of all, or the faith under every aspect.*"—Works, vol. viii., p. 187.

²⁴ John xvii. 1, 11, 20, 21.
²⁵ *Ibid.* ver. 23.
²⁶ *Ibid.* vers. 20, 21, 22.
²⁷ Chap. iv. 1-5.
²⁸ *Ibid.* vers. 11-14.
²⁹ Chap. i. 10. Cf. also Rom. xv. 5, 6.
³⁰ Titus iii. 10, 11.
³¹ Rom, xvi. 17.   ³² Gal. v. 20, 21.   ³³ Gal. i. 9.
³⁴ II. Peter, chap. ii. 1; II. John i. 10.

³⁵ A barbarian chief in New Zealand made answer to a Protestant missionary: "You Europeans are not agreed amongst yourselves as to what is true religion. When you have agreed amongst yourselves which is the right road I may, perhaps, be induced to take it."—Swainson's "New Zealand," p. 36, in Marshall's "Christian Missions," vol. i. p. 452. See also the word "Heathen" in Index VI.

Ninigrat, a celebrated Indian Sachem, replying to an offer of the Pilgrim Fathers to preach to his tribe, sarcastically answered: "If my people should have a mind to turn Christians, *they could not tell what religion to be of.*"—Drake's "History of the Indians of North America," part ii. p. 80, in Marshall's "Christian Missions," vol. ii. p. 348.

"I declare, though with regret," said the Protestant Bishop of Salisbury, in a Charge to his clergy (1842), "that our missions have no success. What is the cause ? *Want of unity.* How can we hope to convert infidel nations, *when we are not in unity ourselves by Jesus Christ ?* By whom can the doctrine of Christianity be accepted, *when every side presents a scene of the wildest division, of heresy, and schism.*"—Gaume's "Catechism of Perseverance," vol. ii. p. 464.

³⁶ The testimony of the learned Protestant Grotius is to the point. Writing to the Calvinist minister, Réretus, he says: "All those who know Grotius are aware how earnestly he has wished to see Christians united in one body. *This he once thought might have been accomplished by a union of Protestants, but afterwards he saw that such a union is impossible.* . . . Therefore Grotius now is thoroughly convinced, as are many others also, that Protestants never can be united among themselves, *unless they join those who adhere to the Roman See,*" *i. e.*, to the Infallible Witness, Guardian, and Teacher of divine truth. Cf. Murphy, "The Chair of Peter," p. 346 (note).

³⁷ "There would," says Cardinal Manning, "be no such sin as heresy if there were not a divine authority teaching among men; no such sin as schism if there were not a divine law of unity. Heresy would be mere error of opinion, and Schism a lawful freedom of separation if it were not for the divine authority of truth, and the divine law of unity."—"Sermons on Ecclesiastical Subjects," vol. iii., p. 6.

³⁸ Hebr. xi. 6. ³⁹ Mark xvi. 16.

⁴⁰ See Cardinal Newman, "Discourses to Mixed Congregations," Discourse x., *Faith and Private Judgment*, and xi., *Faith and Doubt.* According to the First Helvetic Confession (Protestant), faith is "*certain* and *undoubting*"; and the Second calls it "*the most certain comprehension of the truth of God.*" Cf. Schaff, "Creeds of Christendom," vol. iii., pp. 218, 208. "The Scriptures," writes Dr. Hodge (Protestant), "teach that there is a full assurance of faith; a faith *which precludes the possibility of doubt.* . . . The Apostle declares (Hebs. xi. 1) faith to be an ὑπόστασις and ἔλεγχος, than which no *stronger* terms could be selected to express *assured conviction.* . . . That distinction, therefore, which makes the characteristic of faith to be a measure of confidence greater than opinion, but less than knowledge, *cannot be declared satisfactory.*"—"Systematic Theology," vol. iii., pp. 48-49.

⁴¹ Even in Catholic teaching the authority of the Church, though infallible, is not the formal motive of faith. Cf. Mazzella "De Virt. Inf.," nn. 766, 769-772; and below, pages 177-178.

⁴¹ᵃ Cf. Franzelin, "De Traditione," p. 696. Perrone, "De Locis Theologicis," part iii., n. 95.

⁴² II. Cor. x. 5.

⁴³ Until the reason is *certain* there can be no moral obligation to believe; cf. Cardinal Manning, "The True Story of the Vatican Council," p. 131. Cf. also Perrone. "De Locis Theol," Part iii., n. 94.

⁴⁴ Cf. Mazzella, "De Virt. Inf.," nn. 429, 733, 734, 744, 745, 787, 804, 806, 819, 820; Hurter, "Theol. Gen.," vol. i., nn. 617, 622; Perrone, "De Locis Theol.," part iii., n. 95.

⁴⁵ Hebr. xiii. 8.

⁴⁶ "Its [the Bible's] value must consist entirely in the fact that it faithfully records, in an authentic form, what was actually revealed. It is, then, only as a record that it can be adduced as evidence. But a record is no evidence till *authenticated*. It cannot authenticate itself; for till authenticated, its testimony is inadmissible. *It must be authenticated by some competent authority independent of itself.*"—Brownson's Works, vol. v., p. 353.

⁴⁷ Cf. Cardinal Wiseman's "Lectures on the Principal Doctrines and Practices of the Catholic Church," Lecture ii.

⁴⁸ Contra, Epist. Fundamenti, c. 5.

⁴⁹ "England alone is reputed to contain some *seven hundred sects. Each of them proves a whole system of theology and morals from the Bible.*"— The Times, May 13, 1884. Cf. Allnatt's "The Church and the Sects," Ten Letters, p. 65.

⁵⁰ Conference with Claude, "Irish Ecclesiastical Record," March, 1888, p. 223. "It is proverbial," says Dr. Brownson, "among them [Unitarians] that the Bible is like a fiddle on which a skilful performer *may play any tune he pleases.*—Works, vol., vii., p. 332.

⁵¹ *Nineteenth Century*, February, 1884, p. 190. "*Of all the absurd notions* which ever claimed large sway over the human mind, perhaps the most singular is that a Supreme Being, who for ages had spoken to men by direct communication, or by ministers and prophets having a special gift of His own Spirit, who at the last sent His Son with a message, should, when He recalled that Son, have simply *put the record of all these transactions in a book, and given to none any authoritative power of interpretation.*" —Kegan Paul, "Faith and Unfaith," pp. 27-28.

⁵² It is said that Catholics, in making the Church the Witness and Interpreter of the Bible, put the Church above the Bible. In answer I ask, do Protestants, in making Private Judgment the Interpreter of the Bible, thereby put private judgment above the Bible ? Do the people in electing, or the State in appointing a Judge to interpret and apply the law, thereby put the Judge above the law ? A gentleman hands me what purports to be an official letter from the President of the United States. I am not acquainted with the President's handwriting, and therefore cannot say that the letter is genuine. But I know the bearer to be a thoroughly reliable man, and I take his testimony to the fact of its genuineness. Do I thereby put the authority of the witness above that of the letter in question ? The objection is a silly one, and yet it is commonly urged by Protestants. Even the respectable Faculty of the Union Theological Seminary of New York does not deem it unworthy of notice. "Dr. Briggs," says President Hastings and *confrères*, "does not *with the Romanist* exalt the Church above the Bible."—Statement of the Faculty of the Union Theological Seminary," *New York Sun*, May 16, 1891.

⁵³ "Kritischer Geschichte des Urchristenthumes." B. i., p. 15.

⁵⁴ "History of European Civilization," 12th Lecture.

⁵⁵ Compitum. These (last three) quotations are taken from Hecker's "Aspirations of Nature," pp. 239-240.

⁵⁶ Mr. Mallock, after observing of Protestantism that "*Criticism has*

NOTES TO CHAPTER II.

washed away like sand every vestige of its supernatural foundation," writes as follows of the Catholic Church: "With so singular a firmness and flexibility is her frame knit together, *that none of her modern enemies can get any lasting hold on her, or dismember her or dislocate her limbs on the racks of their criticism.*"—"Is Life Worth Living ?" chap. xii., pp. 308-317.

⁵⁶* Job xvi. 19.

⁵⁷ *Marheineke Symbolik*, p. 705, in Hecker's "Aspirations of Nature," pp. 230-240.

⁵⁸ "Essay on Ranke's "History of the Popes."

⁵⁹ "Is Life Worth Living ?" chap. xii., p. 318. The reader will find in Marshall's "Christian Missions," hundreds of Protestant testimonies, "of all classes and creeds—English and American, German and French, Swedish and Dutch; historians and naturalists, civil and military officials, tourists and merchants, chaplains and missionaries," to prove the truth of this statement. He may also consult an article on "The Great Missionary Failure," in the *Fortnightly Review*, Oct., 1888, by Dr. Isaac Taylor, Protestant Canon of York; also Ranke's "History of the Popes," vol. ii., pp. 228-235.

⁶⁰ *North British Review*, May, 1864, p. 433, quoted in Allnatt's "Which is the True Church?" p. 22, note. It is stated that during the present century England and America alone, omitting Germany, Switzerland, and all Protestant states of modern Europe, had before the year 1862 expended in the work of missions, including the distribution of Bibles and tracts, at least $200,000,000. "Upwards of a million [$5,000,000] sterling," writes Dr. Taylor (*loc. cit.*) "is annually raised in this country [England] for Protestant missions, and probably another million [$5,000,000] in America and on the Continent of Europe. About 6000 European and American missionaries, and some 30,000 native agents are employed. *Clearly there is no lack of men or means.*"—In Allnatt, p. 75.

⁶¹ See below, pp. 197-201.

⁶² *Apologia*, p. 271 (2d ed. 245).

⁶³ "He who follows this guidance is neither entangled in the nets of error nor tossed about on the waves of doubt."—Leo XIII., Encyclical Letter, *Aeterni Patris*, 4. Aug. 1879.

⁶⁴ P.S. iv. 9, 10. ⁶⁵ Appendix A, p. 251.

⁶⁶ Cf. Bossuet's "History of the Variations of the Protestant Churches."
"I have been long and greatly tormented by those thoughts which you describe. I see our people wandering, *the sport of every wind of doctrine. . . . What their opinion on religion may be to-day, you may perchance know; but what it may be to-morrow, you cannot with any certainty affirm.*"—Th. Beza, "Epist. ad Andream Dudit," in Murphy's "The Chair of Peter," p. 288.

⁶⁷ de Wette, in "Tributes of Protestant Writers," etc., by James J. Tracy, p. 226.

⁶⁸ "Is Life Worth Living?" chap. xi., p. 275.

⁶⁹ 1 Tim. iii. 15. ⁷⁰ Eph. iv. 14. ⁷¹ II. Tim. iii. 7.

⁷² "Sailing thus without needle, compass, or rudder on the ocean of human opinions, you can expect nothing but a miserable shipwreck."— St. Francis de Sales, "The Catholic Controversy," p. 329.

⁷³ "The Grounds of Faith," Lecture i., p. 8.

NOTES TO CHAPTER II.

⁷⁴ Essay on Mr. Gladstone's "The State in its Relation with the Church." In a speech delivered at Birmingham at the beginning of the year, the Duke of Norfolk stated that "*within twenty years the number of certified religious faiths had increased from less than 100 to 250 in England.*"— *Liverpool Catholic Times*, January 1. 1891.

⁷⁵ Dr. Ryle, Bishop of Liverpool, Charge, 1888.

⁷⁶ "Authority, or, A Plain Reason for Joining the Church of Rome," by Luke Rivington, M. A. Magdalen College, Oxford, pp. 13-14.

⁷⁷ "Is Life Worth Living?" chap. xi. p. 277. Our esteemed contemporary, the *Churchman* (Episcopalian), refers to the remarkable changes that have been brought about in the faith of the various denominations of Protestantism. It says: 'The Thirty-nine Articles of the Church of England were never obligatory on the laity, and now they are not subscribed even by the clergy of the Church which framed them. The Methodists are no longer rigid in their adherence to the modified form of the Articles which they at first adopted. The Congregationalists have virtually abandoned the Savoy declaration and the Cambridge platform. The Continental churches have all laid aside the formulas set forth at the Reformation. Of the Presbyterian churches some have modified the terms of subscription to the Confession of Faith; in others the Confession has been really replaced by the teachings of dogmatic divines, and in this country the Confession itself is in process of revision.'—*The New York Sun*, June 14, 1891.

⁷⁸ Lecture 14, quoted in Hecker, "Aspirations of Nature," pp. 181-182.

⁷⁹ *Arena*, Nov. 1890.

⁸⁰ November, 1890.

⁸¹ "Essays, Ecclesiastical and Social," p. 99.

⁸² "Notes on the German Catholic Church," p. 145.

⁸³ "Berlin under the New empire," vol. ii., pp. 108-111.

⁸⁴ October, 1880, pp. 530, 539. For the last five quotations I am indebted to Mr. Allnatt's excellent pamphlet, "Which is the True Church ?" pp. 66, 67, 68, 69.

⁸⁵ In Tracy's "Tributes of Protestant Writers," p. 227.

⁸⁶ "Apologia," p. 271 (2d ed. 246). "*A book, after all, cannot make a stand against the wild living intellect of man.*"—*Ibid.* p. 270 (2d ed. 245).

⁸⁷ *Op. cit.*, chap. xi. pp. 279-280.

⁸⁸ M. Mallock, *op. cit.*, c. xi. p. 281.

⁸⁹ *Ibid.*

CHAPTER III.

EIGHTH ARGUMENT : THE DOGMA OF INFALLIBILITY IS A FACT OF REVELATION.

Part I.—The Church.

HAVING proved the *necessity* of Infallibility I might fairly conclude, without further argument, the *fact* or actual existence of such an authority, for what the Goodness and Love of God suggest as likely, what the Wisdom and Justice of God, as well as the needs of the soul call for, what Faith and Reason and conscience demand, that we may reasonably conclude, exists in *fact*. But in this important matter we are not left to mere inference, however natural, legitimate, and necessary. We have ample evidence of the fact; and to this we shall now turn our attention.

And, first, let us see what provision our Divine Lord made for authenticating, protecting, and propagating His revelation. To inform ourselves on the divine economy we have only to turn to the pages of the New Testament, where we find it unfolded with sufficient clearness. The writers of the Gospels tell us that soon after entering on His public ministry, our Divine Lord selected from among His disciples twelve, whom He set apart from the rest. "*And when it was day*," says St. Luke,[1] *he called unto him his disciples: and of them he chose twelve, whom also he named apostles.*" He made these twelve His close attendants and special friends; He trained and instructed them with special care, and made known to them "*all things that I have heard of my Father.*"³ The object of our Divine Lord in all this was to prepare them to be the future pastors of His Church, and the preachers of His Gospel. "*And he ordained twelve, that they should be with him, and that he might send them forth to preach.*"³ Later on we find Him sending forth these twelve to preach and giving them the power of miracles,⁴ and finally, when He is about to leave this world,—just before His Ascension—we read that He committed to them the very Mission He Himself received from the Father, "*As the Father hath sent me, even so send I you.*"⁵ And then solemnly appealing to His supreme power in heaven and in earth,⁶ He gives them the great Commission, and bids them "*Go into all the world,*"⁷ "*and teach all nations, baptizing them in the Name of the Father, and of the Son, and of the Holy Ghost; teaching them to observe all things whatsoever I have commanded you.*"⁸

To secure them against error in interpreting and declaring the divine truths they were commissioned to preach, and thus to provide for the success of their mission our Lord expressly promises to ask the Father to send them *the Spirit of Truth to abide with them forever,*⁹ *and guide them into all truth.*¹⁰ Moreover, He expressly pledged to them His own abiding presence and assistance to the end of time. Go, said He, and teach all nations all things whatsoever I have commanded you; "*and lo, I am with you* *always, even unto the end of the world.*"¹¹ Such are the explicit promises, be it remembered, of Him who emphatically declared, "Heaven and earth shall pass away, *but my words shall not pass away.*"¹²

Finally, He added that all who would hear and receive these apostles would hear and receive Himself; because He had committed to them His Gospel and His Mission, and they would speak in His name, and by His authority, and with His assistance. "He that heareth *you*, heareth *me;* and he that despiseth *you*, despiseth *me;* and he that despiseth *me* despiseth *him* that sent me."¹³

Furthermore, the Apostles were empowered to ordain and receive into the ministry others. Hence we find them after the Ascension electing Mathias to fill the place of Judas, and investing him with the same mission and authority.¹⁴ Paul and Barnabas also are selected and given authority;¹⁵ and these in their turn ordained others for the same ministry.¹⁶

So again St. Paul appoints Timothy Bishop of Ephesus,¹⁷ and Titus Bishop of Crete, with instructions to "*ordain priests in every city.*"¹⁸ He cautions the former to guard carefully "*the deposit*"¹⁹ of the faith, and to commit "*the things which he had heard from himself*" to "*faithful men who shall be fit to teach others.*"²⁰ And he gives both instructions as to the kind of men they were to admit into the ranks of the clergy.²¹

Finally, this living, teaching body or society, incorporated and commissioned by our Divine Lord, was to be perpetual, to continue to the end of time. Our Lord's words were not addressed to the apostles personally or individually; they were addressed to them as a corporate body, as the first representatives of an organization that He designed to last to the consummation of all things. This is evident from the words of two of the texts quoted; for in one He promised that the Spirit of Truth would *abide with them forever;*" and in the other that He Himself would be with them *always, even unto the end of the world.*" Now the Apostles could not live "*forever,*" or "*unto the end of the world,*" except in their successors. Our Divine Lord, therefore, must have addressed them not in their individual, but in their corporate capacity; and, consequently, His words refer not only to them, but to their legitimate successors in the apostolate to the end of time. The very terms, then, of the commission implies the perpetuity not only of the commission but also of the body commissioned.

Besides the object of instituting this living ministry was, as we have seen, to preach the Gospel *to every creature,* to teach, or, as the original has it, to make disciples of *all nations.* Well that work, manifestly, could not be accomplished during the lifetime of the Apostles; and hence St. Paul, a safe interpreter of the Divine Counsels, tells us that "*the ministry of reconciliation*"" instituted by Christ Himself would continue until all would be converted to the true faith. "And he gave some, Apostles; .... and some Pastors and teachers; ... *for the work of the ministry,* for the edifying of the body of Christ (the Church) : *till we all come into the unity of the faith and of the knowledge of the Son of God.*"" Thus the object of our Divine Lord in instituting the ministry of living teachers no less than the express terms of His commission to them prove the perpetuity of that ministry.

The divine economy then, as traced out in the texts I have quoted, is plainly this: The Father sent the Son with the Gospel of Salvation. The Son sent the Apostles, committing to them the mission He had received from the Father with full power to continue the great work He had begun, and to appoint others to assist and succeed them in the ministry. These in turn had the power to appoint others to assist and succeed them, and so on from generation to generation to the consummation of all things.

Not by the means of a book, then, but by the ministry of a perpetual succession of living teachers, guarded and assisted by the Holy Spirit of Truth, did Christ ordain that His Revelation should be authenticated, safeguarded, declared, and propagated in all ages; and thus we have fulfilled the prophecy of Isaias, "*This is my covenant with them, saith the Lord; my Spirit that is in thee* [the Church], *and my words which I have put into thy mouth, shall not depart out of thy mouth nor out of the mouth of thy seed, nor out of the mouth of thy seed's seed, saith the Lord, from henceforth and forever.*" [26]

The ministry of the Church being the means ordained by Christ for teaching men the truths of salvation, the question of the Infallibility of this teaching authority now presents itself for examination, and so we shall direct our attention at once to the Scriptural evidence of this fact.

Let us begin with the words of the divine commission as recorded by St. Mark: "*And he said unto them, Go ye into all the world, and preach the Gospel to every creature. He that believeth and is baptized shall be saved, but he that believeth not shall be damned."* [27]

Here we have two things clearly laid down: an express divine commission to the Church to preach the Gospel to every creature, and an express divine command to every creature to accept the Gospel from the Church under the penalty of losing forever his soul. Now I contend that this divine commission to teach, coupled with the divine command to believe, necessarily implies the concession of Infallibility. For who can suppose that God would formally commission anybody to teach in His name and command all to hear and accept His teaching under the severest of penalties, and at the same time not secure that teacher against the possibility of teaching error for truth? Suppose the Church thus commissioned by God did actually teach error, even then would not all (there is no exception made), by reason of the divine command, be bound to believe? And in that case would not God Himself be accountable for the erroneous belief? I conclude, therefore, that the formal commission to teach the Gospel in God's name, and by His authority, joined to the express command to believe carries with it a pledge of the divine assistance of Infallibility as a guarantee to all men that in yielding the obedience of faith, they are perfectly secure against all danger of error.

From St. Mark we turn to the parallel passage in St. Mathew, and here we receive great light on the subject; for here we have the formal promise of Infallibility united with the divine commission. Let us have our Divine Lord's address in full: "And Jesus came and spake unto them, saying, All power is given unto me in heaven and in earth. Go ye, therefore, and teach all nations, baptizing them in the name of the Father, and of the Son, and of the Holy Ghost; teaching them to observe all things whatsoever I have commanded you; *and lo, I am with you always, even unto the end of the world.*"[28]

To the last sentence in this address I ask the reader's attention; and in reference to it I observe: (1) that the Son of God here promises to the pastors of His Church a special and efficacious assistance in the execution of the great work He had just committed to them; (2) that the promise is of perpetual, abiding assistance; and therefore applies not merely to the Apostles but also to their successors throughout all ages; and (3), that the assistance promised is the supernatural assistance of Infallibility.

(1) That there is a promise of a *special* and *efficacious* assistance follows from the Scriptural use of the expression, "*I am with you.*" This phrase, which occurs about one hundred times in the Bible, invariably implies that God will so assist the person to whom the words are addressed, that the success of the work he undertakes, and to which the words have reference, is assured beyond the possibility of failure.[29]

(2) That the promise is of a *perpetual* assistance, and therefore extends to the legitimate successors of the Apostles in the ministry to the end of time, is clear from the words "*always, even unto the end of the world.*" Besides, the commission to preach and teach and the promise of assistance go together, and as the commission was not personal or confined to the Apos-

tles and their times, so neither was the subjoined promise. The promised assistance, therefore, as well as the office of preaching and teaching, passed on to the successors of the Apostles.

Moreover, the very reasons why the assistance in question was promised urge with greater force its continuance. Surely if the Apostles, taught and commissioned directly by our Lord Himself, needed his special assistance, that assistance is much more necessary to those who, taught and commissioned by men hundreds of years after, are to-day charged with their (the Apostles') office and its responsibilities. And if God promised the apostles his special assistance in preaching the Gospel as a guarantee to the faithful of the unerring truth of their teaching, why should He deny the same guarantee to the faithful of to-day, of whom He demands the same faith and who are at the same time more exposed to error and deception?

(3) The assistance in question is the supernatural assistance of Infallibility. The circumstances of the case go to show that there is question of a singular and extraordinary assistance. The occasion: it was on Ascension Day—the day our Divine Lord was to take leave of His Apostles to go to His Father; the form of the address, opening as it did with a solemn appeal to His supreme power in heaven and on earth; then the formal grant of the great commission to teach all nations all things whatsoever He had commanded; and finally the solemn promise to which He calls attention as something of special importance by the significant word "*lo!*" "behold!" These considerations leave no doubt that our Divine Lord here

promises a singular and extraordinary assistance. It only remains then to determine the nature of that assistance, and this the work He had just committed to the Apostles to execute at once determines. "Go," He says, "and *teach* all nations, and lo, I am with you" (plainly) in that work of *teaching*, and will see that you succeed in its execution. The work then for the success of which the divine assistance was formally pledged was the work of preaching and teaching the Gospel. And as, according to what has already been proved, nothing less than the assistance of Infallibility can guarantee the successful propagation of this work, it follows as a consequence that the special supernatural assistance promised by our Lord to the Apostles and their successors is no other, or at least no less, than that of Infallibility. Moreover, this interpretation of the divine promise receives support from the following reflection: Clearly enough, as commentators remark, our Divine Lord, in the words we are considering, is replying to a difficulty that would naturally occur to the minds of the Apostles on hearing the preceding portion of His address. Not having yet received the Spirit of Pentecost, and therefore being still unenlightened, weak, and carnal, they might well become alarmed and say within themselves: "Master, how can we hope to be able to fulfil so great, so extraordinary a mission? You charge us to teach not one nation but all nations, in fact, every creature; and to teach them not a few truths but the whole Gospel, or as you put it, '*all things whatsoever I have commanded you.*' Now how is it possible for poor, rude, illiterate fishermen, such as we are, to succeed in so great a work when you withdraw, as you are about to do, your presence from us, and we are thus deprived of your divine direction and assistance?" To such thoughts the words, "*and lo, I am with you*" are plainly an answer. They are words of encouragement, intended to allay their fears and assure them that, though they were to lose His visible presence, they would still have His special divine assistance in their work as a guarantee of success. The following paraphrase then of our Lord's words gives us their full meaning: It is true that the mission I have charged you with is one of great magnitude and responsibility; it is true that it calls for the preaching and teaching of the Gospel *in all its purity and integrity* to all nations and peoples; it is also true that you are of yourselves altogether unequal to such a work. But notwithstanding these considerations be not discouraged. Be not disheartened because of its magnitude, or because of your unfitness and inability; or because I am about to withdraw my visible presence from among you. Let not these or any other such thoughts cause you anxiety, for I hereby solemnly pledge myself for your success. "*And lo, I am with you*"; as if He said—*lo! behold! I pledge you beforehand my solemn word, I make you this inviolable promise, I give you this unfailing guarantee*—I will be ever present with you, though invisibly, to direct and assist you in teaching the sacred truths I committed to you."[80] Is not this, I ask, the plain, natural, obvious meaning of the words, "*and lo, I am with you*"? And does not this meaning necessarily imply the prerogative of Infallibility?

But if there should remain any doubt on the mind

as to the truth of this interpretation, we have only to turn to the parallel passages in St. John to have it removed. There we have the meaning of the words, "*and lo, I am with you*" determined beyond all doubt. Our Lord is addressing the Apostles for the last time before His Passion; they are sorrowing and in distress over the fact that He is to be taken from them, and they are to be left orphans. He speaks to them words of comfort and consolation: "*Let not your heart be troubled*" " because I am to leave you, for "I will pray the Father, and he shall give you *another* Comforter" " in my place. "When this Comforter is come" " (on Pentecost) He will "*abide with you forever.*" And not only will He "*abide with you, and be in you,*" " but, being "*the Spirit of Truth,*" " "the Holy Ghost" " Himself, "*he shall* (also) *teach you all things, and bring all things to your remembrance whatsoever I have said unto you.*" ".... "*He will guide you into all truth.*" "

What mind that is not clouded by prejudice can fail to see the doctrine of the Church's Infallibility in these texts? If the Holy Spirit of Truth *abides* with the Church, and if the great object of this abiding presence is to "*teach her all things*" and to *guide her into all truth,*" how can she err? And if she cannot err, is she not Infallible? And once Infallible, always Infallible, for the principle, the source, of Infallibility abides with her "*for ever.*" *

There are other texts which contain the doctrine,

---

* "The Bride of Christ," says St. Cyprian, "can never become an *adulteress;* and the promise of Christ (Math. xxviii. 20) extends to *all days, even to the end of the world.*"—De Unit. Eccl., c. vi.

but after what has been said, a few words on each will suffice. After giving to the Apostles the commission to go and teach all nations, our Divine Lord adds, "He that heareth *you*, heareth *me;* and he that despiseth *you*, despiseth *me.*"⁽³⁹⁾ Here our Divine Lord clearly identifies the voice of the Pastors of His Church with His own,⁽⁴⁰⁾ and gives to all men the explicit assurance that their teaching would have the very same authority as His own, and that, consequently, in hearing and believing it, they would be as secure against error or deception as if it came directly from His own lips. Does not this Divine assurance imply the doctrine of Infallibility? Would the Son of God say that in hearing a Church that was fallible, and therefore may actually be teaching error, we hear Himself, the infallible, immutable, eternal truth? The above text then, I submit, pledges, almost in so many words, the Son of God Himself for the truth of the Church's teaching, and, consequently, binds Him to see to it that she teaches the truth, the whole truth, and nothing but the truth.

"If he neglect to hear the Church *let him be unto thee as an heathen man and a publican.*"⁽⁴¹⁾ Here the Divine Founder of Christianity, in unmistakable terms, ordains that the man who does not hear the Church should be regarded as the heathen and the publican. Now would Christ our Lord use such language, and impose upon all men such an obligation, and under such a penalty, if there was the least danger that the Church could mislead or deceive them?

"And I say also unto thee, that thou art Peter, and upon this rock I will build my Church; *and the gates of hell shall not prevail against it.*"[12] Again have we not here a virtual promise of Infallibility? What can be the meaning of saying that "*the gates of hell*" shall never prevail against the Church, but that she would never fall into heresy or error? And is not that equivalent to saying that she is Infallible? Grant her the prerogative of Infallibility, and you can at once see how the gates of hell can never prevail against her. Deny her Infallibility and how is she to be proof against the assaults of error, heresy and schism, symbolized, according to the common opinion of the Fathers, by "the gates of hell"?

Finally, St. Paul distinctly calls the Church "*the pillar and ground of the truth.*"[13] How would she be worthy of this title if she could deceive or be deceived in propounding the Gospel of Salvation?

This completes the Scriptural evidence for the fact of the Church's Infallibility. That evidence, I claim, proves beyond a reasonable doubt that the Church which Christ instituted and commissioned to teach His Gospel to all nations and in all ages was endowed by Him with the prerogative of Infallibility. And now the only question that remains to be determined is, Which of the many Churches we see around us is that divine and infallible Church of Christ? That the Infallible Church, set up at Pentecost, still exists and is engaged on the great mission committed to her by her Divine Founder, there can be no doubt, unless we are prepared to say that He, who emphatically declared that "Heaven and earth shall pass away, *but my words shall not pass away,*"[14] has failed in His promises, which would be blasphemy.

The Infallible Church then exists. But which of those around us is it? The answer to this question is not far to seek. There is only *one* Church in the world *that claims and ever has claimed by divine right* the prerogative of Infallibility; only *one* Church that has ever been looked upon as Infallible, *and that is the Catholic Church.* Every other Church is, *by its own admission*, fallible.

Part II.—*The Pope.*

Leo XIII. claims to be, by divine right, the successor of St. Peter, to hold his place in the Church, and to possess the same powers and prerogatives. Every one of the long line of Popes claimed a like succession, and no other person on earth has ever made any such claim. Neither does history accord the right of succession to anybody else save to the duly elected Bishop of Rome."[**] To learn, then, what the powers and prerogatives of the Pope are, we have only to find out what St. Peter was in the Apostolic Church by the appointment of Jesus Christ its Divine Founder; and for this purpose we shall consult the pages of the New Testament.

The first mention made of Peter is significant. Andrew, his brother, we are told, "*brought him to Jesus, and when Jesus beheld him, He said, Thou art Simon, the son of Iona; thou shalt be called Cephas, which is by interpretation, Peter*,"[**] which again means a Rock. Change of name had a special significance to the Jews. God gave Abram a new name when He made him *the father of many nations,*" and He changed Jacob into Israel because of His designs in reference to him."⁵ So here God promises to change the name of Simon because of the lot He had in store for him, and gives him the name of Peter, which, as we shall see, is indicative of the position he is to hold in His future Church. "Allusively to the name from the rock," observes St. Cyril of Alexandria (A. D. 424), commenting on the above text (John i. 42), "He changes his name to Peter, *for on him He was about to found His Church.*" " This was Peter's first interview with our Lord; he was not yet called to be a disciple.

Later on, the new and significant name here promised to Simon is conferred on him when our Lord selects, from among His disciples, the twelve Apostles. "And Simon He surnamed *Peter.*" Next we come to the memorable occasion when our Divine Lord explains the full meaning of the name, discloses the office which it symbolizes, and officially announces the position and authority the bearer of it is to hold in the Church. "When Jesus came unto the coasts of Cæsarea Philippi," says St. Mathew, "He asked His disciples, saying, Whom do men say, that I, the Son of man, am? And they said, Some say thou art John the Baptist, some Elias, and others Jeremias, or one of the Prophets. He saith unto them, But whom say ye that I am? *And Simon Peter answered and said,* Thou art Christ the Son of the living God. *And Jesus answered and said unto him, Blessed art thou, Simon Bar-jona:* for flesh and blood hath not revealed it unto thee, but my Father which is in heaven. *And I say also unto thee that thou art Peter, and upon this rock I will build my Church; and the gates of hell shall not prevail against it. And I will give unto thee the keys of the kingdom of heaven; and whatsoever thou shalt bind on earth shall be bound in heaven; whatsoever thou shalt loose on earth shall be loosed in heaven.*" [10]

Let us dwell for a moment on this remarkable address. Previous to its delivery our Lord, according to St. Luke,[11] retired to a lonely place to pray, a practice which we learn from the sacred narrative was customary with Him before undertaking a work of special importance. *As he was alone praying,* He asks His disciples the question "Whom do men say that I, the Son of man, am?" They answer that the people are of different opinions, none of which is right. He then puts the question to themselves, "Whom say *ye* that I am?" All are questioned, but only one answers. "*And Simon Peter answered and said,* Thou art Christ the Son of the living God." Hereupon our Lord pronounces Simon Bar-jona *blessed,* because the Father in Heaven had revealed to him His Divinity, and then proceeds to reward him in a singular way for his confession. "*And I say also unto thee.*" Observe the force and solemnity of these words. There is clearly some signal honor, some singular distinction in store for Simon, to whom *alone* our Divine Lord now distinctly addresses Himself. "*And I say also unto thee,*" that is, Simon, you have made a noble confession of My Divinity, and now I, in return for that confession—I who have the power to do all things—make known to you the dignity and office which I will one day confer on you. Thou art

Peter, that is rock, and upon this rock—the name I have given you—I, as Divine Architect, will build *My* Church, and the gates of hell, that is all the powers of error, sin, and Satan, shall not prevail against it. And to thee whom I will make the rock-foundation of My Church, I, as Supreme Lord and Master, will give the keys of the kingdom of heaven, the symbol of Supreme Authority; and whatsoever, in virtue of that Supreme Authority, you shall bind upon earth shall be bound in heaven; and whatsoever you shall loose upon earth shall be loosed in heaven. In other words you shall receive and hold from Me supreme power to guide and govern *My* Church, and every exercise of that power shall be ratified in heaven. This is the plain meaning of our Lord's address.

"*Thou art Peter, and upon this rock I will build My Church.*" Here our Lord plainly reveals the reason why He had given Simon the name of Peter. He was to be to the Church what the firmest of foundations is to the house built on it; he was to support it and be the principle of its unity, strength, and stability.

In the Aramaic or Syro-Chaldaic," the popular Hebrew dialect spoken by our Divine Lord, for "Peter" and "rock" there is but *one* word, viz., Cepha, which means a *rock;* so the text runs thus in the original, Thou art *Cepha*, and on this *Cepha* I will build My Church; and literally translated into English, "Thou art a Rock and on this Rock I will build My Church." Formerly the exigencies of controversy drove Protestants to deny the identity of Peter and rock," but modern commentators generally have abandoned this position as untenable." Some even acknowledge that this text is decisive in favor of the Primacy of St. Peter among the Apostles."

"*And upon this rock I will build My Church, and the gates of hell shall not prevail against it.*" The Omnipotent Architect promises to build His Church on Peter," as upon a rock, and *because*, or *in consequence* of the unity, strength, and stability which it will derive from its rock-foundation, He declares that it will be perfectly secure against the assaults of its most powerful and determined enemies."

"*And I will give unto thee the keys of the kingdom of heaven.*" Here we have a new image drawn from the relation of the Lord to his household and servants. "What," asks Father Bernard Vaughan, "was the obvious and natural meaning of this second part of the passage? In the first part our Lord had spoken of Himself as an Architect, and had compared His Church to a house; now He speaks as a King, and His Church he compares to a kingdom, and He declares that the King will give to Peter the keys of this kingdom. The obvious and natural meaning of all this was that Peter was to be the King's viceroy or vicar over His kingdom, for even in domestic life the tradition of the key of a house meant the house was in the possession of the holder of the key. Again, at the coronation of a Sovereign, the presentation of the keys of the City to him by the Chief Magistrate meant that the Sovereign was to be regarded as having the supremacy over the City. *And so our Lord, who has supreme authority over the Church, by promising to commit the keys of it to Peter, sig-*

nified His intention of investing him with Supremacy under Him of His Church upon earth."⁵⁸

"Keys are, according to all usage, sacred and profane, a symbol of power, administrative, judicial, and legislative: *Clavis* signum est curæ et administrationis, necnon potestatis in ordinando gubernandoque statu totius familiæ" (Rosenmüller)."⁹

"*And whatsoever thou shalt bind on earth shall be bound in heaven; whatsoever thou shalt loose on earth shall be loosed in heaven.*" Between this and the preceding part of the text there is the difference that exists between the *possession* of authority and its *exercise;* between holding the keys and using them. "*It is one thing to exercise authority in a house, and a very different thing to hold the keys thereof.*"⁶⁰ The power here promised to Peter is unlimited (*whatsoever*),⁶¹ and it is a power over the Universal Church (My Church),—the Kingdom of Christ on Earth.

The next most striking instance of the pre-eminence Peter received from our blessed Lord is found in St. Luke. The occasion was the last supper. Our Lord is addressing the whole Apostolic body, when all at once He directs His attention to Peter personally, and speaks to him solely as *Chief* or *Head*. "And the Lord said, Simon, Simon, behold, Satan hath desired to have *you* (ὑμᾶς, *all of you*) that he may sift you as wheat; but I have prayed for *thee* (σοῦ, *thee, Peter, in particular*) *that thy faith fail not.*"⁶² Here our Divine Lord foretells that the faith of *all* would be tried; but though all would be subjected to temptation, yet it is for Peter's faith, and for Peter's faith *alone*, He prays. "But I have prayed for thee that *thy* faith fail not." Who does not see here the pre-eminence of Peter in the mind of our Lord? What more natural interpretation of our Lord's words than that of St. Leo the Great, in the fifth century? "The danger from the temptation of fear was common to all the Apostles, and they equally needed the help of Divine protection, since the devil desired to dismay, to make a wreck of all; and yet the Lord takes care of Peter in particular, and prays specially for the faith of Peter, as if the state of the others would be more sure if the mind of their prince were not conquered. *In Peter*, the fortitude of all, and the help of Divine Grace is so ordered, that the firmness which through Christ is given to Peter may *through Peter* be conferred on the Apostles."[63] St. Francis de Sales beautifully illustrates the meaning of the text: "The gardener who sees the young plant exposed to the continual rays of the sun, and wishes to preserve it from the drought which threatens it, does not pour water on each branch, but having well steeped the root, considers that all the rest is safe, because the root continues to distribute the moisture to the rest of the plant. Our Lord also having planted this holy assembly of the disciples, prayed for the head and the root, in order that the water of faith might not fail to him *who was therewith to supply all the rest, and in order that through the head the faith might always be preserved in the Church.*"[64]

"And thou being once converted," continues our blessed Lord, "*confirm thy brethren.*"[65] Here Peter is distinguished from the others as *confirmer* from the *confirmed*, and the reason why our Lord prayed for him specially is given: for having secured the indefectibility of Peter's faith, He forthwith appoints him the guardian of the faith of the other Apostles, and, therefore, of all "*which shall believe on Me through their word.*" ⁶⁵* Surely, here we have the primacy of faith conferred on Peter. St. Crysostom says that by the words "And thou being converted, confirm thy brethren," Christ "*put all in his hands.*" ⁶⁶ "Peter," says St. Ambrose, "after having been tempted by the devil, *is set over the Church.*" ⁶⁷

"'Confirm thy brethren,' — that is," says St. Cyril of Alexandria, "*become the support and teacher of those who come to me by faith.*" ⁶⁸ "He prays for Peter," says St. Francis de Sales, "as for the confirmer and support of the others; *and what is this but to declare him head of the others?* Truly one could not give St. Peter the command to confirm the Apostles without charging him to have care of them." ⁶⁹

We now pass on to the occasion when our Divine Lord, before His Ascension, formally appoints Peter to take His place on earth, and be to His Apostles and the Church what He himself was to them during His public ministry. "So when they had dined, Jesus saith to Simon Peter, Simon, son of Jonas, lovest thou me more than these? He saith unto him, Yea, Lord, thou knowest that I love thee. He saith unto him, *Feed my lambs.* He saith unto him again the second time, Simon, son of Jonas, lovest thou me? He saith unto him, Yea, Lord, thou knowest that I love thee. He saith unto him, *Feed my sheep.* He said unto him the third time, Simon, son of Jonas, lovest thou me? Peter was grieved because he said unto him the third time, Lovest thou me? And he said unto him, Lord, thou knowest that I love thee. Jesus saith unto him, *Feed my sheep.*"⁷⁰ In other words our Lord here fulfils His promise⁷¹ to Peter by solemnly installing him His chief representative on earth,—Supreme Pastor and Ruler of His Church. "Three times was the question put,—as though a triple profession of love was to repair the triple denial. As in reward of Simon Peter's public profession of faith in the Divinity of his His Master,"⁷² Christ had publicly promised him the Supremacy over His Church, so now in reward for Simon Peter's profession of love of Him, Christ publicly invests him with that Supremacy promised on the former occasion. As before our Lord had spoken as an Architect and then as King, so now He speaks as the 'Good Shepherd,'"⁷³ and He compares His Church to a flock made up of lambs and sheep. Simon Peter is to be, under the 'Prince of Shepherds,'"⁷⁴ the one shepherd commissioned to feed both lambs and sheep. What meant that commission? It meant that Peter was to have the *Supremacy*. It meant that laity and clergy were to be fed upon the Word of Faith by Peter; it meant what in ancient classics, what in the Old and what in the New Testament it obviously meant,—jurisdiction and authority."⁷⁵ "To the whole Church," says Dr. Döllinger, "to the Apostles was given a *Supreme Pastor, one taking the place of our Lord, a Head to rule all.*"⁷⁶

"*Feed my lambs.*" "*Feed my sheep.*" In the original there are two different words for "feed." In the first and third places we have βόσκε, and in the second ποίμαινε, which has a wider signification and means not merely *feed*, but *have charge of, rule over*, *govern*," as a shepherd does his flock. "The unrestricted commission," says Cardinal Wiseman,[18] "to feed the entire flock of Christ implies a primacy and jurisdiction over the whole. For the commission to feed is a commission *to govern and direct*. In the oldest classics, such as Homer, whose imagery approaches the nearest to that of Scripture, kings and chieftains are distinguished by the title of 'shepherds of the people' (ποιμένες λαῶν). In the Old Testament the same idea perpetually occurs, especially when speaking of David, and contrasting his early occupation of watching his father's flocks with his subsequent appointment to rule over God's people."[59] It is a favorite image with the prophets to describe the rule of the Messiah, and of God over His chosen people, after it should be restored to favor."[60] And our Blessed Redeemer Himself adopts it when speaking of the connection between Him and His disciples,— His sheep that hear His voice and follow Him."[61] In the writings of the Apostles we find at every step the same idea. St. Peter calls Christ 'the Prince of Shepherds,'[62] and tells the clergy to *feed* the flock which is among them;[63] and St. Paul warns the bishops whom he had assembled at Ephesus, that they had been put over their flocks by the Holy Ghost, to '*rule* the Church of God.'"[64] "This term, 'of feeding, as a shepherd feeds his flock,'" says the Protestant Arnold, "is one of the oldest and most universal metaphors to express a *supreme*, and at the same time a beneficent *government*."[65]

Finally, it is to be noticed that Peter received the commission to feed not only the *lambs*, but also the *sheep*,—not only the faithful, but also "those who are to the faithful as sheep to lambs, their parents in Christ,"[86] "the pastors and Apostles themselves, who, as sheep, nourish the lambs and young sheep, and are mothers to them."[87]

The many references made to Peter in the sacred writings, and the many incidents recorded in connection with his name, now become perfectly intelligible and full of meaning. We now understand why it is that Peter receives such prominence from the sacred writers; why he figures so conspicuously among the other Apostles, and so often acts as their leader and mouthpiece; why our Divine Lord so closely associates him with Himself, and so often honors him above the others by various tokens of distinction. Thus, to come to the facts, in the New Testament we have four complete lists of the Apostles,[88] and in all four Peter is placed first, while the order in which the others are named, with the exception of Judas, who, on account of his treason, is always placed last, varies considerably. St. Matthew simply calls him "the first," that is, the captain, the leader, the chief[89] of all. "*The first Simon who is called Peter.*" "1. Not first in mere numerical order; for then we should have the corresponding ordinals, *second, third,* etc. . . . 2. Nor first by *calling;* for it appears from John i. 40-42, that Andrew was called before Peter (and brought him to Christ). 3. Nor first in *age,* a meaning that is unexampled, and there is strong reason to believe that Peter was younger than Andrew; but first in dignity and authority—in *dignity;* the word πρῶτος requires, at least, so much; and in authority, because the explanatory clause, 'who is called Peter,' gives the reason why Simon was styled *first,* that is, *because* he was made and called *Peter* the *Rock* (*Petra*) of the Church (John i. 42; Math. xvi. 18)."[90] "*First*, says he, *Peter* and Andrew. From this is derived the name of Primacy. For if he were first (*primus*), his place was first, his rank first, and this quality of his was *Primacy*." "It is answered to this," continues St. Francis de Sales whom I am quoting, "that if the Evangelists here named Peter the first, it was because he was the most advanced in age among the Apostles. . . . But what is the worth of such a reason as this, I should like to know? To say that Peter was the oldest of the society is *to seek at hazard an excuse for obstinacy;* and the Scripture distinctly tells us that he was not the earliest Apostle when it testifies that St. Andrew led him to our Lord. The reasons are seen quite clearly in the Scripture, *but because you are resolved to maintain the contrary*, you go seeking about with your imagination on every side. Why say that Peter was the oldest, since it is a pure fancy, which has no foundation in the Scripture, and is contrary to the ancients? Why not say, rather, that he was the one on whom Christ founded His Church, to whom He had given the keys of the kingdom of heaven, who was the confirmer of the brethren?—*for all this is in the Scripture*. What you want to maintain you do maintain; whether it has a base in Scripture or not makes no difference."[91]

Again, when only some of the Apostles are mentioned with Peter, he invariably gets the most honored,—the first place. Thus, when three witness the raising of the daughter of Jairus to life, the order is, "*Peter*, and James, and John";[92] and when the same

THE DOGMA OF INFALLIBILITY? 109

three are privileged to witness the Transfiguration, the record reads: "Jesus taketh unto him *Peter*, and James, and John."[95] So again in the history of the Agony in the Garden, Peter is one of the witnesses of that tragic event and is named first: "And he taketh with him *Peter*, and James, and John."[96]

Again, while the others are often mentioned in a body, Peter is expressly mentioned by name to mark the difference in rank between him and the others. Thus: "*Simon*, and they that were with him";[95] "*Peter*, and they that were with him";[96] (they) "said unto *Peter*, and to the rest of the Apostles."[97] The form of expression we have here is not applied to any other of the Apostles; it is clearly an expression that denotes superiority,[98] and in this sense we find the Evangelists using it in the case of David and his attendants,[99] and of our Lord and His disciples.[100]

Again, a constant practice with the sacred writers, in narrating anything which concerns all the Apostles, is to represent Peter as speaking and acting for all. Thus when our Lord puts to all the question: "But whom say ye that I am?"[101] it is Peter who answers: "And *Simon Peter* answered and said."[102] He speaks to all of how difficult it is for a rich man to enter into the kingdom of heaven; and again Peter alone speaks: "Then answered *Peter* and said unto him, Behold, *we* have forsaken all, and followed thee, what shall *we* have therefore?"[103] And again, "When Jesus said unto the twelve, Will you also go away?" all save Peter are silent. "Then *Simon Peter* answered him, Lord, to whom shall *we* go?"[104]

The next incident is a remarkable one: "And when they were come to Capernaum, they that received tribute money came to *Peter*, and said, Doth not your Master pay tribute? He saith, Yes. And when he had come into the house, Jesus prevented him, saying, What thinkest *thou*, *Simon?* Of whom do the kings of the earth take custom or tribute? Of their own children, or of strangers? *Peter* saith unto him, Of strangers. Jesus saith unto *him*, Then are the children free. Notwithstanding lest we should offend them, go *thou* to the sea and cast an hook, and take up the fish that first cometh up: and when *thou* hast opened his mouth, *thou* shalt find a piece of money: that take and give unto them for *Me*, and *thee.*"[105] Here you will observe: (1) the taxgatherers address themselves to *Peter* rather than to any of the other Apostles. Why?[106] (2) Our Lord singles out Peter and asks him *alone* for his opinion; and (3) He orders Peter to pay the piece of money not for Himself and all the others, but for Himself and for *Peter:* " Give unto them for *Me*, and *thee.*"[107] Can any one fail to see the very marked manner in which our Lord associates Peter with Himself on this occasion? Assume Peter to be the Chief,—the Leader, and the action of our Lord and of the taxgatherers is most natural,—just what would be expected.[108]

After His Resurrection our Lord shows special concern to have that fact made known to Peter. "Go," says the angel to Mary Magdalen and her companions, " tell His disciples and *Peter.*"[109] He appears to *Peter* first among the Apostles,[110] and to *Peter* alone He foretells his martyrdom.[111]

Once more the frequent recurrence of Peter's name in the pages of the sacred narrative cannot fail to impress the thoughtful reader. " In the whole New

Testament," observes Mr. Allies, "John, who is yet mentioned oftener than the rest, occurs only thirty-eight times; but in the Gospels alone Peter is mentioned *twenty-three* times by Mathew, *eighteen* by Mark, *twenty* by Luke, and *thirty* by John."[112]

After the Ascension, Peter, "without debate, without election, without a formal organization of the Apostolic College," openly takes the lead, and unmistakably acts the Pope in the new-born Church. Of this the Acts of the Apostles supply abundant evidence.

This history may be divided into two parts; the first part, embracing the first twelve chapters, gives the labors of the Apostles in common: the second part, beginning with Chapter XIII., and continuing to the end, is little more than the history of St. Paul, and of the churches founded by him.

Now taking the first part and examining it, what do we find? In these twelve chapters of general history, Peter's name is mentioned more than *twice* as many times as all the others put together. His name occurs *fifty-three* times, while the names of all the others occur only twenty-three times. St. John's name, the next most frequent, occurs only *twelve* times, and that of St. James, the Bishop of Jerusalem, the birthplace of the Church, only *twice*. In a history which professes to record the acts of all the Apostles, this fact, surely, is not without meaning. Then, as was already noted, Peter gets the place of honor whenever he is mentioned with all or any of the others. He is expressly mentioned while the others are mentioned only in a body; he is represented as the mouthpiece of the others; his discourses, his miracles, the number of his converts, his various acts, are carefully noted, while little is said of the others. Hence, as Mr. Allies justly remarks, as the Gospels may be called the history of Christ, so these twelve chapters of the Acts may be called the history of Peter. The position of Peter in the Acts is similar to that of Christ in the Gospels. What Christ was to the Apostolic body while on earth that Peter was after His Ascension.

But to review, briefly, the evidence: The first exercise of Peter's authority is found in the election of a successor to Judas in the Apostolic College. Here he takes the initiative. Rising in the midst of his brethren and addressing them in a tone of authority, he lays down the rules that are to govern the election. "*And in those days Peter stood up in the midst of the disciples and said . . . . Men and brethren, this Scripture must needs have been fulfilled, etc.*"[113] Then, after referring to the treachery and fate of Judas, he defines the circle from which his successor *must* be chosen. "Wherefore of these men which have companied with us all the time that the Lord Jesus went in and out among us, beginning from the baptism of John, unto that same day that he was taken up from us, *must* one be ordained to be a witness with us of His Resurrection."[114]

Next we find Peter, as Head, defending the body against the charge of intemperance. "These men (the Apostles)," charged the Jews, "are full of new wine," whereupon Peter, we are told, rose up and rebuked the calumny. "But *Peter*, standing up with the eleven, lifted up his voice, and said unto them, Ye men of Judæa, and all ye that dwell at Jerusalem, be

THE DOGMA OF INFALLIBILITY? 113

this known unto you and harken to my words: for these men are not drunken, as ye suppose."[115]

Peter is the *first* to preach the Gospel, and instruct the people in the doctrine of the Resurrection.[116] His hearers, struck with compunction for the terrible crime they had committed, " said unto Peter, and the rest of the Apostles, Men and brethren, what shall we do?" The question is put to all, but Peter alone speaks, and authoritatively lays down the law. " Then *Peter* said unto them, Repent and be baptized every one of you in the Name of Jesus Christ."[117] The result of his first sermon is that 3000 are converted to the faith.[118] He preaches a second time and 5000 are converted through his word.[119] He speaks a third and a fourth time, and so far the others had not opened their mouths. Now, let me ask, Why should Peter monopolize the instruction of the people at the outset? and why does St. Luke go so much into detail about him and no other? Is not the answer plain? Because Peter was appointed by our Lord the Supreme Teacher of the new Revelation.

Peter works the *first* miracle, and full particulars of this[120] and two others[121] are given, while the miracles worked by the others are barely referred to.[122] It is Peter who singly pronounces the *first* excommunication, cutting off from the Church Simon Magus, the first heretic.[123] He it is who publicly reproves Ananias and Saphira for lying to him and to the Holy Ghost;[124] he it is who *first* announces Christ before the Sanhedrim,[125] and he it is who makes the *first* visitation of the churches.[126] " Primate, Peter appears in everything: the first to confess the faith, the first to declare his love, the first of the Apostles to see the risen

Lord, the first to witness to Him before the people, the first to confirm the faith by a miracle, the first to convert the Jews, the first to admit the Gentiles, the first everywhere."[127]

The faithful, clearly, recognized the superiority and pre-eminence of Peter, for we are told "that they brought forth the sick into the streets and laid them on beds and couches, that at the least the shadow of *Peter* passing by might overshadow some of them."[128] And—most significant incident—when Peter is cast into prison we are expressly told that "prayer was made without ceasing of the Church unto God for him."[129] The significance of this incident will appear from the following observations: In the same chapter, immediately preceding, it is recorded that James, the brother of John, whom our Lord, it will be remembered, specially favored, was put to death by Herod. In this case there is not a word about any sorrow or concern on the part of the Church. All that is said is simply: "Now about that time, Herod the king, stretched forth his hands to vex certain of the Church. And he killed James the brother of John with the sword."[130] This is all the notice James's martyrdom receives. Now observe the striking contrast: Peter is taken and cast into prison; and what happens? Immediately the Church is filled with anxiety, and the faithful pour forth their hearts in prayer for his safety. "Peter, therefore, was kept in prison, "but *prayer was made without ceasing of the Church unto God for him.*"[131] Observe how the instinct of self-preservation moves the Church to implore the divine protection for her Head!

A few years later the great Apostle of the Gentiles

St. Paul, who "*labored more abundantly than they all,*"[112] was apprehended and cast into prison in the same city, and his life was in momentary danger. Yet we do not read that the Church showed any great anxiety about him, or that she offered up unceasing prayer for his deliverance. And why? Because the Church's safety was not bound up with his, as in the case of Peter, the rock on which it was founded, and from which it derived its firmness and stability.

Two more instances of the exercise of Peter's Supremacy, and we shall have done with the Scriptural evidence on the subject. One is to be found in the call of the Gentiles; the other in the Council of Jerusalem. Both are important.

God's design to call the Gentiles to the faith is kept a secret until after the Ascension; and then it is disclosed to Peter, and to him alone, to be carried into effect. The history of this great event is recorded in the tenth Chapter of the Acts.

Almighty God, we are told, sent an Angel to a certain good and holy man, named Cornelius, with directions that he would "send men to Joppa and call for one Simon, *whose surname is Peter.*"[113] "*He shall tell thee what thou oughtest to do.*"[114] Observe though God sends an Angel, He reserves for Simon, surnamed Peter, the office of declaring His will in regard to the salvation of the Gentiles. As the messengers of Cornelius were nearing the house at which Peter was a guest, we learn that he had a vision in which a voice spoke to him and instructed him that henceforth certain Mosaic observances should be abolished. "While Peter thought on the vision, the Spirit said unto him, Behold, three men seek thee.

Arise therefore, and get thee down, and go with them doubting nothing; for I have sent them."[135] Peter went down to see the messengers, inquired of them the object of their mission, and, learning that Cornelius wanted to see him, he set out with them the next day. On meeting Cornelius he asked him why he had sent for him. Cornelius at once related to him the conversation of the Angel, and concluded thus: "Now therefore are we all here present before God, to hear all things that are commanded *thee* of God."[136] Peter then opening his mouth explained to them the Gospel revelation, and while he was yet speaking "the Holy Ghost fell on all them which heard the word."[137] The Jewish converts who came with him express wonder "because that on the Gentiles also was poured out the gift of the Holy Ghost."[138] Whereupon Peter, in a tone of undoubted authority,[139] asks, "*Can any man forbid water, that these should be baptized which have received the Holy Ghost, as well as we?*"[140] and forthwith "*he commanded them to be baptized in the Name of the Lord.*"[141] How clearly does not this history point to the pre-eminence of Peter! God has a great purpose to be revealed. It is the fulfilment of the "Good Shepherd's" prophecy: "Other sheep I have that are not of this fold: them also I must bring . . . . and there shall be *one* fold and *one* shepherd."[142] And the duty of announcing to the world and *to the Apostles themselves* the divine purpose, and of actually receiving into the Church the first Gentile converts, is committed to Peter. And why? Because he had been appointed the Supreme Pastor on earth of the Church, the Shepherd of Christ's fold.

The action of Peter in the first council of the Church, is perhaps the most convincing point in the Scriptural evidence of the exercise of the Primacy. The council was held in Jerusalem in the nineteenth year after the Resurrection, and about the fifty-first of the common era; and its history is recorded in Chapter XV. of the Acts. There we read that a bitter controversy arose at Antioch as to whether the Gentile converts should submit to circumcision and the other observances of the Mosaic law. Paul and Barnabas having failed to settle the matter in dispute, it was determined that they "and certain other of them, should go up to Jerusalem unto the Apostles and elders about this question."[143] At Jerusalem "the Apostles and elders came together for to consider of this matter."[144] After the question is fully discussed by the Council, Peter, we are told, rose and delivered judgment, in which all acquiesced without a murmur. "And when there had been much disputing, *Peter rose up and said unto them*, etc."[145] If Peter were not acknowledged the Supreme Arbiter in the case, why are we told that he rose up rather than any of the others,—rather than, for instance, James, in whose Diocese the Council was held, and whose place it would be to deliver judgment, if Peter was not his Superior? In his address Peter reminds his hearers that God made choice of him to make known the Gospel to the Gentiles and receive them into the Church;[146] and that He made no distinction between Jew and Gentile in the matter of salvation.[147] Then, using the words of authority, he definitively pronounces judgment on the subject of the controversy. "*Now, therefore, why tempt ye God to put a yoke upon the neck of the disciples*, which neither our fathers nor we were able to bear?"[140] How does the Council receive this strong language? Without one word of dissent or remonstrance. Though "there had been *much disputing*,"[149] though the controversy had aroused strong passions, and involved a question of the greatest importance in the eyes of the Jewish converts, yet we read that "all the multitude (the whole assembly) kept silence.[150] It was a case of *Roma locuta est; causa finita est*. Who does not see the Pope here in the very first Council of the Church? Did Pius IX. claim more authority in the Vatican Council?[151]

St. Francis de Sales sums up the Scriptural evidence for the Primacy thus: "Whoever will read the Scriptures attentively will see this Primacy of S. Peter *everywhere*. If the Church is compared to a building, as it is, *its rock and its secondary foundation is S. Peter* (Math. xvi.). If you say it is like a family, it is only our Lord who pays tribute as head of the household, *and after Him S. Peter, as his lieutenant (Ib.* xvii.). If to a ship, *S. Peter is its captain*, and in it our Lord teaches (Luke v.). If to a fishery, *S. Peter* is the *first* in it; the true disciples of our Lord fish only with *him (Ib.* and John xxi.). If to draw nets (Math. xiii.), it is *Peter* who casts them into the sea, *S. Peter* who draws them; the other disciples are his coadjutors. It is *S. Peter* who brings them to land and presents the fish to our Lord (Luke v., John xxi.). Do you say it is like an embassy?— *S. Peter* is the *first* ambassador (Math. x.). Do you say it is a brotherhood?—*S. Peter* is the *first*, the *governor* and *confirmer* of the rest (Luke xxii.). Would you rather have it a kingdom?—*S. Peter* receives its *keys* (Math. xvi.). Will you consider it a flock or fold of sheep and lambs?—*S. Peter* is its *pastor* and *shepherd-general* (John xxi.) *Say now in conscience how could our Lord testify his intention more distinctly.* Perversity cannot find use for its eyes amid such light. . . . But let us continue. When our Lord ascends to heaven, all the holy Apostolic body goes to *S. Peter*, as to the *common father* of the family (Acts i.). *S. Peter* rises up among them and speaks the *first*, and teaches the interpretation of weighty prophecy (*Ib.*) *He* has the *first* care of the restoration and increase of the Apostolic College (*Ib.*) It is *he* who *first* proposes to make an Apostle, which is no act of light authority. . . . The Apostles have no sooner received the Holy Ghost than *S. Peter*, as *chief* of the Evangelical Embassy, being with his eleven companions, begins to publish, *according to his office*, the holy tidings of salvation to the Jews in Jerusalem. *He* is the *first* catechist of the Church, the preacher of penance; the others are with him and are all asked questions, but *S. Peter alone* answers for all as *chief* of all (Acts ii.). If a hand is to be put into the treasury of miracles confided to the Church, though S. John is present and is asked, *S. Peter alone* puts in his hand (*Ib.* iii.). When the time comes for beginning the use of the spiritual sword of the Church, to punish a lie, it is *S. Peter* who directs the *first* blow upon Ananias and Saphira (*Ib.* v.). . . . *He* is the *first* who recognizes and refutes heresy in Simon Magus (*Ib.* viii.). . . . *He* is the *first* who raises the dead, and he prays for the devout Tabitha (*Ib.* ix.). When it is time to put the sickle into the harvest of paganism, it is *S. Peter* to whom the revelation is made, as the *head* of all the laborers, and the *steward* of the farmstead (*Ib.* x.). The good Italian centurion, Cornelius, is ready to receive the grace of the Gospel; he is sent to *S. Peter*, that the Gentiles may by *his* hands be blessed and consecrated; *he* is the *first* in commanding the pagans to be baptized (Acts x.). When a General Council is sitting, *S. Peter* as *President* therein opens the gate to judgment and definition; and *his* sentence is followed by the rest (*Ib.* xv.). . . . S. Paul declares that he went to Jerusalem expressly to see *Peter* and stayed with him fifteen days (Gal. i.). He saw S. James there, but to see him was not what he went for,— *only to see S. Peter.* What does this signify? Why did he not go as much to see the great and most celebrated Apostle, S. James, as to see S. Peter? Because we look at people in their head and face, and *S. Peter* was the *head* of all the Apostles. When S. Peter and S. James were in prison the Evangelist testifies that *prayer was made without ceasing by the Church to God for S. Peter* as for *the general head and common ruler* (Acts xii.). If all this put together does not make you acknowledge S. Peter to be the head of the Church and of the Apostles, I confess that Apostles are not Apostles, pastors are not pastors, and doctors not doctors, *for in what other more express words could be made known the authority of an Apostle and pastor over the people than those which the Holy Ghost has placed in the Scriptures to show that Peter was above Apostles, pastors, and the whole Church."* [143]

There are a few objections urged against the supremacy of St. Peter, and based on texts of Scripture, which it may be well to consider here before entering on the question of the Pope's Infallibility.

"*Other foundation*," says St. Paul,[163] "can no man lay than that is laid, which is *Jesus Christ.*" Therefore Christ, not Peter, is the foundation of the Church. To this we answer that Christ, to be sure, is the foundation of the Church; but that does not prevent St. Peter also being its foundation. Christ is the *primary*, St. Peter the *secondary* foundation, so made by Christ Himself. St. Leo the Great well explains the relation of Christ and Peter as foundations of the Church in a paraphrase of our Lord's words.[164] He had in mind clearly the objection and the words of St. Paul on which it is based. "As my Father has manifested my divinity to thee," says St. Leo, "I make known to thee thy excellencies; for thou art Peter, that is, as I am the inviolable Rock, who maketh both one, I the foundation, other than which no one can lay; nevertheless, thou also art a Rock, because thou art strengthened by my power, so that those things which belong to me by *nature* are common to thee with me by *participation.*"[165] That St. Paul did not mean to exclude such a relation on the part of St. Peter to the Church is plain from the fact that he says, elsewhere, that the Church is built on "the foundation of the Apostles and Prophets."[166]

There was nothing given to Peter that was not afterwards given to the rest. If Peter was made the foundation of the Church, so were the others.[167] If Peter received the power of binding and loosing, so did the others.¹⁵⁸ If Peter received universal jurisdiction—jurisdiction over the entire world—so did the others.¹⁵⁹ Peter therefore was not superior in authority.

In answer I observe (1), that whatever the Apostles received, Peter, as one of the body, shared, for "nothing passed unto any one else without his participation in it."¹⁶⁰ (2) That whatever the others received they received in a body, of which Peter was a member, and therefore in union with Peter; whereas, what Peter received he received singly,—*alone*. (3) It is true that whatever power Peter possessed, the whole body of the Apostles possessed, inasmuch as it included Peter, just as it is true to say that the whole Episcopate of the Catholic Church possesses all the powers and prerogatives of the Pope because it includes the Pope. But, as in the latter case, it does not follow that every member of the Episcopal body has the same authority as the Pope; so neither does it follow in the former case that every one of the Apostolic body had the same authority as Peter. (4) It is not true to say that Peter received nothing that was not afterwards given to all. For (*a*) Peter *alone* received a new name, and that, as we have seen, so significant; (*b*) Peter *alone* was made the *petra ecclesiæ*,—the Rock of the Church; (*c*) Peter *alone* received the keys, the symbol of supreme authority; (*d*) Peter *alone* received the office of confirming his brethren; (*e*) Peter *alone* received the commission to feed the lambs and sheep,—to shepherd the whole flock. There was just one promise made to Peter that was afterwards made to all, Peter included; that was the promise of binding and loosing.

But in reference to this I ask, Is there nothing meant by first bestowing this power on Peter *singly?*[1] No greater, no higher degree of this power imparted? "It was, then," remarks Bossuet, "clearly the design of Jesus Christ to put first in one alone, what afterwards He meant to put in several; but the sequence does not reverse the beginning, nor does the first lose his place. That first word, 'Whatsoever thou shalt bind,' said to one alone, has already ranged under his power each one of those to whom shall be said, 'Whatsoever ye shall remit'; for the promises of Jesus Christ, as well as His gifts, are without repentance; and what is once given definitely and universally, is irrevocable: besides, power given to several carries its *restrictions* in its *division*, whilst power given to one alone, and over all, and without exception, carries with it *plenitude;* and, not having to be divided with any other, it has no bounds save those which its terms convey."[102]

And now to the proofs of the objection. The Apostles were not made the foundation of the Church; for it is not said that it was built on the Apostles, but on the foundation of the Apostles,"[103] *i. e.*, on the doctrine they preached. This is clear from the fact that it is said to be built also on the foundation of "the prophets,"[104] who were the foundation of the Church only by their doctrine. A comparison with Chapter IV., 11-14, makes it plain that there is question of doctrine. So in the Apocalypse the twelve are called foundations[105] of the heavenly Jerusalem, because they were the first to convert the world by their preaching, and thus, as it were, lay the foundations of Christianity. But Peter was not merely made the *foundation;* he was made the *rock* of the Church,— the support even of the foundation; for the universal Church (*My* Church), and therefore the Apostles themselves, was built on him. The two metaphors differ very materially. The metaphor of the *Rock* points to the support of the entire building; it involves the idea of firmness, strength, and stability, and implies that the rock will communicate these qualities to the superstructure raised upon it. This is plain from what follows: "and the gates of hell shall not prevail against it"; and especially from Math. vii. 24-25, where our Lord Himself explains the import of the metaphor. On the other hand, the metaphor of the foundation necessarily implies no more than the beginning of anything, and thus aptly typifies the relation of the Apostles to the Church, who were its beginning and the first preachers of its Gospel. As *Apostle*, then, Peter with the rest was the foundation of the Church; but as *Primate* he was, moreover, the *Rock* whose office was to sustain the foundation or corner-stones of the superstructure as well as the others.

It is true that the Apostles, like Peter, had universal jurisdiction; but in them it was extraordinary and subordinate, while in him it was ordinary and supreme. They received it in *union* with him, to be exercised in subordination to his authority."[188]

Peter's prerogative was no other than that of being the first to open the gates of the Church and receive into it the first converts—Jews and Gentiles. The Church, for this reason, may be said to take its rise and spring from him, and in this sense he was the rock of the Church.

Would our Lord have changed Simon's name to Rock and said "Upon this rock I will build my Church" if He meant nothing more than the objection contends for? What propriety would there be in calling the first preacher of Christianity, in any country, the rock on which the Church of that country was founded? "Had our blessed Saviour said, 'Thou shalt *lay* the foundation of my Church,' this sense might have been given to His words. But is there no difference between such a phrase and 'Thou shalt be the rock on which I will build it'? In other words, can this figure imply nothing more than that he should give a beginning to the edifice; that he should lay the first stone? Would any one give to another the name of a *rock* to signify *this* relationship between him and a building? Is there no idea of stability, of durability, of firmness, conveyed by the name, but only one of simple commencement?"[167]

Had the Apostles known that Peter had, or was to have, any supremacy over them by reason of the promises contained in Matthew (xvi. 18-19), they would not have disputed among themselves as to who was the *greatest*.[168]

On this objection I have four remarks to make: (1) The dispute referred to does not necessarily imply that the Apostles were not aware of the Primacy. (2) Even if they did not understand our Lord's words to Peter to contain a promise of the Primacy, it could not be justly inferred that therefore there was no Primacy; for we know that before the descent of the Holy Spirit—and He had not yet come—they were slow of apprehension. Our Blessed Lord repeatedly refers to their dulness of understanding,[169] and when He spoke of His Passion,[170] though His meaning seemed to be quite clear, yet we read that "they understood not this saying."[171] There would be nothing then to be wondered at, if they did not understand the promises concerning the Primacy. But, (3) the context would seem to point to the fact that they did know of the Primacy, for they do not ask our Divine Lord "Will there be a *greater?*" but, "Who is the greater?"[172] They saw that Peter was often honored by our Lord, and specially so in the incident of the tribute which had just taken place. From this they inferred his Supremacy; and to settle the matter they asked the question, "Who is the greatest (greater)?" "'In that hour,'" says St. Chrysostom, "when He had honored him (Peter) above all. For of James, too, and John, one was a first-born, *but no such thing had he done for them.* They being ashamed to acknowledge the feeling which they experienced, they do not say, indeed, openly, On what account hast thou honored Peter above us? and, Is he greater than we are? for they were ashamed; but they ask indefinitely, Who, then, is greater? For when they saw the three honored[173] above them they suffered nothing of this kind, but because this matter of honor had come round to one, then they were vexed. And not this only, but putting together many other things, that feeling was kindled. For to him also He had said, 'To thee will I give the keys,' and 'Blessed art thou, Simon Barjona,' and here 'give to them for Me and thee.'"[174] And (4) our Lord, it will be observed, in His answer to their question, does not deny that there was or would be a "greater"; but rather, taking that for

THE DOGMA OF INFALLIBILITY? 127

certain, goes on to say how that greater, that chief and leader (ἡγούμενος) should act,—what his character should be."[5]

"*Now when the Apostles, which were at Jerusalem heard that Samaria had received the Word of God, they sent unto them Peter and John.*"[6] The sender is not inferior in authority to the sent; but here Peter is sent by the other Apostles; therefore the other Apostles were not inferior in authority to Peter.

I observe, in reply, that it by no means follows as a necessary consequence that because Peter was here sent by the other Apostles, therefore he was not their Superior. In the Book of Joshua we read that "the children of Israel *sent* unto the children of Ruben.... Phenehas, the son of Eleazar, the priest, and with him ten *princes*, of each chief house *a prince* throughout all the tribes of Israel; and each one was *an head* of the house of their fathers among the thousands of Israel."[7] Were not the sent here superior to the senders? Again it is related in the Acts[8] that the faithful of Antioch "*determined* that Paul and Barnabas .... should go up to Jerusalem, etc." Were not Paul and Barnabas superior to the faithful who sent them? Josephus[9] relates that the Jews living in Jerusalem, in order to settle some differences between themselves and Agrippa, *sent* their *High Priest*, Ismael, to Rome to Nero; and St. Ignatius[10] tells us that the Churches *sent* their *Bishops*. Was not the High Priest, and were not the Bishops, superior to those who sent them? It is not true, then, to say that the sent is never superior to the sender. "The sender who sends as having authority to send in such a manner that the sent is not free not to obey; such a sender is not inferior to the sent; but the sender who cannot call for obedience may be inferior to the sent, over whom he is not in authority. Peter was sent because, being *Superior*, he was considered the fittest adversary against an opponent like Simon Magus, especially when aided by the eloquence of 'the disciple whom Jesus loved.'"[181]

"*When Peter was come to Antioch I withstood him to the face, because he was to be blamed.*"[182] Were Peter his Superior, Paul would not have acted thus.

On this I observe—(1) That there are commentators[183] who maintain that the Peter or Cephas here referred to was not the Apostle, but another of the same name, who was one of the seventy disciples. (2) That fraternal correction is a christian duty binding on all, even on inferiors in regard to superiors: and therefore if one should exercise this office of charity towards another it does not necessarily follow that the latter is inferior in authority to the former. (3) That the incident rather proves than disproves the Primacy of Peter: for why did Paul withstand him *to the face* and *before all?* and why is the incident considered worthy of special notice? Simply because of the high position and authority of Peter, whose example, therefore, would be more calculated to influence and mislead others. "Though St. Peter," says Bossuet, "was imitated in his conduct by St. James, St. Paul did not blame St. James, but he blamed St. Peter, *because the government of the Church was confided to him.*"[184] (4) That there was question of a matter of conduct, not of doctrine; for what was the reason for Paul's resistance?

Peter had already admitted the Gentiles into the Church, and had declared that converts were no longer bound to live according to the Jewish observances. On this occasion he was enjoying the company of the Gentile converts, and eating with them, when suddenly, on learning of the arrival of some Jewish converts from Jerusalem, out of consideration for their prejudices against the Gentiles and all association with them, and to avoid giving them offence, he withdrew from the company of the latter. Paul, the special Apostle of the Gentiles, seeing that Peter's conduct was inconsistent with the great principle of Gospel liberty he himself had shortly before maintained at the Council of Jerusalem, and fearing the evil influence which his example might have, publicly protested against his action, which he afterwards characterizes as *dissimulation*. "Paul reproved Peter," says Tertullian, "for no other reason, however, than change of his mode of living, which he varied according to the class of persons with whom he associated, not for any *corruption of divine truth.*"[185] And again he says, "If Peter was blamed, *certainly it was for a fault of conduct, not of preaching.*"[186] (4) That the Fathers of the Church saw nothing in this incident prejudicial to Peter's authority, while the humility with which he bore Paul's rebuke calls forth their admiration. "Peter," remarks St. Augustine,[187] "received with the piety of a *holy and benighted humility* what was with advantage done by Paul in the freedom of charity. And so he gave to posterity a rarer and holier example that they should not disdain, if perchance they left the right track, to be *corrected even by their youngers*, than Paul, that *inferiors* might confidently venture to resist *superiors* maintaining brotherly charity in the defence of evangelical truth." And St. Jerome,[188] "If any one thinks that Paul really withstood the Apostle Peter, and for the truth of the Gospel intrepidly did an injury to one that was *over him*, this will not stand for him, that Paul also himself was made a Jew to the Jews, and will be held guilty of the *same dissimulation*." "Behold," cries St. Gregory the Great,[189] "he is reproved by his *inferior*, and he does not disdain to receive the reproof: he does not remind him, *that he has received the keys of the kingdom of heaven*." "Peter," says the same St. Gregory,[190] "was silent, that he who was *first in Apostolic dignity* might be first in humility." (5) That the very epistle from which this objection is taken shows that St. Paul acknowledged the Supremacy of St. Peter. "Then after three years I went up to Jerusalem *to see Peter*, and abode with *him* fifteen days. But other of the Apostles saw I none, save James, the Lord's brother."[191] Now why does St. Paul go to Jerusalem specially to see Peter and none other? Why does he so speak of the others as if he had no anxiety to see them, but only Peter? The Greek and Latin Fathers, commenting on the text, tell us that the reason was that St. Paul acknowledged Peter's Primacy, and therefore felt bound to visit him, and testify to his respect for his office, just as at the present day bishops go from all parts of the world to Rome to visit the Pope. "He (Peter)," says St. Chrysostom, "was chosen one of the Apostles, and the mouth of the disciples, and the leader of the choir. *On this account*, Paul also went upon a time to see him rather than the others."¹⁹² And again, "He (St. Paul), who was so disposed with respect to all, knew *how great a prerogative Peter ought to enjoy*, and reverenced him most of all men, and was disposed towards him as he deserved. *And this is a proof.* The whole earth was looking to Paul; there rested on his spirit the solicitude for the Churches of all the world. A thousand matters engaged him every day; he was besieged with appointments, commands, corrections, counsels, exhortations, teachings, the administration of endless business; *yet giving up* all these, *he went to Jerusalem*. And there was no other occasion for his journey save to see Peter, as he himself says: 'I went up to Jerusalem to see'¹⁹³ Peter.' *Thus he honored him and placed him before all men.*" "Paul," says St. Jerome, "came to see Peter. . . . *to pay honor to the Primate of the Apostles.*"

Peter's Primacy was one of honor, not of authority or jurisdiction; he was simply *primus inter pares*. In reply, we answer a mere Primacy of honor would give Peter no right or title to speak and act for all as he so often did. Did he then assume to himself a right to which he had no claim? And did the other Apostles, who knew him to be only their equal, silently allow so presumptuous a usurpation on his part?

Our Divine Lord, as we have seen, made him the Rock of the Church, the Bearer of the Keys, the Confirmer of his brethren, the Shepherd of His flock. Were these all empty titles? and are we to believe that He, who was so much opposed to mere pomp and display, gave nothing more, and that his words meant nothing more? To ask the question is to solve at once the difficulty.

Lastly, it is said, that the supremacy we claim for the Pope is derogatory to the authority and headship of Christ over the Church. To meet this difficulty, it is merely necessary to ask,—Is the authority of a viceroy derogatory to the sovereignty of the King who appoints him? A King, an Emperor, sends a plenipotentiary into the Council of Nations with the fullest powers to act in his name; would the unlimited powers of such a representative be derogatory to the sovereignty of his master? Then why should the supremacy of Peter, of the Pope, be derogatory to the power of Christ? He is Christ's plenipotentiary, he is His viceroy, His vicar on earth, acting in His name and by virtue of His own divine institution.

The Primacy of Peter with all its powers and prerogatives passed on to his successors in the See of Rome. "The image of a foundation presents the idea of permanent support, since no fabric can subsist if the foundation be removed; the kingdom of Christ must always have a ruler, bearing the keys, and exercising sovereign power under Christ; the brethren must always be confirmed in faith; the lambs and sheep of Christ at all times need the care, guidance, and protection of a shepherd, to keep them all in one sheepfold. Since the powers of hell cannot prevail against the Church, the fundamental authority of Peter can never cease: since the visible kingdom of Christ shall endure to the end of time, there must be always a viceroy governing in His name: since the prayer of Christ is always heard for His reverence, the faith of Peter can never fail: there shall be always one fold, and there shall be likewise one shepherd."¹⁰⁴ "Say not, think not," says Bossuet, "that this ministry of Peter terminates with him; that which is to serve for support to an eternal Church can never have an end. Peter will live in his successors, Peter will always speak in his chair. That is what the Fathers say. That is what six hundred and thirty bishops at the Council of Chalcedon (A. D. 451) confirm."¹⁰⁵ "And in truth," says St. Francis de Sales, "all the reasons for which our Lord put a head to this body (the Church) do not so much require that it should be there in the beginning when the Apostles who governed the Church were holy, humble, charitable lovers of unity and concord, as in the progress and continuation thereof, when charity having now grown cold, each one loves himself, no one will obey the word of another, nor submit to discipline.

"I ask you," he continues, "if the Apostles whose understanding the Holy Spirit enlightened so immediately, who were so steadfast and so strong, needed a confirmer and pastor as the form and visible maintenance of their union, and of the union of the Church, how much more now has the Church need of one, when there are so many infirmities and weaknesses in the members of the Church? And if the wills of the Apostles, so closely united in charity, had need of an exterior bond in the authority of a head, how much more afterwards when charity has grown so cold is there need of a visible authority and ruler? And if, as St. Jerome says, in the time of the Apostles, 'one is chosen from amongst all, in order that a head being established, occasion of schism may be taken away,'¹⁰⁶ how much more now, for the same reason, must there be a chief in the Church? The fold of our Lord is to last till the consummation of the world, in visible unity: the unity then of eternal government must remain in it, and nobody has authority to change the form of administration save our Lord who established it."[197]

I will add one more testimony on this head; it is that of a Protestant,—the great Leibnitz. To him the Primacy and its perpetuity was a plain necessity; and that it was held by the Bishop of Rome as successor of St. Peter he did not doubt. "Since, therefore, our merciful and sovereign God has established His Church on earth, as a sacred *'city placed upon a mountain,'* His immaculate spouse, and the interpreter of His will,—and has so earnestly commended the universal maintenance of her unity in the bonds of love, and has commanded that she should be heard by all who would not be esteemed *'as the heathen and the publican'*; it follows that He must have appointed some mode by which the will of the Church, the interpreter of the Divine Will, could be known. What this mode is, was pointed out by the Apostles, who, in the beginning, represented the body of the Church. For at the Council which was held in Jerusalem, in explaining their opinion, they use the words, *'It hath seemed good to the Holy Ghost and to us.'* Nor did this *privilege of the assistance of the Holy Ghost cease in the Church with the death of the Apostles;* it is to endure *'to the consummation of the world,'* and has been propagated throughout the whole body of the Church by the Bishops, as successors of the Apostles. Now as, from the impossibility of the Bishops frequently leaving the people over whom they are placed, it is not possible to hold a council continually, or even frequently, while at the same time the person of the Church must always live and subsist, in order that its will may be ascertained, it was a *necessary* consequence, by the Divine law itself, *insinuated* in Christ's most memorable words to Peter (when he committed to him specially the keys of the kingdom of heaven), as well as when he thrice emphatically commanded him to '*feed His sheep,*' and *uniformly believed* in the Church, that *one among the Apostles, and the successor of this one among the bishops, was invested with pre-eminent power;* in order that by him, as the visible centre of unity, the body of the Church might be bound together; the common necessities be provided for; a council, if necessary, be convoked, and when convoked, directed; and that, *in the interval between councils,* provision might be made lest the commonwealth of the faithful sustain any injury. And as the ancients *unanimously attest* that the Apostle Peter governed the Church, suffered martyrdom, and appointed his successor, in the City of Rome, the capital of the world; and as *no other bishop has ever been recognized under this relation, we justly acknowledge the Bishop of Rome to be the chief of all the rest.* This, at least, therefore, must be held as certain, that in all things which do not admit the delay necessary for the convocation of a general council, the power of the chief of the Bishops, or Sovereign Pontiff, is, during the interval, the same as that of the whole Church. *We are to obey the Sovereign Pontiff as the only vicar of Christ on earth.*"[108]

The last point of our thesis is: The Pope is Infallible; and now for the proof of this proposition. For all who admit the Infallibility of the Church, the Infallibility of the Pope is a logical necessity. This is plain. The Church is infallible; and the Church, in the exercise of her Infallibility, has defined and declared the Pope to be infallible. Consequently the Infallibility of the Pope is unquestionable.

Moreover, what would an Infallible Church with a fallible Pope mean? An Infallible body with a fallible head and mouthpiece,—an absurdity. Suppose for a moment the Pope were fallible; that means that he may err in teaching the Universal Church. Suppose, further, that he does actually teach error, what would follow? This—the Church would be obliged to accept his false teaching, or reject his authority; that is, she would cease to be Infallible or cease to be subject to her Supreme Head; she necessarily, then, errs or rebels,—falls into heresy or into schism, and (in either case) the gates of hell prevail against her contrary to the explicit promise of Him whose word shall never pass away. The Infallibility of the Pope, then, is necessarily implied in the very idea of an infallible Church subject to him, as its Supreme Head, in matters of faith.

But to come to the Scriptural evidence of this truth. Math. xvi. 18, was adduced to prove the Infallibility of the Church. "And I say also unto thee, that thou art Peter, and upon this rock I will build my Church; *and the gates of hell shall not prevail against it.*" From these words it is plain that the reason why the gates of hell can never prevail against the Church is because she is built on Peter.'"

Therefore, if the Divine promise that the gates of hell shall not prevail against her, implies the Infallibility of the Church, it also and necessarily implies the Infallibility of Peter, her divinely laid foundation. For if they could prevail against the rock-foundation, how could the superstructure be proof against them? The firmness and stability of a building can be no greater than that of the foundation on which it rests for support.

What was implied in Matthew is explicitly promised in Luke. "And the Lord said, Simon, Simon, behold, Satan hath desired to have you (*all*), that he may sift you as wheat; but I have prayed for *thee* (Peter), that thy faith fail not; and when thou art converted, confirm thy brethren."[200] Our blessed Lord, as is plain from the context, speaks of trials of faith to which all the Apostles alike would be exposed. Against the danger to their faith arising from such trials and common to all, He, as is also plain, proposes to safeguard them; and how does he do this? Simply by making Peter, whom he had already chosen to be the Rock of His Church and the Key-Bearer of His kingdom, infallible in faith, and then charging him to confirm the faith of the others. All this is clear from the texts quoted: (1) All were to be tried: "Behold, Satan hath desired to have you (ὑμᾶς, *all of you*). (2) Though all were equally exposed to danger, yet our Lord does not pray for all or for the Church, but directly, expressly, and specifically for Peter: "But I have prayed for thee (σοῦ, *thee in particular*). Not that He had no concern for the others who were equally in need of protection; but, as the Fathers[201] explain the text, because by securing the faith of the Head He thereby made ample provision for that of the body. (3) The object of our Lord's prayer is the indefectibility or Infallibility of Peter's faith: "I have prayed for thee that *thy faith fail not.*" (4) Our Lord prays for the Infallibility of Peter's faith *because* He was to commit to him, as Chief or Leader, the office of confirming the others in the faith. "And when thou art converted,"[202] *confirm thy brethren.*" The prerogative of Infallibility, then, was not *personal*, but *official*. It was bestowed on Peter, not for his own benefit, but for the benefit of the Church which was to be built on him as its foundation, and over which he was to be placed as Supreme Pastor. Consequently, it was to pass on with his office to his successors, and continue to be their prerogative as long as there were brethren to be confirmed in the faith. Dr. Döllinger, commenting on this text, once wrote: "The See of Peter was to remain a place of truth, *a citadel of firm faith*, conducing to the strength of all; for the words, as well as the prayers, of our Lord were addressed not merely to the individual person, and for the immediate moment, but were meant to lay an *enduring* foundation; their significance was, above all, *for the Church*, and for her *future* needs beheld by Christ in spirit."[203]

"So when they had dined, Jesus saith to Simon Peter: Simon, son of Jonas, lovest thou Me more than these? He saith unto him, Yea, Lord, thou knowest that I love thee. He saith unto him, *Feed my lambs.* He saith to him again the second time, Simon, son of Jonas, lovest thou me? He saith unto him, Yea, Lord, thou knowest that I love thee. He saith unto him, *Feed my sheep.* He said unto him the third time, Simon, son of Jonas, lovest thou me? Peter was grieved, because he said unto him the third time, Lovest thou me? And he said unto him, Lord, thou knowest all things; thou knowest that I love thee. Jesus saith unto him, *Feed my sheep.*"[204] Here our Lord, as we have seen, formally committed to Peter the office of Pastor of His whole flock,—lambs and sheep, people and pastors alike. Now would our divine Lord intrust the care of the flock "which he hath purchased with his own blood,"[205] to one who would be liable to lead them into, and feed them on, the poisonous pastures of error? Is it not clear, on the one hand, that His love for His lambs and sheep provided them with a Shepherd who would, beyond the possibility of failure, feed them on the sound doctrines of the true faith? And, on the other hand, is it not equally clear, that any man, to be equal to the duties of the great charge here committed to Peter by the "Prince of Shepherds," requires a special unfailing divine assistance? "St. John xxi, 15-17, 'Feed my lambs, feed my sheep.' Christ, who calls Himself the Good Shepherd (St. John x. 11), appoints St. Peter to be His representative as Shepherd of His whole flock, of His lambs, and of His sheep. The Shepherd must guard His flock from destruction; he must protect it from the wolf that goeth about in sheep's clothing—that is, from false teachers (St. Math. vii. 15); he must lead it into good pastures, and must maintain it in unity of faith. . . . But unless the word of the Shepherd were infallible, *it would be impossible to accomplish the charge and obligation undertaken as Vicar of Christ.*"[206] "The word 'to feed' obviously means," remarks Cardinal Manning, "to feed with the word of God, which is the food of the soul. But how shall he feed the Universal Church with this pasture of life if he cannot discern what is food and what is poison—if instead of bread he be liable to give not only a stone, but the virus of falsehood?"[207].

NOTES TO CHAPTER III.

¹ VI. 18. See also Math. x. 1.
² John xv. 15.
³ Mark iii. 14.
⁴ Math. x. 1-8; Mark ix. 1-2; Luke vi. 7.
⁵ John xx. 21. See also xvii. 18.
⁶ Math. xxviii., 18.
⁷ Mark xvi. 15.
⁸ Math. xxviii. 19, 20. See also Acts i. 8; ix. 15.
⁹ John xiv. 16, 17. See also xv. 26.
¹⁰ John xvi. 13. See also xiv. 26; Luke xxiv. 49; Acts ii. 1-4; 1 Peter i. 12.
¹¹ Math. xxviii. 20.
¹² Math. xxiv. 35; Mark xiii. 31.
¹³ Luke x. 16; Math. x. 15, 16. Believers in "The Bible and the Bible only" would do well to reflect on these texts, and to ask themselves whether they can point to any as clear and as cogent in support of their theory. The texts quoted above clearly show that our Divine Lord was deeply interested in the Church and in its pastors. He gave an express commission to the pastors of the Church to preach His gospel to all nations. Did He anywhere give this commission to the Bible? Did he appoint it to be the organ of His Revelation, the means of propagating its teaching? To the pastors of His Church He said, he that hears *you* hears *me*. Did He anywhere say anything like this of the Bible? Did he constitute it His mouthpiece? He said expressly that he who did not "*hear the Church*" should be regarded as a heathen and a Publican (Math. xviii. 17). Did He anywhere say that he who did not *hear the Bible* should be regarded in the same light?
¹⁴ Acts i. 26.
¹⁵ Acts xiii. 2-4.
¹⁶ Acts xiv. 22.
¹⁷ I Tim. i. 3.
¹⁸ Titus i. 5.
¹⁹ II. Tim. i. 14.
²⁰ II. Tim. ii. 20.
²¹ I. Tim. chap. iii., and Titus, chap. i.
²² John xiv. 16.
²³ Math. xxviii. 20.
²⁴ II. Cor. v. 18.
²⁵ Eph. iv. 11-13.

NOTES TO CHAPTER III.

[26] Chap. lix. 21.

[27] Chap. xvi. 15, 16. There is no *vicious* circle involved in this argument, as is frequently charged. We do not make the Bible prove the infallible authority of the Church, and then turn to the Church to establish the authority of the Bible. In the above argument we abstract altogether from the inspiration and divine authority of the Bible and use it merely as a historical narrative, whose trustworthiness (at least in the parts quoted) can be proved in the same way as that of any other history, sacred or profane. We get our argument, then, for the institution, mission, and authority of the Church from the Bible as a mere human record of the sayings and doings of our Divine Lord and His Apostles. And having thus established the Church's authority, we then take its infallible testimony to the divinity and inspiration of the Bible. In this there is no circle, for in both cases the Bible is taken, not in the same, but in different senses; in the first case it is used as a historical document, *of no more than human authority;* in the second case it is taken to mean *the inspired* word of God. Cf. Cardinal Wiseman's "Lectures on the Principal Doctrines of the Church," Lecture iii. But while we use this argument from the Bible to prove the Church's divine and infallible authority, let not the reader conclude that the Church depends on or needs the support of the Bible. The Bible, it must be remembered, is not the charter of the Church. The Church with its constitution, mission, powers, and prerogatives, came directly and immediately from God, and not from the Bible. We know as a matter of history that the Church was founded, had received its commission, and was actually engaged in the work of teaching and converting the world *years before a single word of the New Testament was written.*

The Church entered on its mission on Pentecost; the first part of the New Testament, St Mathew's Gospel, was not written for seven or eight years after; and the last part, the Apocalypse of St. John, was not added until above sixty years after. The Church, therefore, being antecedent to the Bible, at least to that portion of it of which there is question—the New Testament—it can in no way be dependent on it. Those who say, as the New York *Sun*, in discussing the case of Professor Briggs, has lately said, that "the personality of God, Adam and Eve, and the fall of man, the atonement, the scheme of redemption by the crucifixion of God's Son, *and the divine establishment of the Church* are the mere imagings of men if they are not facts and truths declared by God himself, *through the inspiration of the Scriptures,*" would do well to note this important fact. To such we say, with St. Irenæus (A.D. 135-202): "*And supposing that the Apostles had left us nothing in writing,* should we not follow the rule of doctrine *which they delivered to those to whom they entrusted the churches?* Advers Haeres, l. iii. c. 4.

[28] Math. xxviii. 18-20.

[29] "Now what," asks Cardinal Wiseman, "is the meaning in Scripture of 'God's being with any person.' It signifies a more special providence in regard of that individual than is manifested towards others—a particular watchfulness on the part of God over his interests, in such a way *that what he undertakes shall infallibly succeed.* This is the signification

NOTES TO CHAPTER III.

which this phrase always bears in Scripture."—"Lectures on the Principal Doctrines and Practices of the Catholic Church," Lecture iv., where he proves his statement from a number of texts.

³⁰ "On examining the practice of Scripture we find that when God gives a commission of peculiar difficulty, one which to those that receive it must appear almost, nay entirely, beyond man's power, He assures them that it can and will be fulfilled, by adding, at the end of the commission, 'I will be with you.' As if He would thereby say, 'The success of your commission is quite secure *because I will give my special assistance for its perfect* fulfilment."—Cardinal Wiseman, *ibid.*, where he adduces in proof Gen. xl. 3, 4; Exodus iii. 11, 12; Jerem. i. 17, 19.

³¹ John xiv. 1.
³² *Ibid.* V. 16.
³³ xv. 26.
³⁴ xiv. 16.
³⁵ xiv. 16; xv. 26.
³⁶ xiv. 26.
³⁷ *Ibid.*
³⁸ xvi. 13.
³⁹ Luke x. 16.—Compare Math. x. 40; John xiii. 20; Thess. iv. 8.
⁴⁰ "How," asks Cardinal Manning, commenting on this text, "should these things be true, or, rather, how should not these words *be most illusory and false*, if the perpetual living voice of the Church in all ages were not identified with the voice of Jesus Christ?"—"Temporal Mission of the Holy Ghost," chap. l., p. 81.
⁴¹ Math. xviii. 17.
⁴² Math. xvi. 18.
⁴³ 1 Tim. iii. 15. To evade the force of the argument for the Church's infallibility drawn from this text, some Protestant controversialists refer the words, "the pillar and ground of the truth," to "the mystery of Godliness," (v. 16,); while others refer them to Timothy. Of the former interpretation, Bloomfield, a Protestant commentator, says that it lies open to *insuperable objections*, as stated by Poole, Benson, and Scott." "The "Speaker's Commentary" calls it "an interpretation which, if not positively ungrammatical, is singularly harsh, obscure, and feeble." And of the latter interpretation this same authority says that it "could scarcely be borne by the Greek, and is little in harmony with the context." "In this sentence thus arranged and understood," writes Dean Alford, "there are weighty and, I conceive, *fatal objections.*" "The natural connection of the words," writes Bloomfield, "is certainly *not*, as some imagine, to Timothy, for that would be an *utter violation of the construction*, and involve somewhat of an incongruity.... There can be no doubt that the true reference is to ἥτις ἐστὶν ἐκκλέσια (*which is the Church*, etc.), as was maintained *by almost all the ancient* expositors, and many eminent Protestant commentators, as Grotius, Bishop Hall, Calvin, Hammond, Gothofred, Weber, Schmid, Dayling, Whitby, MacKnight, and Bishop Van Mildert; and of the recent expositors, Dr. Peile; and of the foreign, Wiesing, Huther, and Mack, who understand it of the *Church Universal*, administered under an external form of government, and which, *by main-*

taining the revelation of God and His religion, upholds it as a foundation does a building, or as pillars support an edifice. . . . Any other mode of explanation is, both philologically and otherwise, quite untenable." Wiesinger and Bengel acknowledge that, until the 16th century, all commentators refer the words to the Church.

⁴⁴ Math. xxiv. 35; Mark xiii. 31.

⁴⁵ "Never was it said, either *certainly* or *doubtfully*, of any bishop in the first five hundred years, that he was head or superior over the rest, except of the *Bishop of Rome*. About him, indeed, it was never doubted, but was held as *settled* that he was such."—St. Francis de Sales, "The Catholic Controversy," p. 284. The limits of this work do not allow me to enter into the proof of this statement, nor do I deem it necessary to do so, for the fact is undeniable. A few non-Catholic testimonies, then, will suffice.

"If anything," says Dr. Nevin, a former President of Marshall College, Mercersburg, Pa.—"If anything in the world can be said to be *historically* clear, it is the fact that, with the close of the fourth century and the coming in of the fifth, *the Primacy of the Roman See was admitted and acknowledged in all parts of the Christian world.*" And this universally acknowledged Primacy of the Roman See was not a Primacy merely of *honor;* it was a primacy of *jurisdiction*, a Supremacy. For this writer goes on to say: "Examples of the actual exercise of *supreme power* on the part of the Popes, in the fourth and fifth centuries, are so frequent and numerous, that *nothing short of the most wilful obstinacy* can pretend to treat them as of no account. In every great question of the time, whether rising in the East or in the West, *all eyes show themselves ever ready to turn towards the Cathedra Petri, as the last resort for* counsel and adjudication; all controversies, either in the way of appeal, or complaint, or for the ratification of decisions given in other quarters, are made to come directly or indirectly, in the end, before this tribunal, and reach their final and conclusive settlement only through its intervention. The Popes, in these cases, take it for granted themselves, that the power which they exercise belongs to them of right, *in virtue of the prerogative of their See;* there is no appearance whatever of *effort* or of *usurpation* in the part they allow themselves to act; it seems to fall to them as naturally as the functions of a magistrate or judge in any case are felt to go along with the offices to which they belong. And the *whole world apparently regards the Primacy in the same way, as a thing of course, a matter fully settled and established* in the constitution of the Christian Church. *We hear of no objection to it, no protest against it, as a new and daring presumption, or as a departure from the earlier order of Christianity.* The whole nature of the case implies, as strongly as any historical conditions and relations well could, that this precisely, and no other order, had been handed down from a time *beyond which no memory of man to the contrary then reached.*"—"Early Christianity," *Mercersberg Review*, Sept. 1851, in Kenrick's "The Primacy of the Apostolic See," pp. 148, 155.

"The opinion of the Roman See's *supremacy*," says Hallam, "seems to have prevailed very much in the fourth century. Fleury brings *remarkable* proofs of this from the writings of Socrates, Sozomen, Ammianus,

Marcellinus, and Optatus."—"Middle Ages," chap. vii., p. 270; see also note to this chapter (vii.).

"At the commencement of the fifth century," writes Dean Milman, "*the lineal descent of the Pope from St. Peter was an accredited tenet of Christianity.*"—"History of Latin Christianity," book ii., ch. i., vol. i "Before the end of the third century," says the same author, "the lineal descent of her [Rome's] Bishops from St. Peter *was unhesitatingly claimed, and obsequiously admitted by the Christian world.*"—"History of Early Christianity," vol. iii., p. 370. And again, he admits that "Cyprian [Bishop of Carthage from A. D. 248-257] *acknowledged the hereditary descent of the Roman Bishop from the great Apostle.*"—"Hist. of Latin Christ.," b. ii., c. 4., p. 248, vol. i. And that "the succession of the Bishop of Rome from St. Peter was now, near 200 years after his death, *an accredited tradition.*"—*Ibid.* b. 1, c. 1, p. 66.

The Church historian, Neander, tells us that "Optatus of Milevis, who wrote in the last half of the fourth century, represents the Apostle Peter as the head of the Apostles—as representative of the unity of the Church and of the Apostolic power, who had received the Keys of the kingdom *for the purpose of giving them to others.* . . In the Roman Church he perceives *the indestructible Cathedra Petri. This stood in the same relation to the other Episcopal Churches as the Apostle Peter stood to the rest of the Apostles.* The Roman Church represents the one Visible Church, the one Episcopate," vol. iii., pp. 236-237. "*It is impossible to doubt,*" continues this author, "*as to what the Popes, even as early as the fifth century, believed themselves to be, or would fain be, in relation to the rest of the Church, after having once listened to the language which they themselves hold on the subject.*—*Ibid.*, p. 242. He admits that "Cyprian looked upon the Roman Church *as really* the *Cathedra Petri*, and as the representative of the outward unity of the Church," vol. i., p. 299; and again remarks that "*very early indeed* do we observe in the Roman Bishops traces of the assumption that to them, *as successors of St. Peter*, belonged a paramount authority in ecclesiastical disputes; that the *Cathedra Petri*, as the source of Apostolic tradition, must take precedence of all other *ecclesiæ apostolicæ*. . . . In the Montanist writings of Tertullian (A. D. 150-220) we find indications that the Roman Bishops *already issued preemptory edicts on ecclesiastical matters*, endeavored to make themselves considered as the Bishops of Bishops—Episcopos Episcoporum—*and were in the habit of speaking of the authority of their "antecessors."*—Vol. i., p. 298. Here he is referring specially to the conduct of Pope Victor, A. D. 190, Pope Zephyrinus, A. D. 200, and Pope Stephen, A. D. 250.

M. Ernest Renan, the well-known French savant and skeptic, admits in the *Hibbert Lectures*, delivered in London in 1880, that "the Pope of Rome has made it [Christianity] the religion of the world" (p. 122); and after mentioning the attempt of Valentinus to establish a Gnostic school in Rome, and his excommunication by Pope Hyginus, he goes on to say, "*The centre of a future Catholic orthodoxy was plainly here.* Pius, who succeeded Hyginus, showed the same firmness in defending the purity of the faith. Cerdo, Marcion, Valentinus, Marcellinus, are removed from the Church by the sentence of Pius. *In the reign of Antoninus* (A. D. 138 seq.) *the germ of the Papacy already exists in a very definite form*" (p. 148). "Rome," he continues, "was the place in which this great idea of Catholicty was worked out. *More and more every day it became the capital of Christianity*, and took the place of Jerusalem as the religious centre of humanity *Its Church claimed a precedence over all others, which was generally recognized.* (Iren. iii. 3 ; Tertull. Præscript, 21, 30; Cyprian, Epist. 52, 56, 67, 71, 75; Firmilian). *All the doubtful questions which agitated the Christian conscience came to Rome to ask for arbitration, if not decision.* Men argued, certainly not in a very logical way, *that as Christ had made Cephas the corner-stone of His Church, the privilege ought to be inherited by his successors.* . . . The Bishop of Rome became the Bishop of bishops, *he who admonished all others.* Rome proclaims her right— a dangerous right—of excommunicating those who did not walk step by step with her. . . . *At the end of the second century we can recognize, by signs which it is impossible to mistake, the spirit which in 1870 will proclaim the infallibility of the Pope.* . . . Irenæus (A. D. 135-220) refutes all heresies by reference to the belief of this Church [of Rome], '*the greatest, the oldest, the most illustrous, which possesses, in virtue of an unbroken succession, the true tradition of the Apostles Peter and Paul, and to which, because of its Primacy, all the rest of the Church ought to have recourse.*' (Lib. iii. 3)"—pp. 172-174. And going farther back and speaking of "the last years of the first century," he says: "Already the idea of a certain primacy belonging to his [Pope Clement's, A. D. 91-101] Church was beginning to make its way to the light. *The right of warning other churches, and of composing their differences was conceded to it.* Similar privileges—*so at least it was believed*—had been accorded to Peter by the other disciples (Luke xxii. 32)."—pp. 124, 125. For these extracts I am indebted to Mr. Allnatt's works, "Which is the True Church ?" pp. 35, 36, 37, 40, and "Cathedra Petri," pp. 60, 62, 63, 105. The reader would do well to consult the latter work for the traditional teaching of the Church on the Supremacy of St. Peter and his successors, or one of the following: Waterworth's "The Faith of Catholics," vols. i., ii; "The Supremacy of the Apostolic See," two lectures by the late eminent German theologian, Dr. Franz Hettinger; M. Allies, "The See of Peter"; Cardinal Gibbons, "The Faith of Our Fathers," or "The True Faith of Our Forefathers," by a professor of theology in Woodstock College; "Catholic Dictionary," article on the "Pope"; Hurter, "Theol. Gen., "vol. i., nn. 504-540; Mazzella, "De Ecclesia," nn. 901-947.

⁴⁶ John, i. 42.

⁴⁷ Gen. xvii. 5.

⁴⁸ Gen. xxxii. 28.

⁴⁹ Cf. "Cathedra Petri," pp. 24-25. "Peter was to be the πέτρα of the building of the Church."—Olshausen, "Commentary on the Gospels," translated by Rev. Thomas Brown. "This name of Peter," observes St. Francis de Sales, "was not a proper name of a man, but was only (then) appropriated to Simon Bar-jona.—"The Catholic Controversy," p. 241.

⁵⁰ Math. xvi. 13-19. Compare Mark viii. 27-29; Luke ix. 18-20.

⁵¹ Luke ix. 10, 18.

⁵² In all the ancient versions the Greek and Latin (which followed the

Greek) excepted, the word is the same in both clauses. See Walton's Polyglot. "Πέτρος or Κηφᾶς means not *stone* (as some affirm), but rock, *saxum*, as Πέτρος often does in the best classical writers."—Bloomfield. So also Meyer, *in locum*.

"The change of Πέτρος into Πέτρα, in Greek, is easily accounted for: because the masculine termination is properly chosen as the *man's* name, and the feminine as more closely indicating its *import*."—McCarthy, "The Gospel of St. Matthew." Benô autem Mathæi interpres vocis Hebraicæ genus mutavit, quia neque vir πέτρα dici *salva Græci sermonis regula* poterat, neque πέτρος id usitate significabat quod Christus volebat indicatum nempe *saxum firmum super quo aliquid ædificari soleat.*"—Grotius, *ibid.* Cf. also Mazzella, "De Ecclesia," n. 854.

⁵³ Some referred the word "rock" to Christ Himself; some to Peter's *confession*; some to the College of the Apostles; some understood it of the body of the faithful; some of Peter himself, but only as the first living stone in the Church, and the first through whose ministry large numbers were converted to the faith.

⁵⁴ "That Christ here promised to build His Church upon St. Peter, seems evident."—Whitby, "A Critical Commentary," p. 123. "Building on Peter is explained, by some, as contrary to the faith that Christ is the only foundaton (I. Cor. iii. 2), and as favoring the succession of Peter and his successors; but the connection shows that *Peter is here plainly meant.*" —Gerard's "Institutes of Biblical Criticism," canon 511. "The rock is neither the confession of Peter, nor Christ, pointing out Himself by His finger or by a shake of the head (*which interpretations the context does not admit*), but Peter himself."—Rosenmuller, "Scholia in Novum Testamentum," tom. i., p. 336. "Certainly when the expositors above alluded to conjecture that in pronouncing the words, Christ pointed to *Himself*, as the great foundation, *they argue upon a wholly gratuitous supposition.* . . . Indeed, the first interpretation (referring πέτρα to Christ), and the second *probably* (referring to Peter's confession),—however plausible— seem to have been *forced* upon the passage *for the purpose of avoiding the difficulty thought to arise from taking it in its obvious sense*, which is: Thou art by *name Rock* (*i. e.*, thy name means Rock), and *suitable to that shall be thy work and office;* for upon *thee*, etc."—Bloomfield, "Comm." *in locum*. "It would be a *desperate undertaking* to prove that Christ meant any other person than Peter."—Bishop Marsh, "Comparative View," App., p. 227. "Protestants have betrayed unnecessary fears, and have, therefore, used all the *hardihood of lawless criticism* in their attempts to reason away the *Catholic* interpretation."—Thompson, "Monotessaron," p 194. Finally Bloomfield (Comm. *in locum*) testifies that "almost every modern [Protestant] *expositor of note*" maintains the identity of Peter and rock. To the names of those already given may be added Kuinoel, Alford, Bengel, Hammond, S. Clare, Schleusner, Parkhurst, (ad. v. Κηφᾶς), Stanley, "Sermons and Essays on the Apostolic Age," p. 118. Cf. Mazzella, *op. cit.*, n. 856.

⁵⁵ So Schelling, Meyer, and Holtzman. Cf. Hettinger, "The Supremacy of the Apostolic See," pp. 20, 130.

⁵⁶ "The evasion," says Meyer, who is considered one of the most emi-

nent Biblical scholars of modern times,—"The *evasion* often taken advantage of in controversy with Rome—viz., that the rock means not St. Peter himself, but the firm faith and the confession of it on the part of the Apostle—is incorrect, since the demonstrative expression, 'on *this* rock,' can only mean the Apostle himself."

"If some of the Fathers," observes Cardinal Hergenröther, "call faith the foundation of the Church, so this they take not in an absolute and abstract sense, but by it understand the living faith of Peter, which was the reason wherefore he was chosen to be the foundation-stone of the Church. Hence theologians say the faith of Peter is *causaliter*, his person *formaliter*, the basis of the Church."—"Anti-Janus," p. 63. Dr. Dollinger was of the same opinion. "Not," says he, "*en* his confession, but on the *man* himself, with his rock-like character *on account* of his confession, the Church was built; being made up of persons, living beings, she required and will ever require a living foundation, a personality."—"Christenthum und Kirche," p. 32, in Hettinger, *op. cit.* It is worthy of note that, previous to the rise of Arianism, no Father interpreted rock to mean Peter's confession of faith. The literal interpretation was universal. It is also to be remarked that one interpretation does not exclude the other; rather one complements the other. Again the argument for the Primacy holds good in either interpretation; for if the 'rock' be taken to mean Peter's faith it is that faith *as believed and professed* by Peter, and, therefore, inseparably connected with the person of Peter.

⁵⁷ "Πύλαι ᾅδου (gates of Hell) pro fortissimo quoque et quod omnia devincat memorari."—Fritzsche. For the Fathers on this expression see Hettinger, "The Supremacy," etc., pp. 21, 131.

⁵⁸ Lecture delivered in Manchester, England.

⁵⁹ McCarthy, "The Gospel of St. Mathew," p. 331. Referring to the Protestant explanation that the words "and I will give unto thee the keys of the Kingdom of Heaven" only implied that Peter should *open* the gates of the Church to the Jews and Gentiles, Cardinal Wiseman remarks: "But can any bring himself to believe in so cold and, I might almost say, so paltry a signification as this? *Where, on any occasion, among profane or sacred writers, was the image used in such a sense?* The delivery of keys has always been a symbol of the intrusting with supreme authority to command. It is so used in Scripture" (Cf. Is. xxii. 2; Apoc. iii. 7. See also Apoc. i. 18; ix. 1; xx. 1; Job xii. 14; Is. ix. 6). *Op. cit.*, lecture viii.

⁶⁰ Kent Stone, "Invitation Heeded," p. 231.

⁶¹ "*Ligandi et solvendi* verbis comprehendunter omnia ea, quæ Petrus in virtute nominis Jesu Christi et per fidem in illud nomen apostolica potestate gessit, docendo, prohibendo, permittendo, puniendo, remittendo."—Bengel in McCarthy's "The Gospel of St. Mathew," p. 333.

⁶² Luke xxii. 31-32.

⁶³ Serm. iv., c. 3, 4, in Allnatt's "Cathedra Petri," pp. 37-38.

⁶⁴ "The Catholic Controversy," pp. 258-259.

⁶⁵ Luke, *ibid.*

⁶⁵* John xvii. 20.

⁶⁶ *In locum.*

⁶⁷ Hom. iii., in Act. Apost., tom. ix., p. 26.

NOTES TO CHAPTER III. 149

⁶⁸ In Ps. xliii., n. 40, p. 1109.
⁶⁹ *Op. cit., ibid.* The Protestant Bengel admits that "this whole speech of our Lord pre-supposes that Peter is the first of the Apostles on whose stability or fall the less or greater danger of the others depended."
⁷⁰ John xxi., 15-17.
⁷¹ Math. xvi. 18, 19.
⁷² Math. xvi., 17, 18, 19.
⁷³ John x. 11.
⁷⁴ I. Pet. v. 4.
⁷⁵ Father Vaughan, *loc. cit.*
⁷⁶ "Christenthum und Kirche," p. 32, in Hettinger, *op. cit.*
⁷⁷ Cf. II. Kings, v. 1-2; Ps. ii. 9, xlvii. 15., lxxix. 2; Is. xl. 10, 11; Ezech. xxxiv. 23, 24; Mich. v. 2, 4; Math. ii. 6; Apoc. xii. 5; xix. 15, "βόσκε denotes simply, 'Feed, give nourishment'; ποιμαινε embraces *all the cares* which a watchful shepherd bestows on his flock, guiding it, guarding it from all danger, watching over it with tireless vigilance."— Abbé Fouard, "Life of Jesus," foot-note, p. 370, vol. ii.
⁷⁸ *Op. cit..* lecture viii.
⁷⁹ II. Kings (Sam.) v. 2; Ps. lxxvii. 71, 72; Ezech. xxxii. 1-10; Jer. lii. 15, xxiii., 1, 2, 4; Nah. iii. 18.
⁸⁰ Is. xl. 11; Mich. vii. 14; Ezech. xxxii. 10-23.
⁸¹ John x.
⁸² I. Pet. v. 4
⁸³ *Ibid.* 2.
⁸⁴ Acts xx. 28
⁸⁵ "Fragments on the Church," p. 26.
⁸⁶ Kenrick, "The Primacy of the Apostolic See," p. 58.
⁸⁷ St. Francis de Sales, "The Catholic Controversy," p. 262.
I am tempted to make a few extracts here from Mr. Allnatt's work to show the reader how the great lights of the Early Church—the Fathers— understood this address (John xxi. 15-17) to Peter:
Origen (A. D. 185-254)—"When the *chief authority* as regards feeding the sheep was delivered to Peter, and *upon him* as on the earth the *Church was founded.*"—Lib. v., in Epist. ad Rom. n. 10, tom. iv., p. 568.
St. Cyprian (A.D.—258)—"Peter to whom the Lord commends his sheep to be fed and guarded."—"De Habitu Virginum," n. 10.
St. Basil (A. D. 329-379)—The spiritual "ruler is none else than one who represents the person of the Saviour, and offers up to God the salvation of those who obey him; and this we learn from Christ Himself, *in that He appointed Peter to be the Shepherd of His Church after Himself.*" —Const. Monast. c. 25, n. 5.
St. Ambrose (A.D. 335-397)—"*Set over the Church. . . . The Pastor of the Lord's flock*" (In Ps. xliii., n. 40).—"Him whom, as He is about to be raised to heaven, He was leaving to us, as it were, *the Vicar of His love.* . . . And now he is not ordered, as at first, to 'feed His lambs' . . . . but 'His sheep,' *that the more perfect might govern the more perfect.*"—"In Lucam," lib, x., p. 1848, tom. ii.
St. John Chrysostom (A.D. 347-407)—"And why, then, passing by the others does He converse with Peter on these things? *He was the chosen*

NOTES TO CHAPTER III.

one of the Apostles, and the mouth of the disciples and the leader of the choir. On this account, Paul also went upon a time to see him rather than the others. And withal, to show him that he must thenceforward have confidence, as the denial was done away with, *He puts into his hands the presidency over the brethren.* And He brings not forward the denial, nor reproaches him with what had past, but says, ' If thou lovest Me *preside over the brethren.*' . . . And a third time He gives him the same injunction, showing at what a price *He sets the presidency over His own sheep.* And if any one should say, How then did James receive the throne of Jerusalem? This I would answer, that He appointed this man (Peter) *Teacher,* not of that throne, *but of the world.*—" In Joan Hom. lxxxviii., n. 1, tom. viii., pp. 526-7. "Peter," says this same great doctor in another place—"Peter so washed away that denial as *to be even made the first Apostle, and to have the whole world committed to him.*"—Tom. i., orat. viii., n. 3. And again: "Why," he asks, "did He shed His blood? That He might gain possession of those sheep which *He intrusted to Peter and to his successors.*"—De Sacerdotio, lib. ii., p. 371.

St. Asterius (contemporary of St. Chrysostom)—"He intrusts to this man *the universal and œcumenical Church,* after having thrice asked him, ' Lovest thou Me?' . . . Peter received *the world in charge;* as it were for *one fold, one shepherd,* having heard ' Feed My lambs.' "—Hom. viii., in SS. Pet. et Paul, tom. i., p. 147.

St. Augustine (A.D. 354-430)—"I am held in the communion of the Catholic Church by . . . . the succcession of priests from the very Chair of the Apostle Peter, *to whom the Lord, after His Resurrection, committed His sheep to be fed, even to the present Episcopate.*"—Tom. viii., Epist. Cont. Manich. Fund., n. 5., p. 269. Again: "Peter was made *the pastor of the Church,* as Moses was made *the ruler* of the Jewish people."—Cont. Faustum, lib. xxii., c. 70. And again: "Peter, *to whom He commended His sheep as another* self."—Tom. v., serm. xlvi., n. 30., p. 345.

St. Leo the Great (A.D.—461)—"*Out of the whole world the one Peter is chosen to be set over both the calling of the Nations, and over all the Apostles, and all the Fathers of the Church;* that although in the people of God, there be many priests and many shepherds, *Peter may rule all as made his, whom Christ also rules by Supreme Headship.*"—Serm. iv. in Natal. Ora., c. i., p. 14.

St. Gregory the Great (A.D. 520-604)—"By the voice of the Lord, *the care of the whole Church* was committed to Peter, *the head of all the Apostles;* for to him it was said, ' Peter, lovest thou Me? Feed my sheep.' "—Lib. iv., Epist. 32.

Were these fathers to appear to-morrow on earth, *to what Church would they point you?* St. Ambrose could speak for all: "*Ubi Petrus, ibi Ecclesia: Where Peter is, there is the Church,*" (In Ps. xl., n. 30., tom. i., p. 879.) And St. Jerome (A.D. 340-420) would tell him, where Peter unmistakably was, "*I,* following none as the first but Christ, *am linked in communion with thy blessedness* [Pope Damasus], *that is, with the Chair of Peter. Upon that rock I know that the Church is built. Whoso shall eat the Lamb outside this house is profane. If any one be not in the ark of Noah, he will perish when the deluge prevails.* . . . *Whoso gathereth*

NOTES TO CHAPTER III. 151

not with thee, scattereth, that is, he who is not of Christ, is of Antichrist."
—Epist. xv., ad Damas., tom. i., 38.

⁸⁸ Math. x. 2-5; Mark iii., 13-19; Luke vi., 13-16; Acts i. 13.

⁸⁹ The Greek word (πρῶτος) for "first" is rendered *chief*, later on in xx. 27, also in I. Tim. i. 15; Acts xvi. 12, xxviii. 7, and in Old Testament in II. Chron. xxvi. 20, Nehem. xii. 46.

⁹⁰ McCarthy, "The Gospel of St. Mathew," p. 212.

⁹¹ "The Catholic Controversy," p. 268.

⁹² Mark v., 37; Luke viii. 51.

⁹³ Math. xvii. 1. Comp. Mark ix. 1; Luke ix. 28.

⁹⁴ Mark. xiv. 33. Comp. Math. xxvi. 37; Mark xiii. 3. Cf. also Math. iv. 18; Luke xxii. 8; John xxi. 2; Acts iii. 1, 3, 4, 11, iv. 6, 13, 19, viii. 14. The text from Gal. ii. 9., which is objected and made so much of, is not a *clear* exception to the rule. The distinguished Protestant critic, Tischendorf, gives the names of no less than *eight* of the oldest MSS., or *Codices* of the Holy Scriptures, in which Peter's name is written first in the text, and he quotes the old Syriac, the Coptic, the Armenian, and the Ethiopic old versions as giving the same order. "In that most ancient of MS.," writes the Protestant Grotius, "the name of Cephas is not placed between that of James and John, and *this I consider the more correct.* Nor is it according to usage that he who is the Head of the College (Apostolic) be named in the middle place. . . . Besides, the *ancient* writers when treating of this place (the text in question) name Peter in the *first* place." (Comm. *in loc.*) Among the ancient writers who read "Peter, James, and John," are Tertullian, Chrysostom, Ambrosiaster, Augustine, and Jerome. Cf. "The True Faith of Our Forefathers," pp. 173-175, where the references are given. In John i. 44, Andrew and Peter are named not as Apostles, but as citizens; and in I. Cor. i. 12, iii. 22, the order is that of the *ascending* scale, and therefore Peter holds the place of honor.

⁹⁵ Mark i. 36.

⁹⁶ Luke viii. 45.

⁹⁷ Acts ii. 37. Comp. Math. xxvi. 37; Mark xvi. 7; Luke ix. 32; Acts v. 29.

⁹⁸ "You know well," observes St. Francis de Sales on these texts, "that to name one person and put the others all together with him, is to make him the most *important* and the others his *inferiors.*—"The Catholic Controversy," p. 266.

⁹⁹ Math. xii. 3; Luke vi. 3.

¹⁰⁰ Mark iii. 14; xvi. 10.

¹⁰¹ Math. xvi. 15.

¹⁰² *Ibid.* ver. 16.

¹⁰³ Math. xix. 23.27. Comp. Mark x. 23-28.

¹⁰⁴ John vi. 67-68. See also Luke xii. 41; Acts i. 15; ii. 14. 29, 38; iii. 6, 12; iv. 8; v. 3; viii. 19; x. 39, 42. If Peter were not the Superior, would it be becoming in him to make himself the spokesman on all occasions?

¹⁰⁵ Math. xvii., 24-27.

¹⁰⁶ "The enemies of the Papacy," says Mr. Allies, to whose work, "St. Peter, His Name and Office," I am much indebted for this summary of Scriptural evidence,—"The enemies of the Papacy will say, by chance,

NOTES TO CHAPTER III.

but men of good will will answer, because it was apparent *even to strangers* that Peter was their *leader*." "As Peter seemed to be the first of the disciples," says St. John Chrysostom on the text, "they go to him."

[107] "Dost thou see the exceeding greatness of the honor?"—St. Chrysostom (*in loc.*)

[108] "In very many circumstances our Lord by His actions signified the special power of Peter. From *his* bark He teaches the multitude; to *him* He gives the command to let down the net, and rewards his obedience by a miraculous draught of fishes; to *him* He promises that he shall henceforth catch men. He commands *him* to walk to Him on the waters, and stretches forth His hand to support *him*, when the weakness of the Apostle's faith causes *him* to sink. He pays tribute for *him* as well as Himself."—Kenrick, "The Primacy of the Apostolic See," pp. 58-59.

[109] Mark xvi. 7.
[110] I. Cor. xv. 5.
[111] John xxi., 18, 19.
[112] "St. Peter, his Name and Office," p. 93.
[113] Acts i., 15, 16.
[114] *Ibid.* ver. 21, 22. "Could not Peter himself," asks St. John Chrysostom," have chosen the individual?" To which he answers, "*By all means;* but he abstains from doing it, lest he should appear to indulge partiality. He is the *first* to proceed in the affair, because *all have been delivered over into his hands ;* for to him Christ said, "Thou being once converted confirm thy brethren."—Hom. iii., in I. Cap. Act.

[115] Acts ii. 14-15.
[116] *Ibid.*, ver. 22 *et seq.*
[117] *Ibid.*, ver. 38.
[118] *Ibid.*, ver. 41.
[119] *Ibid.*, iv. 4.
[120] *Ibid.*, Acts ii. 2-8.
[121] *Ibid.*, ix. 34, 40, 41.
[122] *Ibid.*, ii. 43; v. 12.
[123] *Ibid.*, viii., 20.
[124] *Ibid.*, v. 3-10.
[125] *Ibid.*, iv. 7-12.
[126] *Ibid.*. ix. 32. "Like a General he went surveying the ranks," says St. John Chrysostom.
[127] Bossuet, *Disc. sur l'Unité de l'Eglise*, in McCarthy's "The Gospel of St. Mathew," p. 336.
[128] Acts v. 15.
[129] Acts xii. 5.
[130] *Ibid.*, vers. 1, 2.
[131] *Ibid.*, ver. 5.
[132] 1 Cor. xv. 10.
[133] Acts x. 5.
[134] *Ibid.*, ver. 6.
[135] *Ibid.*, ver. 19, 20.
[136] *Ibid.*, ver. 33.
[137] *Ibid.*, ver. 44.
[138] *Ibid.*, ver. 45.
[139] "Words," remarks St. John Chrysostom, "of one almost assaulting any that should forbid and say, That should not be."
[140] *Ibid.*, ver. 47.
[141] *Ibid.*, ver. 48.
[142] John x. 11, 16.
[143] Acts xv. 2.
[144] *Ibid.*, ver. 6.
[145] *Ibid.*, ver. 7.
[146] *Ibid.*
[147] *Ibid.*, ver. 9.
[148] *Ibid.*, ver. 10.
[149] *Ibid.*, ver. 7.
[150] *Ibid.*, ver. 12.
[151] See Appendix B.
[152] "The Catholic Controversy," pp. 269-272.

NOTES TO CHAPTER III. 153

[153] 1 Cor. iii. 11.
[154] Math. xvi. 18.
[155] Serm. iv., "de Assumpt ad Pontificatum."
[156] Eph. ii. 20. [157] Eph. ii. 20: Apoc. xxi. 14.
[158] Math. xviii. 18. [159] Math. xxviii. 19; Mark xvi. 15.
[160] St. Leo, *loc. cit.*
[161] God's words are "*not idle and inoperative.*"—*St. Jerome.*
[162] "Discours sur l'Unité de l'Eglise." "What before was granted to Peter," says Origen, a Father of the third century, and of the Greek Church, "seems to have been granted to all,—but as something *peculiarly excellent* was to be granted to Peter, it was given singly to him. 'I will give thee the keys of the kingdom of heaven.' This was done before the words 'whatsoever ye shall bind on earth' were uttered. And truly, if the words of the Gospel be considered, we shall there find that the last words were common to Peter and the others, but that the former, spoken to Peter, *imparted a great distinction and superiority.*"—Comm. in Math., t. iii., p. 612.

"Here we come at last," says the author of "The Invitation Heeded," "to a grant which was afterwards extended to the other Apostles also. But that God chose to make it to Peter first *means something.* To Peter *singly* was given in promise what was subsequently so bestowed upon the rest *collectively and with him. It is one thing to exercise authority in a house, and a very different thing to hold the keys thereof.*"—pp. 230-231.

[163] Eph. ii. 20. [164] *Ibid.*
[165] xxi. 14.
[166] Cf. St. Francis de Sales, "The Catholic Controversy," pp. 248-249.
[167] Cardinal Wiseman; *op. cit.*, Lecture viii.
[168] Math. xviii. 1; Mark ix. 33-34; Luke ix. 46., xxii. 24.
[169] Math. xv. 16., xvi. 8-11; Of. also Mark iv. 13; vii. 18; viii. 17-21.
[170] Luke ix. 44; xviii. 31-33.
[171] Luke ix. 45; xviii. 34.
[172] Math. xvii. 24-27; xviii. 1. In the original it is $μειζων$, greater.
[173] When He privileged them to be witnesses of the raising to life of Jairus's daughter, of His Transfiguration, and Agony in the Garden.
[174] *In loco.*
[175] Math. xviii. 2-4; xx. 26-27; Mark ix. 35; x. 42-44; Luke ix. 47-48; xxii. 25-27.
[176] Acts viii. 14.
[177] xxii. 13-14.
[178] xv. 2.
[179] Antiq. Heb., b. 20., c. 8.
[180] Ad Philad., c. 10.
[181] "The True Faith of Our Forefathers," p. 178.
[182] Gal. ii. 11.
[183] Cf. Allies, "St. Peter, His Name and Office."
[184] "Disc. sur l'Unité de l'Eglise."
[185] L. V. Contra Marcion, c. iii.
[186] "De Præscript.," c. 23. Peter erred "non falsi prædicatione sed imprudenti conversatione,"St. Aug. Ep. 9 et 19 ad Hieronymum.

[187] Cf. Allies, "St. Peter, His Name and Office."
[188] *In locum.*
[189] Lib. ii. in Ezech. Hom. xviii.
[190] *Ibid.*, Hom. vi.
[191] Chap. i. 18, 19.
[192] In Joan. Hom. lxxxviii.
[193] Rev. A. R. Fausset, in "The Portable Commentary," admits that the Greek word (ἱστορῆσαι) for "to see," may mean "to visit a person *important to know.*
[194] Kenrick, "The Primacy of the Apostolic See," p. 60.
[195] Discours sur l'Unité de l'Eglise."
[196] Adver. Jov., i. 26.
[197] "The Catholic Controversy," pp. 276-277.
[198] *Systema Theologicum* in Tracy's "Tributes of Protestant Writers," pp. 23-25. See also extract from Grotius, *ibid.*, pp. 26-29.
[199] Compare chap. vii. 24, 25.
[200] Luke xxii. 31-32.
[201] See the words of St. Leo the Great, quoted above, p. 103.
[202] There are eminent commentators, and they not a few, who take the original (ἐπιστρέψας), which is translated above "when thou art converted," to be a Hebraism signifying "*in turn.*" The text then would run thus: "And thou *in turn* confirm thy brethren;" as if Our Lord said: "Peter, I have made provision for the security of your faith as Chief; and now I charge you in turn to do for your brethren what I have done for you,—Confirm their faith." Among the Protestant commentators who hold this interpretation are Grotius, Kwindel, Bengel, and Ewald. Two reasons are assigned for this rendering: 1st, the parallelism of both parts—I have prayed for you and confirmed your faith, now do you the same for the others—favors it; and, 2d, because a reference to his denial which the first interpretation contains, would not be understood by the Apostles, seeing that up to the present Our Lord had given them no intimation of such an event. Besides, Our Lord's Prayer could not refer to the temptation which led to Peter's denial during His Passion; for in that case, we would be forced to admit that the *unconditional* prayer of Him *who knew that the Father always heard Him* (John xi 42) failed to attain its object. The argument for the Primacy, as is obvious, becomes clearer and stronger in this interpretation.
[203] "Christianity and the Church," p. 32, in "Anti-Janus," p. 59.
[204] John xxi. 15-17.
[205] Acts xx. 28.
[206] Cardinal Hergenröther, "Catholic Church and Christian State," vol. i., p. 89.
[207] "The True Story of the Vatican Council," p. 176. For the teaching of Tradition on Papal Infallibility, see Cardinal Mazzella, "De Ecclesia," nn. 1072-1080; Cardinal Manning, "The Vatican Council and Its Definitions" ("Petri Privilegium," part iii.), pp. 85-90, 145-158; Cardinal Hergenröther, "Catholic Church and Christian State," vol. i., pp. 91-113, and "Anti-Janus," pp. 62-69; Ryder, "Catholic Controversy," pp. 12-21; "The True Faith of Our Forefathers," chap. xi.

CHAPTER IV.

How do Catholics Meet the Objections to Infallibility?

Objection: The dogma of Infallibility makes the Pope a despot, and the authority of the Church a despotism; to believe in and submit to it is to believe in and submit to intellectual bondage,—to become, mentally and morally, a slave.

Answer: This objection is specious, catching, and very popular. It is one of those that is specially calculated to bring the Church into odium with the unthinking masses; and hence it is that we so often find it, in one form or another, made the subject of impassioned declamation by her enemies. In the following pages I will endeavor to examine it fully and fairly; and for that purpose I will present it under its most popular aspects.

At the outset I will lay down and assume the truth of the following principles:

1. That the authority of God is not a despotism or a tyranny; and that He has a supreme and absolute right to command the obedience of man's reason, will and conscience.

2. That it is not slavery, mental or moral, but a most reasonable act on the part of man to yield an unconditional obedience of his reason, will, and conscience to God's teaching and command.

3. That the authority of God is not derogatory to the dignity of man; nor are its claims irreconcilable with the rights of man's reason, or with the freedom of his will, or with the liberty of his conscience.

4. That it is not an act of mental slavery, or of intellectual bondage, to submit one's reason to the truth, however known and to whatever order it may belong, whether of reason or of revelation, of science or of faith.

5. That to believe on sufficient authority, be there question of divine or of human faith, is not an unreasonable act, or one that in any way reflects on the dignity of man.

6. That it is not tyranny or despotism in a divinely constituted and Infallible Teacher to demand the obedience of man's reason, will, and conscience in matters of religion; nor is it, consequently, slavery, mental or moral, on the part of man to allow the justice of such a demand, and yield obedience accordingly.

7. That no *merely human* authority can rightfully demand of man the obedience of faith in matters of religion; that to claim any such right would be a monstrous act of usurpation, and to exercise it would be an intolerable act of tyranny, on the part of any human authority; and that, on the part of man, to submit to it would be an act of slavery degrading to his manhood.

Taking for granted these principles—and I think that no professing Christian can seriously question them—I now proceed to answer the objection. If, then, the Church is what she claims to be; if, as was proved above,[1] the Son of God Himself founded her;[2] if He to whom *all power in heaven and in earth* was given⁸ directly and expressly commissioned her to *teach all nations,*⁴ to *preach the Gospel to every creature,*⁵ and to do so with the same authority with which He Himself preached it during the years of His public ministry;⁶ if, moreover, He expressly pledged His word that He Himself would be ever present with her,⁷ to assist in teaching all that He had commanded her to teach;⁸ if the Holy Spirit of Truth, by formal promise, *abides with her forever,*⁹ to *guide her into all truth;*¹⁰ if, consequently, she is *the pillar and ground of truth,*¹¹ the infallible organ of God's voice, so that whoever *hears* her *hears* Him¹²— if all this is true, how can her authority be a despotism unless God's own authority is such? and how can submission to her teaching be intellectual bondage or mental slavery unless it is intellectual bondage and mental slavery to submit to the teaching of God,—the teaching of truth itself. Despotism or tyranny consists not in the exercise of authority, but in the exercise of usurped authority; and slavery consists not in submission, but in submission to an authority that has no right to exact it. If the Church did not claim to be, and were not, a divine and infallible, but only a human and fallible, authority, then, indeed, to submit to her in matters of religion, as Catholics do, would be a mental slavery unworthy of man, and the claim on her part to the obedience of faith would be wholly unjustifiable. For no merely human authority has or can have the right to dictate what man must believe in religion, or to interfere between his conscience and God. But the Church is not a mere human authority; she is a divine and infallible authority,—God's direct representative on earth, clothed with His authority, and specially commissioned and aided by Him to teach man the truths and principles of salvation; and it is only because she is all this that she claims the right to speak to the reason and conscience of man, and to demand their obedience in matters of religion."

This objection is strangely inconsistent in the mouths of some of those who are most eager in urging it against Catholics. Orthodox Protestants give to the Bible as great and as absolute an authority in matters of religion as Catholics give to the Church. If, then, the objection is good against the Church and the Catholic, how is it not also good against the Bible and the Protestant? If the authority of the Church be a despotism or a tyranny, how is the case of the Bible different? If obedience to the authority of the Church be an intellectual bondage, a mental slavery, how is it otherwise with obedience to the Bible? If Protestants in submitting to the Bible be free men, how are Catholics in submitting to the Church miserable slaves? Protestants object to us and say, 'Oh, you have to believe the Church; you cannot think for yourselves; you are slaves.' We answer, We believe the Church because God commanded all men to do so, and the Bible registers this command;" but you—you believe the Bible, though neither God nor the Bible commands you to do so. 'But,' you say, 'the Bible is the Word of God.' And I rejoin, according to the Bible, the Church is the work of God," and her voice is the voice of God." I believe the Church because my reason tells me that she is what she claims to be—a teacher appointed by God with authority to declare infallibly to me what He wills me to believe and do to gain eternal life; and you believe the Bible, though your reason cannot possibly prove" to you that it is what it claims to be and what you admit it to be,—not only a divine and infallible, but an *inspired*, Teacher of the will of God in your regard. The reader will pardon me for making some lengthened extracts from Dr. Brownson, who presses home this retort with invincible logic.

"The Protestant makes in his own mind, perhaps, and in the minds of the unreflecting, a point against us in assuming that he is free in his belief, while we, being bound to believe whatever authority commands us to believe, are slaves in ours. But can he believe the Bible is the word of God, and yet hold that he is free to disbelieve it, or to believe anything contrary to what it teaches? If not, how can he be more free in his belief, or in his faith than we? Is the authority of the Bible, in his opinion, less authority or less stringent than the authority of the Church? If he believes that in the Bible he has the word of God, he has no more right or liberty to contradict it, than we have to contradict the Church. Supposing, then, that he really believes the Bible to be what he alleges, he believes in principle on authority just as much as we do."[8]

"God in the Bible says so, is for him a final answer to all questions. If God in His Church says so, which is final for us in all cases, is spiritual despotism, how does he escape the charge of asserting a like despotism? What, *in relation to mental freedom*, is the difference in principle in saying that we are to believe what the Church teaches, or that we are to believe what the Bible teaches? The rule is as absolute in the one case as in the other; and the only difference is that in the one case we have a living teacher, with regard to whose teaching there is no obscurity or uncertainty, while in the other we have a dead book whose teachings after our best efforts remain dark and doubtful. In the one case we may have certain truth, in the other we can have only uncertain opinions or mere guesses; *but the submission demanded to authority is precisely the same in both cases.* It is singular that Protestants, who are continually asserting the authority of the Bible, and at the same time denouncing the authority of the Catholic Church as a spiritual despotism, never appear to be aware of this."[19]

"It is a curious fact that the *soi-disant* orthodox Protestant reasons against us Catholics with apparent unconsciousness that every objection he brings against faith by infallible authority bears equally against his professed rule of faith—the infallible authority of the written word. If the authority of the Church is incompatible with the rights of reason, how can the authority of the written word, of a book, be less so? He, as well as we, has to meet all the objections of the Rationalists, the interior light men or Quakers, and Sceptics, and he has far less with which to meet them; *for while he has all the disadvantages of the principle of authority to overcome, he has none of the advantages to offer.* Of all the men in the world he is the most unreasonable; for, as to the Bible, he has to meet all the objections, in order to assert its authority, that we have to meet in order to assert the authority of the Church; and when he has asserted it, it avails him nothing, since it speaks only as he gives it tongue."²⁰

" The Protestant is fond of calling us slaves because we recognize the Papal Supremacy, and forgets that, unless he is fibbing, he is, to say the least, as great a slave as we. He is no more at liberty to believe or to do anything contrary to the teachings and precepts of the Bible than we are to believe or to do anything contrary to the definitions and rescripts of the Holy Father. He is as much bound, according to his own confession, to conform in all things to the Bible as we are to the Church. He asserts for all men and nations, statesmen and individuals, an authority as supreme and as inflexible as that which we assert. How, then, are we less free than he? The only difference between us in respect to authority is that he places it in the record of what God said by men in ancient times, and we in what He teaches and commands through the voice of a living Pontiff. If the authority we assert is human, because it comes through a human organ, then must the authority he asserts be human, for that comes to him only through a human organ. The prophets and Apostles were men in the same sense that the Pope is a man, and if God's voice through *them* is divine and authoritative, it may be equally divine and authoritative through *him*. If he holds that in believing and obeying the Bible he is believing and obeying God's word, so we hold that in believing and obeying the living Pontiff we are believing and obeying God. He asserts an apostolic authority that was, and we an apostolic authority that was and is. If we hold a doctrine incompatible with freedom, he holds one equally so, and every argument he uses to prove that the Papal Supremacy is incompatible with freedom, civil or religious, and favorable to civil or spiritual despotism, may be urged to prove the same of the Scriptural Supremacy which he asserts. He would do well to remember this."[21]

"The Protestant always assumes that in submitting to the authority of the Church we submit to a purely human authority. Can he tell us why the authority of the Church is any more human than that of the Bible? In either case the divine reaches us only through the medium of the human, and if the human medium through which the teachings of the Church reach us makes them human, the same must be said of the Holy Scriptures, for they come to us only through a human medium. If you say that the Bible is the word of God, notwithstanding the human medium through which it comes to us, then why not the teachings of the Church? The same facts and arguments that establish the authority of the men who wrote the Bible to speak in the name of God establish the authority of the Church to speak in His name."[22]

"The same God who inspired the written word lives and teaches in and through her, and can no more deceive or be deceived in teaching in and through her than in teaching in and through the written word itself."[23] The voice of the Church, then, is, equally with the Bible, the voice of God, with this difference—the one is divinely *inspired*, the other is divinely *assisted*.

Objection: The Church with her Infallibility is the enemy of reason; she denies reason, and substitutes for it authority; she will not allow reason to question her authority, or to inquire into and test the truth of her teaching; she demands of reason a blind obedience to dogmas sometimes wholly incomprehensible; in short, her claims are simply irreconcilable with the rights of reason.

Answer: I will take the propositions of this objection separately, and reply to them in the order given.

(*a.*) '*The Church with her Infallibility is the enemy of reason.*' The simplest and most effective answer to this proposition is a brief statement of Catholic teaching on reason and its rights. The Church then teaches that reason is a divine gift, and the greatest of man's natural endowments;[14] that whatever sins against reason sins against God, its Author; and that whatever contradicts it cannot be true, and must be rejected as false and incredible. The Church teaches that reason, in the logical order, comes before faith; that faith presupposes reason, and is impossible without it, because an act of faith necessarily involves an act of the highest reason, and is itself primarily, though not exclusively, an intellectual act. She teaches that reason has a perfect right to investigate according to its own methods all truths of the natural order—every truth that belongs to its province and falls within its reach; that, moreover, it belongs to reason to demonstrate the *preambula fidei*[15] or the foundations of faith—to prove, *scil.*, that there is a God; that He is infinitely knowing and truthful; and therefore that He can neither deceive nor be deceived. She teaches that reason cannot be bound to give its assent to any proposition, whether of the natural or supernatural order, without a sufficient motive for doing so; that therefore before it can be under an obligation to believe a teaching of faith to be the word of God it must be convinced beyond all prudent doubt or reasonable fear of error, (1) that God has spoken, and (2) that what is proposed for its acceptance is what He said; that, consequently, it has a perfect right to examine the credentials of Revelation, and to judge whether or not the proofs or evidence of the fact that God has spoken, or that a revelation has been made, are satisfactory."[26] Moreover, she (the Church) teaches that reason, before it is bound to allow *her own claim* to its obedience, must be satisfied that her title-deeds are good and fully justify the claim; that, therefore, reason has a strict and unquestionable right to examine the question and judge whether or not she is truly and rightfully what she professes to be—God's representative on earth, commissioned by Him to teach man, in His name, and by His authority, and with His special supernatural assistance, the truths of salvation. All this the Catholic Church teaches on reason and its rights. How, then, is she the enemy of reason? And how can she reasonably be accused of being such?"[27]

Furthermore, the Church has put this teaching into practice, and that more than once; for when the powers and rights of reason were denied or belittled we find that she came forward to defend them. When the Reformers of the sixteenth century asserted that man's reason, through the fall, became so obscured that without the light of Revelation he could not attain to any truth, even of the natural order, the Church at once anathematized the teaching as false, and in opposition to it taught that man's natural intellect and reasoning faculty are, after the fall, essentially and substantially what they were before it."

Again when, some years since, she saw a tendency in a Catholic professor in a Continental University, and later on in a Catholic publicist, to undervalue reason and to deny its rights, the Church again came to the defence of reason, expressed her disapproval of the opinions in question, and compelled their authors to repudiate them."

Once more, the Agnostics of our day, the would-be champions of reason and of its rights, the Apostles of free-thought, deny to reason the power or ability to prove the existence of God, its Author; and again the Church, in the Vatican Council,"" condemns the error and proclaims it to be infallibly certain that reason has this power, and, consequently, can prove to its own entire satisfaction the existence of its Divine Author. No; the Church is not the enemy of reason, but, emphatically, its friend. She could not be its enemy without being the enemy of God.

(b.) '*She denies reason, and substitutes for it authority.*' The Church insists on authority in matters of faith, but in this she merely demands for faith what is absolutely essential to it. For faith, as distinguished from knowledge or science, is, of its very nature, belief on authority. Therefore, where there is faith there must be authority; and, consequently, in insisting on authority in matters of faith, the Church acts not in denial of, or in contradiction to, but perfectly in accordance with, reason.

Moreover, the authority which the Church demands is one which challenges the approval of reason,—one that unbiased reason, on examination, is obliged to declare altogether sufficient as a motive of faith. "Non-Catholics," says Dr. Brownson,[30] "object to us that we demand belief on authority; but this in reality is an objection in their minds chiefly because they suppose we substitute authority for reason, and do not recognize in belief on authority a real act of reason. Nothing, of course, is more unreasonable than to substitute authority for reason (in the sense of the objection), or to suppose that any authority can be a good ground of faith after reason is denied. Faith is an assent of the intellect as well as a consent of the will, and is and must be, in order to be faith, an act of reason. To deny reason is to deny both faith and the possibility of faith; and hence without the act or exercise of reason there is and can be no faith. The unbeliever sees this more or less clearly, and supposing that we, like Calvinists, assert authority only as a substitute for reason, he refuses to entertain any argument in behalf of the authority of the Church. He sets us down as offering, in the very outset, an affront to reason for the very proposition of authority in matters of faith he looks upon as the denial of reason." As this writer points out elsewhere,[31] those who object to faith or belief on authority as belief without reason, do so from a misapprehension of the meaning of authority in matters of faith. They take authority to mean merely an order addressed to the will commanding its obedience without any accompanying reason or motive to justify the assent of the intellect. But in this they greatly err; for authority in matters of faith, as understood at least by Catholic theologians, is authority for the intellect as well as for the will. It means not only an order for the will, but also a reason for the intellect; not only a command *to* believe, but an adequate motive *for* believing. The command of the Church then is addressed both to the intellect and to the will; as the legitimate order of a superior placed over us by God, with authority to command, it is a sufficient reason for the will to give its consent and obey; and because of the necessary and unfailing connection between the truth and her teaching which her Infallibility guarantees, it is a sufficient reason for the intellect to give its full and unwavering assent. That is, in other words, the Church, while she commands the will, enlightens the mind and convinces the reason; and consequently commands us to believe *only through the conviction of our understanding.* Faith, then, is a reasonable act, and if it were not it would not be faith.

(c.) ' *She will not allow reason to question her authority or to inquire into and test the truth of her teaching.*' Before the Church demands your obedience she is ready to satisfy your reason that she has a right to .it. She freely allows the justice of the principle, "Whoever exacts faith ought to furnish a reason for faith, *Qui exigit fidem rationem supplere debet.* Addressing reason accordingly, she says, ' I claim to come from God with an express commission to teach you His law in His name, by His authority, and with His infallible assistance. Here are my title-deeds; here are my credentials; here are the grounds on which I base this claim to a divine origin and mission, and to an infallible teaching authority. Take and examine them carefully and fairly in the full light of reason and science. I am willing that you should subject them to the severest criticism; for I am confident that you will find them all that you require or can reasonably demand;—that they prove beyond all reasonable doubt my claim to be just, and therefore my right to your obedience to be perfectly legitimate.' Now, if after examination the verdict of reason is for the Church, what right has reason from that forward to question her authority, or to demand that the truth of its teaching be submitted to its test, or to hesitate before giving to that teaching its unconditional and unwavering assent? Once the Church has established to the satisfaction of reason the fact that she is God's representative, possessed with authority direct from Him to declare infallibly His will to man, reason has henceforth no more right to question her authority, or to examine her teaching with a view to see whether or not it is true, or to refuse or waver in its assent to it, than it has to question the authority of God Himself, or to test the truth of His word, or to deny or waver in assenting to its teaching. Two questions then have to be carefully distinguished and kept apart in this matter: (1) 'Has God appointed the Church the infallible Witness, Teacher, and Guardian of His Revelation?' and the other (2) 'Is what she, in the exercise of her infallible authority, proposes for our belief true?' The first question falls within the province of reason, and is therefore one for reason to examine and decide; the second lies outside the province of reason and belongs to an order which transcends its reach. The Church freely acknowledges, or, rather, teaches the right and competency of reason to judge in the first case; in the second case she allows to reason no such right or competency, for the following reasons: (1) Because her Infallibility (already *ex hypothesi* established) is an ample guarantee to reason that what she proposes for its assent is the word of God, and, therefore, necessarily, absolutely, and wholly true. (2) Because the dogmas of her teaching, if truths at all, are truths not of reason or of the natural order, but truths of the supernatural order—truths of Revelation, and, therefore, as such, truths not to be known by science but to be believed by faith. If reason were competent to examine into and pass judgment on the *intrinsic* truth of the contents of Revelation, or of the dogmas of the Church; and if it accepted and assented to them simply because it saw the *intrinsic* evidence of their truth, it would in that case have knowledge or science, but not faith; there would be no room for faith there. (3) Because if she allowed to reason the right to raise the question: ' Is what the Church teaches as a dogma of faith true or revealed? ' she would virtually admit that God may reveal what is not true, and that she may teach as revealed truth what may be false,—that is, she would virtually confess that God may lie, and that she herself, while claiming to be infallible, may after all be fallible in her *ex-cathedra* judgments; that is, again contradict and stultify herself." In allowing, then, to reason the right to examine and pass judgment on the credentials of Revelation, and on her own credentials as the divinely appointed and infallible Teacher of its contents, the Church allows reason all that reason has a right to,—*all* that it can reasonably demand. In denying to reason the further right to test the truth of what Revelation, and she as its organ proposes for reason's acceptance, she denies it no right which belongs to it. She simply says to it: This truth pertains to an order in which you have neither competency nor authority. And in this she is but following the example of her Divine Founder. Our Lord did not allow His hearers to question the truth of His teaching; neither did He seek to give intrinsic evidence of its truth. He deemed it sufficient to give proof of the Divinity of His mission; and having established that fact, He required His hearers to believe without examination or question, hesitation or doubt. For the truth of His mission and Divinity He gave proof;" for the truth of His doctrine He merely gave His word." So, too, acted St. Paul. He gave proof to his hearers of his divine mission to teach, and then demanded of them unquestioning and undoubting faith in his teaching as the infallible word of God. Hence it is he calls faith an "obedience,"" a "captivity of the understanding.""" Well, the Church's authority to teach is the same as St. Paul's, the same as Jesus Christ's; for it is written, " As my Father hath sent me, *even so send I you.*""

(*d.*) '*She demands of reason a blind obedience to dogmas sometimes wholly incomprehensible to it.*' There is no authority in the world that can rightfully command reason to yield to its teaching a blind obedience; not even God Himself could make such a demand on reason; for it is not in the power of reason to give its assent to a proposition without a reason for doing so. This is the teaching of Catholic philosophy and theology;" and in accordance with this teaching the Church does not ask, much less demand, of reason obedience to her authority until she has given it sufficient grounds for believing that in yielding such obedience it is acting not blindly but knowingly and reasonably. She submits to reason the proofs of her authority, fully confident that if reason is free to examine them fully and fairly, it will pronounce them most reasonable and conclusive." Of course reason may be blinded by prejudice, or prevented by sin or other cause from seeing the full force of the argument in her favor, and consequently refuse to acknowledge her authority as just or from God. This is no more than happened in the case of her Divine Founder. Our Lord gave to the world proofs sufficiently convincing of His Divinity and Mission; and yet we know that there were those who did not believe in Him, and that in doing so they were inexcusable." So, too, it has been, is, and I suppose ever will be with His Church; she gives to the world all the proof that can reasonably be demanded of her claim to a divine mission and to infallible authority in its discharge. To be sure the proof is not compelling—no moral proof ever is—but it is fully sufficient; and being so the question is—and it is a serious question for each and every one of those who refuse or fail to see its force, and on that account deny the Church's rightful claim to their obedience—'Will my action be excusable before God?'

And as to the objection that her dogmas are incomprehensible; and, therefore, that it is unreasonable to demand faith in them. It cannot surely be maintained that it is always unreasonable to believe what is incomprehensible, or if so, then we have no one in the world, save God Himself, who is not unreasonable; for there is no one in the world who does not, every day of his life, believe what is utterly incomprehensible to him. To find out this, any one has but to put himself the question: 'How many of the facts of nature, which I see and know and assume to be true, can I fully explain? In how many cases do I comprehend the *why* and the *wherefore* of them? The truth is, nature as well as religion, is full of mysteries, and all reflecting minds admit the fact. A distinguished writer" has observed that it is only weak minds that believe they can explain all and understand all.

To believe what is incomprehensible without a sufficient reason for doing so, would indeed be unreasonable; but to believe it when God teaches it and when the believer has infallible testimony to this fact, would be not unreasonable but most reasonable, for reason knows that God is infinitely knowing and infinitely truthful—that He can neither deceive nor be deceived—and consequently that what He says must be true, and, even when above reason, ought to be believed on His mere word, without further evidence of its truth." Well, the Church demands our assent to what is incomprehensible in her teaching only because it is God's teaching; and to this fact her testimony is altogether sufficient, because she is an Infallible Witness.

(e.) '*In short, her claims are simply irreconcilable with the rights of reason.*' Though what has already been said contains a sufficient answer to this proposition, I will add a few words expressly to the point. The rights of reason, briefly yet truly stated, are (1) to investigate fully and freely all truths of the natural order—all truths that fall within its reach and province; (2) to demand an adequate motive for its assent whenever, and to whatever, it is claimed; and (3) to reject what is evidently or certainly error, taking care, however, not to condemn as error what is merely above it or incomprehensible to it." More than this reason has not a right to,—more than this it cannot reasonably claim. Now the Church, as we have seen, freely allows these rights to reason; nay, more, she upholds and proclaims them as a portion of her teaching. And what are the demands she makes on reason? Simply (1) that reason shall submit to the authority of God and believe firmly His teaching; (2) that it shall render the same homage to the duly authenticated authority and teaching of her whom God Himself has directly instituted and commissioned to govern and teach in His name and with His special supernatural and infallible assistance; (3) that it shall, as it every day is in most important worldly matters, be satisfied with moral certainty both of the fact of Revelation and of her divine mission to interpret it; and (4) that it shall not *rashly* seek to investigate the mysteries of Revelation or the dogmas of her teaching, much less to grasp the intrinsic evidence of their truth; because such mysteries and dogmas lie beyond the province of reason and belong to an order that is above reason and transcends its reach." Now what contradiction is there or can there be between these respective rights and demands? What is there irreconcilable in them?"

A word to those who honestly urge this objection: You may have examined some systems of religion, and found them unsatisfactory to your reason, perhaps their claims irreconcilable with its rights; and you may have concluded that all systems of supernaturalism being essentially—being in principle at least—the same, there was no use in examining any other. Now if this be your case I wish to say that your conclusion is not the conclusion of reason, nor does it exonerate you from the obligation of further investigation. The fact you assume is not true. All systems of supernaturalism are not the same in principle. The system of Catholicism differs essentially and in principle from all others; and whatever contradiction or conflict you may have found to exist between the natural and supernatural as embodied in other systems, you may rest assured you will find none in Catholicism. There, as an examination will prove, you will find both the principle and guarantee of perfect harmony between both orders and their respective rights in the dogma of Infallibility; and you will find the harmony itself in the complete accord that exists in the bosom of the Church between science and revelation, reason and faith, nature and grace, liberty and authority. Hear the testimony of one whom Lord Brougham styled the "master-mind of America," one who examined and had actual experience of many systems of religion, and, as a result, was, for many years before he became a Catholic, of your way of thinking. I mean the great Dr. Brownson."

"Whoever has been a Protestant knows well that he experiences a constant struggle between reason and what he terms faith. . . . This struggle between faith and reason is something *wholly foreign* to the Catholic mind, and the real Catholic finds it hard, unless he has been bred a Protestant, even to conceive of it, because Catholicity, though it requires us to do violence to the flesh, never requires us to do violence to reason. Catholicity is not a rationalistic, but it is a rational religion, and at every step satisfies the demands even of the most rigid reason. We were told so before we came into the Church, but we could hardly believe it, and even when we were permitted to enter, we did not doubt but we should still find something of that interior struggle between faith and reason *which had rendered us so miserable as a Protestant*, so hard is it for a Protestant mind to conceive the possibility of perfect harmony between faith in the supernatural and the dictates of reason. We have not thus far been troubled with any struggle of the sort, and we are unable to conceive how, as long as we remain a Catholic, we can be, because in Catholicity all has a sufficient reason, is sure to have a purpose worthy of itself, and nothing is required to be believed but on an adequate authority, and thus the demands of the highest reason are satisfied."[47]

Objection: The Catholic creed is a tyrannical creed, and the Catholic's faith in it is not a rational or reasonable faith; the Catholic has no voice in formulating the creed he believes; he cannot use on his creed the faculty God gave him for his direction; he cannot reason on it, for the Church dreads reason. All that is left him is to sit at the feet of the Pope, listen attentively and submissively to what he has to say, and then give forth his *Credo*—I believe. He is not free in his faith.

Answer: (a.) '*The Catholic creed is a tyrannical creed.*' To call any creed tyrannical is, to say the least, a thoughtless misuse of words. A rule or government may be tyrannical, but a creed, that if believed at all must be believed by the free assent of the mind, cannot. There is no species of tyranny that can reach the mind and *compel* its assent. The consent of the will may be extorted, but the assent of the intellect—no. We may be forced to simulate belief in a certain creed, but interiorly and actually to assent to it—into that no man can be forced. The only coercion the mind and its acts are subject to is the coercion of God and of truth. Men often speak of "spiritual tyranny," and by that "they mean, for the most part, the restraining influence upon license of opinion, of established and accepted doctrines, the control of systems which address themselves to the intellect, and hold to fixed beliefs the understanding that has assented to them. Now if the phrase means this, and this only, how can the term 'tyranny' find place in it? In what sense can the word 'tyrannical' be applied to a system which holds men only by the assent of their own understandings—by a bond which they have themselves formed, and which they are at any time free to dissolve? *How can a man be tyrannized over by his own convictions, or by any system to which only conviction binds him?* The invidious phrase 'spiritual tyranny' is, we know, most frequently employed in discrediting criticism of religious beliefs. We are well-nigh tired of the jargon in which Christian faith is denounced as a thraldom of the mind. But why should that be called by names significant of oppression which is freely submitted to by those whom it affects? It is but a self-inflicted grievance, if it be a grievance at all; no tyrant is responsible for the wrong, if wrong there be. It is quite true that the Christian system once accepted, opinions at variance with it cannot be received by the believer. *But this restraint is imposed only as long as the faith with which these opinions are incompatible is submitted to, and this submission is dependent wholly on the will of the believer himself.* Clearly we must change our definition of things if the word 'tyrannical' is to find justifiable application in such a case as this."[18]

(b.) '*The Catholic's faith is not a reasonable faith.*' Nothing is or can be more reasonable than to believe what God teaches; for what He, who is Truth itself, teaches is necessarily and absolutely true. This reason itself well knows and freely allows. Now if the Church is the divinely constituted organ of God's voice; if God has committed to her keeping the truth, and is ever present with her to assist and preserve her from all liability to err in teaching it to us, what is more reasonable than to believe that what she teaches as God's revealed truth is really so? If she is infallible in witnessing and declaring God's word, how can faith in what she teaches be unreasonable unless it is unreasonable to believe the Word of God Himself?"

The Catholic's faith unreasonable! Why, if faith is at all reasonable the Catholic faith is so; for it recognizes no authority in religion but the authority of God, no proper object of faith but God's supernaturally revealed word, and no adequate motive of faith but the infinite knowledge and veracity of God revealing (its object or) the truth to be believed. The reader must bear in mind that Catholics believe the dogmas of their religion, not because they are the authoritative teaching of the Church or of the Pope, but simply and solely because they have been revealed by God and are his teaching. Two things have always to be considered in connection with a dogma of Catholic faith; namely, its *truth* and the *fact* of its revelation; for a dogma of Catholic faith must be not only *true*, but must, moreover, be *revealed*,—a truth contained in the original revelation made by God through Christ and His Apostles. Now the *fact* of its revelation—the *fact* that God has supernaturally revealed it—that *fact* we take on the testimony of the Church which, being infallible, is a sufficient authority for it; but the intrinsic *truth* of the dogma we believe solely on the authority of God, who has revealed it. That is, in other words, we believe on the authority of the Church that each article of our faith has been supernaturally revealed by God, and we believe the articles themselves to be severally true on the authority of God revealing them. "The ultimate authority, then," says Cardinal Manning, "on which we believe is the voice of God speaking to us through the Church. We believe not in the Church, but through it; and through the Church, in God."[60] In other words, the Church is the *medium*, and the authority of God the *motive* of our faith.

(c.) '*The Catholic has no voice in formulating the creed he believes.*' What right has he to a voice in formulating what he is to believe by *divine* faith, and what must be of God's ordination, not of man's formation? Moreover, what use would a voice be in the matter? His voice, at most, is but the voice of reason, the voice of nature; but his creed, to be of any value, must come, not of reason, but of revelation, and be supernatural—above reason and above nature—and purely the work of God and of His grace. The reason, then, is plain why the Catholic has not and does not claim to have a voice in formulating what he has to believe by Divine Faith.

(d.) '*He cannot use on his creed the faculty God gave him for his direction.*' And why? Simply because that faculty (reason) was not given him to construct his religious creed. It was given him to direct him in the natural order, the order to which it belongs. In reference to the supernatural order, the order not of nature but of grace, its part is merely to examine and judge of the proofs of its existence, and, on finding sufficient evidence of that fact, to believe accordingly.

(e.) '*He cannot reason on his creed.*' The Catholic, it is true, cannot inquire into or reason on the question whether his creed or the articles of which it is composed be true or not; for such an act would imply a doubt about its truth; and where there is a doubt there is and can be no faith. The Catholic, therefore, who would require to institute any such inquiry would have already lost his faith and ceased to be a Catholic."

Besides, what consistency, or sense, or reason would there be in the action of such a man? If he believes the Church to be Infallible—and he is not and cannot be a Catholic unless he does—how can he in reason doubt the truth of what she teaches? And if her teaching is true beyond the possibility of error, what would be the sense, or meaning, or use of raising the question whether it is so, and of instituting an inquiry with a view to determine the matter? Such a proceeding surely would not be an act of reason, or one the credit of which any reasonable man would ambition."

But though the Catholic may not inquire into or reason on his creed with a view to determine whether or not it is true, at the same time, while he accepts and holds to its truth with a firm and unwavering faith, and observes in his investigations the respect and reverence due to its sacred authority, he is perfectly free to exercise his reason on its teachings as much as he may please, in order to gain a fuller and clearer knowledge of them, whether for his own instruction, edification, or satisfaction, or for the instruction and edification of others, or with a view to be able to illustrate and defend them against the objections of unbelievers." "Catholics, in fact," writes Dr. Brownson, "are the only people in the world who do, can, or dare to reason in matters of religion. Indeed, they are the only people who have a reasonable faith, and who believe only what they have an adequate reason for believing. They are also the only people who recognize no human authority, not even one's own, in matters of Christian faith and conscience."" And, in reply to the Protestant's boast that he is free in faith, because he admits no authority but reason, he goes on to observe: "As a fact, no man is less free than he who has for his faith no authority but his own reason; for he is, if he thinks at all, necessarily always in doubt as to what he ought or ought not to believe; and no man who is in doubt, who is unable to determine what he is or is not required to believe in order to believe the truth, is or can be mentally free. From this doubt only the Catholic is free; for he only has the authority of God, who can neither deceive nor be deceived for his faith."⁵⁵

(f.) '*The Church dreads reason.*' How, then, is it that she is every day converting men through their reason? During the past fifty years hundreds of the most cultivated minds of England, of Germany and of America have abjured Protestantism to submit to her authority and become Catholics. Take up " *Converts to Rome*,"⁵⁶ by W. Gordon-Gorman, a Protestant, and you will see there the conquests she has made among the graduates of the two most cultured Universities in the world—Oxford and Cambridge. You will find there some of the greatest names that these Universities can boast of, and how were they converted from Anglicanism to Catholicism if not through their reason and at its bidding? The celebrated author, M. De la Harpe, once said, "I am a Catholic *because I have examined; do you the same, and you will be one too.*" A recent distinguished convert, Mr. George Parsons Lathrop, writing to a friend on the reasons which induced him to become a Catholic, says: "The attempt to inform myself about the Church began with the same impartiality, the same candor and receptiveness that I should use towards any other subject on which I honestly desired to form a just conclusion. Notwithstanding that education had surrounded me with prejudice, *my mind was convinced* as to the truth, the validity and supremacy of the Roman Catholic Church *by the clear and comprehensive reasons on which it was based.* And, while the reasoning of other religious organizations continually shifts and wavers, leaving their adherents—as we now see almost every day—to fall into rationalism and agnostic denial, the reasoning of the Church, I found, led directly to sublime and inspiring faith. *This union of solid reasoning and luminous faith I cannot find elsewhere.*" The fact of the matter is, outsiders who read and think and reason impartially are daily learning to look upon the Church with favor and admiration.

"The thing," says Dr. Brownson, "the Church dreads is not reason, but *unreason*, not logic, but sophistry, for all her principles, nay, all her dogmas are Catholic, universally true; and if they transcend the reach of reason, *no reason can ever get beyond them, upset them, or find, so long as it is reason, any ground for doubting them.*"⁵⁷

(g.) '*All that is left to him* [the Catholic] *is to sit at the feet of the Pope, listen attentively and submissively to what he has to say, and then give forth his Credo, I believe.*' The Catholic sits, or, if you will, kneels, at the feet of the Pope, and he deems it a great privilege—a signal grace from above —to have the faith to do so. He listens attentively and submissively to the teaching of the Pope; because his reason is convinced that God appointed the Pope to be the Shepherd of His flock and the Pastor of His people;⁵⁸ and to what the Pope proposes to him as the word of God he is ready to say *Credo*, because he knows full well that the Pope can teach for his belief nothing but what God commissioned him to teach. Is there anything ignoble, or degrading in this? any "sacrifice of the intellect"? anything unworthy of man in submitting to a divine and infallible Teacher, and taking the truth from his lips? Is it not an advantage and a blessing, to be proud rather than ashamed of, to have an unerring Teacher of the truths of salvation and an unerring Guide to the way of salvation? So, at least, think two hundred and thirty millions of Catholics.

(*h.*) '*He* [the Catholic] *is not free in his faith.*' In answer to this suffice it to say that faith, in Catholic teaching, to be of any value, must be perfectly free. Any other is not acceptable to God or beneficial to man."

Objection: The dogma of Infallibility extinguishes liberty of thought, bans free inquiry, stands in the way of intellectual development, and tends to weaken, cripple, dwarf, and enslave the mind. In truth, the mind, that is under the rule of Infallibility, is held in an enfeebling, ignoble, and degrading bondage.

Answer: (*a*) '*The dogma of Infallibility extinguishes liberty of thought.*' Three assumptions underlie this objection, to each of which it is necessary to direct attention. They are: (1) that it is possible to tyrannize over thought and coerce it; (2) that thought is governed by no law and is subject to no restraint, save the good pleasure of the thinker; and (3) that liberty of thought is an unqualified blessing which every man should be proud of, which all men should possess, and of which no man can rightfully be deprived. Now a little reflection will suffice to show that these assumptions, so far from being true, as the objection supposes, are all three grave errors.

1. As was observed before, no power on earth—no such power as the objection contemplates—can tyran-

nize over, coerce, or restrain, much less extinguish, liberty of thought. This is impossible, for the simple reason that no such power can reach one's thoughts, or even know of them against his will. Man may be deprived of physical liberty, of political liberty, of social liberty, of the liberty to profess and openly practise his religion and do the bidding of his conscience; he may be deprived of liberty of body, of limb, of tongue,. of the liberty to express his thoughts in words, but of the liberty of thought itself he cannot be deprived. No government, no Church, no organization, no power on earth, can deprive him of the liberty to think as he pleases, or force him to think thoughts, or to adopt convictions other than those he wills, or to assent to a creed which his reason refuses to accept. This is perfectly plain; and, therefore, to talk of tyranny of thought, or of intellectual despotism, is to talk nonsense; for, from the very nature of the case, there can be no such thing. It is an absolute impossibility.

2. Thought, as well as act, has its law and is subject to its restraint. The law of thought is the law of truth; and the law of act is the law of duty; and man, being capable both of thought and of act, owes obedience to the one law as well as to the other. We have no more right to believe what is false than we have to do what is wrong. Law and reason forbid licentiousness of thought and belief as well as of desire, word, and act; for error as well as vice is to be avoided. Thought, then, is under the dominion of truth, and is subject to its restraints. Where the truth is distinctly known, there liberty of thought can have no place; for no man who knows the truth is at liberty to dissent from it, or to assent to its opposite.

To claim such liberty would be irrational, it would be in direct and gross violation of the laws of reason itself. There is, therefore, no such thing as universal, unrestrained liberty of thought—unrestrained intellectual liberty. It follows, consequently, that as God made thought subject to truth, the greater our knowledge of the truth is—the more truth or truths we know—the more restricted necessarily becomes our liberty of thought, or, to put the matter in another way, liberty of thought is allowable and can exist only in the absence of knowledge of the truth,—that is, only where it is doubtful or uncertain on which side the truth lies. The greater, therefore, our ignorance is, the greater is our liberty of thought—a fact surely sufficient to disprove assumption (3) mentioned above, and to convince the ordinary mind that "liberty of thought" is not exactly a privilege to be proud of, or to boast very loudly about.

It is so fashionable, at the present time, to sound the praises of "free thought," "liberty of thought," "intellectual liberty"; and the enemies of religious faith so frequently make these dazzling phrases do duty against belief in Christian truth, that it is well we should have true and clear ideas of their value. For this purpose I feel justified in making a lengthened extract from a learned address on "Liberty of Thought," from which I have already quoted. After defining thought to mean "the act of the mind by which we form to ourselves ideas and opinions regarding the objects which come under our notice," and "liberty of thought" to mean "liberty to do this act—freedom to form ideas and opinions on the objects before us without let or hinderance"—the distinguished lecturer proceeds as follows: "In the minds of the speakers and writers whose language we are now discussing, it is assumed that this 'liberty of thought' is a privilege of which men can only wrongfully be deprived. It is taken for granted that it is an advantage to be able to think as we will upon any and every subject, that freedom to hold any opinion we choose upon any question whatever is an unqualified blessing. That these assumptions underlie the praises of 'free thought,' with which we are familiar, is evident from the nature of the case. It is not a privation to lose that which it is not an advantage to possess. The proceeding that would interfere with our liberty of thought could not be stigmatized as 'tyranny,' if liberty of thought were not reputed a benefit.

"And yet, what are the advantages of this much exalted liberty? Liberty of thought, in the only sense in which the words bear their rightful meaning, *is of its very nature the mark and misfortune of defective knowledge; it is an evidence of intellectual weakness*, and it must necessarily be restricted as knowledge grows in range and definiteness, and the mind gets a clearer view of the objects presented to it. Wherever and whenever we are free to hold opposite opinions on a question we are free to hold a wrong opinion or a right opinion; we are placed in a position in which we can give assent to error as well as to truth. Liberty of thought implies, in the very notion of it, the liberty to hold what is false as well as what is true. To enjoy this liberty, then, to be free to take either side on any question, *we must be ignorant enough not to discern clearly on which side lies the truth.* If we see the truth, and see it clearly, we are no longer free. The assent of our understanding is at once determined by the manifestation of the truth; we cannot without a violence to ourselves, worse than any which tyranny could inflict, put the manifest truth aside and assent to what is false. A savage may hold that two sides of a triangle are not, together, greater than the third; or a fanatic admirer of the wisdom of the ancients may contend that the earth does not move round the sun; but the one, as the other, *owes his peculiar freedom of opinion to a condition of mind on which he is hardly to be congratulated. His liberty of thought is in exact proportion to his ignorance or prejudice.* If he knew a little more, or were a little less blinded, he would find himself tied to one opinion.

"*The fact is that every accession to our stock of exact knowledge, every new addition to the sum of truth we possess, diminishes our liberty of thought. It binds us to fixed views on the points on which the truth has been made known to us, and it is but to quarrel with the laws of our own understanding to struggle against this restriction.* We have lost much liberty of thought enjoyed by the sages of three centuries ago, and are we anything the worse for this? We have not now the privilege to differ from Kepler and Copernicus as to the movements of the planets; *are we, in this, less favored than were the men who lived when the theories* of Kepler and Copernicus *were still open questions,* and philosophers took sides with or against them according to their lights or their prejudices? It is hardly possible for us now to uphold the view that the ultimate constituents of the material world are the four elements, earth, air, fire, and water; have we gained or lost by the circumstances which preclude a choice of opinions on this question? Our knowledge on all these points has grown; astronomy has traced the orbits of the planets, and chemistry has resolved material substances into many elements, and with the progress of these sciences has come *a proportionate restriction upon the opinions we are at liberty to entertain* on the questions they have solved. *Surely thinking men are not distressed because of the loss of liberty involved therein.*

" What is here said of the sciences of astronomy and chemistry, is applicable to truth in every form. Whenever truth is revealed distinctly to us, be the manner of the revelation what it may, the effect is to fix our opinions, *and, in so far, to restrict our liberty of thought.* Should truth revealed take the form of a religious creed, its effect for the purpose before us will be the same as when it is addressed to us as a science. When we are satisfied of the truth of the system, and, on the strength of this assurance, have given it our honest assent, it is idle to complain that it interferes with our liberty of thought. *It would not be truth at all, or at least it would not be truth worth the knowing, if it did not.* If we doubted its guarantees, and therefore distrusted its tenets, we committed a folly in accepting it; but if we cordially received it in the conviction that it was wholly true, we are committing an equally great folly in complaining that it does not leave us free. We have accepted it as a well-established theory that fire is but the heat and light produced by the chemical union of combining material substances; and, being satisfied of this, we do not find it a hardship that we are not any longer free to regard fire as a semi-celestial substance struggling upwards towards the sphere which is its native abode. In the same way we have received it for true that the Universe is the work of a Great Intelligent Being whose Omnipotent Will is the ultimate and adequate cause of all things that are. Why should we find it a hardship that we are not free to take sides with, or even to entertain, certain current theories which represent the Universe as forming itself by innate forces out of some primeval chaos? What greater prejudice does our liberty suffer in the one case than in the other? Granting that the religious tenet and the scientific theory are alike established truths, *what ground of complaint have we against the one more than against the other?* In both cases we yield to the truth, and are controlled by it. We do not adopt a theory merely because it is religious, nor merely because it is scientific, *but because it is truth.*

"We have come, then, to this: that liberty of thought, in any sense in which the words have meaning, *is wholly out of place where the truth has, by any means, been established;* that to assert the privilege under such circumstances is an effort to suppress truth while conscious of its existence, to exalt it by recognizing it for what it is, and at the same time depreciate it by claiming the right to dissent from it."[60]

Now to return to the point of the objection. If the dogma of Infallibility deprives us of liberty of thought, it does this only by imparting truth to the mind; and, therefore, only in the same sense and to the same extent that the knowledge and possession of the truth deprives us of it. The dogma of Infallibility, then, and its teaching, are no more open to reproach or to objection than truth and its teaching; for the dogma itself is a truth, and the only restraint it can put on our thoughts is the restraint of truth.

(b) "*Infallibility bans free inquiry.*" What I have already said of Catholic faith is equally true of the dogma of Infallibility. It allows reason full play in all questions that fall within the province of reason." As long as reason confines itself to inquiry into the truths of reason and of nature, and does not encroach on the domain of faith, neither the dogma of Infallibility nor any other dogma of Catholic faith will ever interfere with its freedom; and a better guarantee for this than is contained in that very dogma of Infallibility, which is supposed to be its enemy, reason could not have. "Infallibility," writes Cardinal Newman, "is a supply for a need, and it does not go beyond the need. Its object is, and its effect also, *not to enfeeble the freedom or vigor of human thought, but to resist and control its extravagances.*" [62]

(c) "*Infallibility is a hinderance to intellectual development, and tends to weaken, cripple, dwarf, and enslave the mind.*" How so? Is the knowledge (and possession) of truth a hinderance to intellectual development? or does it tend to weaken, cripple, dwarf, and enslave the mind? Is not truth the food and strength of the mind, the life and light of the intellect? and what but truth can Infallibility teach or ask the intellect to assent to? And being incapable of teaching anything but the truth, or of demanding assent to, or belief in anything but the truth, how, I ask again, can it be said with truth, or with reason, that the dogma of Infallibility obstructs or hinders intellectual development, or tends in any way to weaken, cripple, dwarf, or enslave the mind? Just think the matter over for yourself; use a little "liberty of thought" and private judgment on the subject, and don't be too ready to accept for gospel truth the catching phrases and statements of those who do not want you to believe in Infallibility, or in any other Christian truth.

(d) "*In a word, the mind that is under the rule of Infallibility is held in an enfeebling, ignoble, and degrading bondage.*" Is it enfeebling, ignoble, or degrading to submit to the authority of God? Well, the authority of Infallibility is the authority of God." Is it enfeebling, ignoble, or degrading to believe the truth? The teaching of Infallibility is and can be nothing else than the truth pure and simple. Where, then, is the enfeebling, ignoble, and degrading bondage of those who believe in Infallibility, and submit to its teaching? "If," says Dr. Brownson, "it is the truth that liberates us and makes us free, what harm does the Church do us when she presents to us infallibly the truth? If man is necessarily under the law of his Creator, how does she harm us in teaching that law?" " True, the Church does not tolerate liberty of thought on points clearly of faith, but this is no more than saying that she will not allow Catholics to deny or doubt what they have already accepted, and firmly believe to be the absolute and undiluted teaching of God's word. The Catholic, who would claim such a right, would be no more reasonable, or consistent in his action than the geometrician who, while accepting the axioms of geometry as absolute truths, would yet claim the right to deny or doubt them whenever the thought occurred to do so; or of the logician who, after accepting the principle of contradiction, as it is called, would still claim the right to hold and to argue that a thing may be and not be at the same time.

For strength, energy, and activity of mind, for vigor, boldness, and fearlessness of thought, few men of this century can compare with Dr. Brownson. His testimony, therefore, on the effect of the Church's authority on his mental freedom is both valuable and pertinent. "I have been," he wrote, "during the thirteen years of my Catholic life, constantly engaged in the study of the Church and her doctrines, and especially in their relations to philosophy or natural reason. I have had occasion to examine and defend Catholicity precisely under those points of view which are the most odious to my non-Catholic countrymen, and to the Protestant mind generally; *but I have never, in a single instance, found a single article, dogma, proposition, or definition of faith which embarrassed me as a logician, and which I would, so far as my reason was concerned, have changed or modified, or in any respect altered, from what I found it, even if I had been free to do so. I have never found my reason struggling against the teachings of the Church, or felt it restrained, or myself reduced to a state of mental slavery. I have, as a Catholic, enjoyed a mental freedom which I never conceived possible while I was a non-Catholic. This is my experience.*" **

Ten years later, after contrasting "the peace and serenity of Catholic faith" with "the interior struggles" and restless dissatisfaction which he experienced as a Protestant, he adds the significant words: " And yet the period of our life since we became a Catholic *has been with us the period of our freest and most active and energetic thought.*" **

Objection: Infallibility and its teaching are in conflict with science, and a constant impediment to the Scientist in his pursuit of truth.

Answer: The assertion that Infallibility and its teaching are in conflict with science has been made and repeated times without number, but nobody has ever yet succeeded in proving the truth of it. The Church has, over and over, challenged the authors of it for proof; and, though she has at the same time admitted that one single case of contradiction between a teaching of Infallibility and a demonstrated truth or fact of science would conclusively disprove and effectively dispose of her claim to be the infallible organ of God's Revelation; yet there has so far appeared among her enemies—and they have been not a few— no one who has succeeded in making good the assertion, even to the extent of a single case. This, it must be admitted, is a remarkable fact, and one worthy of the attention of thoughtful minds. Just think of it! One case of conflict between an utterance of Infallibility, *in the whole course of the Church's existence,* and a proved truth or fact of science, and, on her own admission, there was an end at once and forever to the dogma of Infallibility, and to her pretensions to be a divine institution. And yet this one case cannot be found, though non-Catholic Scientists, believers and unbelievers, have sighed for it and have spared no effort to discover it. I repeat it, this is a remarkable fact. "We demand of our advanced thinkers, champions of modern thought, and boasters of modern civilization—in a word, of our unbelieving Scientists, the Huxleys, the Tyndalls, the Spencers, the Comtes, the Littrés, the Darwins, the Lyells, the Youmans, the Fiskes, the Drapers, *to name a single doctrine the Church teaches that science has demonstrated or proved to be untrue; or a single scientific truth, or truth scientifically demonstrated to be truth, that the Church forbids or has ever forbidden to be held or taught.*" [67]

Here I will state two principles of Catholic teaching which are also, clearly, dictates or conclusions of reason:

I. There can be no real contradiction between the supernatural and the natural, between a truth of revelation and a truth of reason, between a fact of faith and a fact of science; for truth cannot contradict truth, neither can God, the Author of all truth, be in conflict with Himself. What is true, therefore, in theology cannot be untrue in philosophy; what is true in religion cannot be untrue in science, or *vice versa*. "Although faith," says the Vatican Council, "is above reason, there can never be any real discrepancy between faith and reason, since the same God who reveals mysteries and infuses faith has bestowed the light of reason on the human mind, and God cannot deny Himself, nor can truth ever contradict truth. *The false appearance of such a contradiction is mainly due, either to the dogmas of faith not having been understood and expounded according to the mind of the Church, or to the inventions of opinions having been taken for the verdicts of reason."* [68]

II. The Catholic, accordingly, holds that what really contradicts, or is in any measure at variance with, a dogma of faith, or a clear teaching of Infallibility on the one hand, or a proved truth of reason or dictate of natural justice or morality, or an established fact of science on the other hand, cannot be true;[69] and that, consequently, the religion that teaches any such contradictory or contrarious doctrine must, so far at least, be false, is incredible, and has to be rejected. Moreover, the Catholic holds that the religion that would claim to speak with divine and infallible authority, and in the exercise of that authority would profess to teach such a doctrine, would stand self-condemned.

Now, as truth cannot contradict truth, and as Infallibility can teach only the truth pure and simple, how, I ask, can Infallibility or its teaching be in conflict with science, or with reason, or with the progress or development of either? If the dogmas of the Church are, beyond the possibility of error, true, how can they be an impediment in the way of the Scientist, or an obstacle to the inquirer after truth, whoever he may be?

Rails do not obstruct the progress of the locomotive; landmarks are not considered a grievance to the liberty of the mariner, nor danger-signals to that of the engineer, nor finger-posts to that of the traveller; neither is Infallibility, nor the dogmas (the landmarks) of faith, a grievance to the liberty of the Scientist or other truth-seeker. "The divine teaching of the Church," says Leo XIII., "so far from being an obstacle to the pursuit of learning and the progress of science, or from retarding in any way the advance of civilization, in reality brings to them the *guidance of a shining light.*"[10]

The truth is, Infallibility and its teaching, so far from being an impediment to the Scientist, are, on the contrary, the greatest help and advantage to him. And, from the very nature of the case, this must be so; for truth must be a help to the attainment of truth; what is known must be an aid to the discovery of what is unknown. The Scientist who believes in Infallibility, and enters on his investigations under the direction of its teaching, has over the unbelieving Scientist an advantage somewhat similar to, but greater than, that which the sea Captain, who, with needle and compass, undertakes a voyage on unknown waters, has over him who, without the directing aid of these instruments, would undertake the same voyage. What the needle and compass are to the Captain, Infallibility is to the Scientist; the indications of the needle are not more valuable to the one (they are less) than is the guidance of Infallibility to the other. The dogmas and other teaching of Infallibility are so much known country, so many landmarks; they not only tell him the truth, but they point out to him, and warn him off, the rocks and quicksands of error." He knows that nothing can be more certain than that the dogmas of his faith and the teaching of Infallibility are true; he knows also that what is true in faith cannot be false in science; and, as truth cannot contradict truth, he knows, consequently, that what contradicts a clear teaching of faith or of Infallibility, or is condemned by either, must be false. The result is, because of his faith—because of the safe guidance of Infallibility and its teaching—he is able to reserve for the pursuit of truth much time and labor which might otherwise be wasted in the pursuit of error."

The teaching of Infallibility may sometimes conflict with the theories, speculations, hypotheses, and guesses of Scientists, but never with the truths or facts of science. The Church, in the exercise of her infallible authority, never has and never can teach anything contradictory of or in conflict with a real truth or fact of science; that, from the very nature of the case, is absolutely impossible."

Hitherto, in discussing this objection in its various and most popular phases, I have, for the most part, contented myself with proving that what is charged against Catholic faith and Infallibility is not true; that faith implies neither injury, nor affront, nor any unfriendliness to reason, or to its rights; and that Infallibility is not and could not be the foe of mental freedom. I will now go a step farther, and conclude by briefly showing the very contrary to be the truth; namely, that faith is the friend and helper of reason, and that Infallibility positively gives and guarantees mental freedom.

Faith helps to strengthen, develop, elevate, and ennoble reason; (1) because, while it in no way curtails the legitimate province of reason, withdraws no truth of reason from its jurisdiction, it opens up to its gaze a higher and wider circle of knowledge, and enlarges its field of view by making known to it a body of truths which it never would or could, of itself and by its own innate power, discover or know, or the existence of which it could not even so much as suspect; (2) it stimulates the ambition of reason to investigate those truths, to acquire a clearer knowledge of them, and to explain, illustrate, prove, and defend them against the assaults and objections of unbelievers; (3) it imparts to reason a ready, full, clear, and certain knowledge of many of the truths of its own province which, though it could know, it would not know so fully, or so clearly, or so certainly, or at all events which it would know only at the expense of much time and great labor spent in the pursuit of them; (4) faith frees reason from all doubt and fear and anxiety on the great problems of human life—its origin, destiny, and the means to attain it—and thus leaves it wholly free to investigate all matters within its reach; (5) faith acts as a guide and corrective to reason by supplying it with the landmarks of truth, the safety-posts pointing to the rocks and quicksands of error, and the signals warning it of the danger ahead, and of the wisdom of caution and reserve, or of the fruitlessness, the waste of time and labor, in pursuing its investigations in a direction in which it can find only error, or only meet with disappointment. These considerations are surely sufficient to prove that revelation and faith are really friends and helpers of reason." "And not only can faith and reason," says the Vatican Council, "never be opposed to one another, but they are of *mutual aid* one to the other; for right reason demonstrates the foundations of faith, and, enlightened by its light, cultivates the science of things divine; while faith frees and guards reason from errors, and furnishes it with manifold knowledge."[16] And Pius IX., in an Encyclical Letter[16] to "the Patriarchs, Primates, Archbishops and Bishops of the Catholic World," thus combats the opinion of those who say that faith gainsays reason. "It is certain that there is nothing more foolish, nothing more impious, and that nothing *more contrary to reason* can be imagined or thought of, than the opinion which supposes that the Christian faith gainsays reason. Although faith is above reason, nevertheless no discord, no opposition can ever be found betwixt them, since both faith and reason spring from one and the same unchangeable and eternal fountain of truth, the Almighty and Eternal God; and therefore they afford mutual help to each other, so that right reason demonstrates, upholds, and defends faith; and faith, on the other hand, emancipates reason from all errors, wonderfully enlightens, confirms, and perfects reason with the knowledge of divine things."

"We do not," writes Dr. Brownson, "by asserting that God has made a revelation to man, supersede reason, or forbid him to exercise it. The revelation assists reason, it does not annul it. It brings to reason a higher and a purer light than its own, but removes none of its laws, abridges no sphere of its activity, and impedes in no respect its free and full exercise. It elevates it, it clarifies it, and extends its vision, but does not deny, enchain, or enslave it. The authority which the Catholic claims for revelation, or for the Church in teaching or defining it, does not enslave reason, or require it to *surrender a single one of its original rights;* it enables it to retain and exercise all its rights, and to attain lovingly to a truth higher and vaster than its own." "Revelation gives us the principles and causes of the Universe — the principles and causes which lie above reason, above nature, and which must guide and assist us in our study of nature — but it leaves the whole field of nature to our observation and scientific investigation. *There is, to say the least, as much work for reason under revelation as there would be if no revelation had been given.* Revelation only does that which reason cannot do, and which is beyond the reach of science. What would be within the reach of science if there were no revelation is equally within its reach under revelation. *The field of science is not restricted by revelation, but enlarged rather;* for revelation places the mind of the Christian in a position, an attitude, that enables it to see more clearly and comprehend more fully rational or scientific principles, and things as they really are in God's own world. As is often said, revelation is to reason what the telescope is to the eye." Again, "Revelation was not given to silence reason, to overwhelm it, to puzzle it, or to supersede it; but to aid it, strengthen it, enlarge its scope, and to supply its defects. It brings to man's understanding the superintelligible, and is a sort of telescope added to the natural eye of reason. But the telescope does not supersede the natural eye, for it is the natural eye that sees in or through it, and it would be of no use to a blind man. So of revelation. It does not supersede or even lessen our natural intelligence, for it is our natural intelligence, after all, that understands and believes in it or by it." And again, "Faith is not opposed to reason. No, faith is to reason what the telescope is to the naked eye. The eye with the telescope sees what it could not perceive alone. It penetrates into regions that are inaccessible without that aid. Will you say that the telescope is opposed to the eyesight? Faith, then, but regulates and extends reason. It leaves it free exercise in all that comes within its range, *and when its natural powers have reached its limits, faith comes to its aid, raises it higher, and causes it to penetrate into new supernatural divine truths, even into the secrets of God."* [17]

Infallibility gives and guarantees mental freedom! How does this appear? Error alone enslaves the mind and keeps it in bondage. On the other hand, truth frees, develops, and ennobles the mind. "And ye shall know the truth, and the truth shall make you free." [18] Again, uncertainty and doubt about the truth are what disturb the peace of the mind and rob it of its liberty. The man who is uncertain or in doubt about the truths of salvation, and in fear of falling into error regarding them—that man has not and cannot have mental freedom or intellectual peace. On the other hand, certainty in regard to the truth and security against error are what restore intellectual peace, and with it mental liberty or freedom. Now Infallibility gives, beyond question or doubt, truth, certainty, and security, and, therefore, mental freedom and repose; and as long as we believe in Infallibility, so long will it continue to guarantee to us this great blessing in all its integrity. Infallibility, then, truly frees the mind by putting it in certain and secure possession of the truth in its purity and plenitude.

From what has been said, it is clear that mental freedom and liberty of thought are not one and the same thing. The more truth I know the more real mental freedom I have; while the less truth I know the more liberty of thought I have. That is, mental freedom and liberty of thought, like knowledge and ignorance, increase and decrease in inverse ratio.

NOTES TO CHAPTER IV.

¹ Page 84 *et seq.*
² Math. xvi. 18.
³ Math. xxviii. 18.   ⁴ *Ibid.*, v. 19.
⁵ Mark xvi. 15.
⁶ John xx. 21; Luke x. 16.
⁷ Math. xxviii. 20.   ⁸ *Ibid.*
⁹ John xiv. 16.
¹⁰ John xvi. 13.
¹¹ 1 Tim. cap. iii. 15.
¹² Luke x. 16.
¹³ The truth is, the Church, instead of being a spiritual despotism, actually saves us from it. "It is not the Church that establishes spiritual despotism; it is she who saves us from it. Spiritual despotism is that which subjects us, in spiritual matters, to a human authority, whether our own or that of others—for our own is as human as another's; and the only redemption from it is in having in them a divine authority. Protestants themselves acknowledge this when they call out for the pure word of God. The Church teaches by divine authority; in submitting to her we submit to God, and are freed from all human authority. She teaches infallibly; therefore, in believing what she teaches, we believe the truth, which frees us from falsehood and error, to which all men without an infallible guide are subject, and submission to which is the elemental principle of all spiritual despotism. Her authority admitted excludes all other authority, and therefore frees us from heresiarchs and sects, the very embodiment of spiritual despotism in its most odious forms."—Brownson's Works, vol. x., p. 128.
¹⁴ Math. xviii. 17; Mark xvi. 15.
¹⁵ Math. xvi. 16.
¹⁶ Luke x. 16.
¹⁷ See above, pp. 57-59.
¹⁸ Brownson's Works, vol. vii., pp. 382-383.
¹⁹ Brownson's Works, vol. vii., p. 301.
²⁰ Works, vol. iii., pp. 265-266.
²¹ Brownson's Works, vol. vii. pp. 537-538. "We have all the freedom a Protestant who really holds himself bound to believe the Bible can pretend to have; and the authority we assert for the Church tends, to say the least, no more to enslave the mind than that which the Protestant asserts for the written Word."—*Ibid.*, p. 589.
²² *Ibid.*, pp. 586-587.   ²³ *Ibid.*, p. 464.
²⁴ "This most tender mother, the Catholic Church, recognizes and justly proclaims that among the gifts of heaven *the most distinguished is*

NOTES TO CHAPTER IV.

that of reason, by means of which we raise ourselves above the senses, and present in ourselves a certain image of God."—Pius IX., Letter to the Bishops of Austria, 1856, in Hecker's "Aspirations of Nature," p. 201.

[25] Cf. Vatican Council, "Constit. Dogmat. de Fide Catholica," cap. iv.

[26] Writing to "the Patriarchs, Primates, Archbishops, and Bishops" of the Catholic World, Pius IX. says: "Lest human reason should be deceived in a matter of so great moment, it *behoves* it to inquire diligently concerning Divine Revelation, in order that it be made certain that God has spoken, and also in order that it may exercise, according to the most wise teaching of the Apostle, a 'reasonable obedience' (Rom. xiii. 1)."— Encyclical *Noscitis*, Nov. 9. 1846, in "Aspirations of Nature," p. 209.

[27] Any theological treatise on Reason and Faith contains what is here stated. Cf. Franzelin, "De Traditione," Appendix, De Habitudine Rationis Humanæ ad Divinam Fidem; Perrone, "De Locis Theologicis," Part iii., De Analogia Rationis et Fidei; Mazzella, "De Virtutibus Infusis," Disp. iii. Art. vi-ix., Disp. iv. Art. vii-ix. Hurter, "Theologia Generalis," vol. i., n. 616, and 645 *et seq.* Cardinal Newman, "Discourses to Mixed Congregations," pp. 231-237.

[28] Cf. Council of Trent, Sess. vi. Cans. iv.-vi.; Hecker's "Aspirations of Nature," chaps. xvii., xviii., xxiii.-xxv.

[29] Cf. Denzinger, "Enchiridion," nn. 1488-1493, 1505-1508. Among the propositions here given and to which those referred to above were obliged to subscribe, is the following one: "The exercise of reason precedes faith, and with the aid of revelation and grace leads to faith."

[29*] Cf. "Const. Dogmat. De Fide Catholocia," cap. ii., and can. i.

[30] Brownson's Works, vol. iii., p. 215.

[31] "The Convert," chap. xix. (in Works, vol. v.) Cf. also Works, vol. viii., p. 574 *et seq.*, and 592 *et seq.*; vol. x., p. 127.

[32] Cf. Cardinal Newman, "Discourses to Mixed Congregations," pp. 214-229.

[33] Math. ix. 6; Mark ii. 10; Luke v. 23; John x. 37, 38; xiv. 10, 32.

[34] John iii. 3-12; vi. 51-60.

[35] Rom. i. 5.

[36] 2 Cor. x. 5. Cf. also Bishop Hedley, "The Spirit of Faith," pp. 41-48.

[37] John xx. 21. Cf. also Luke x. 16.

[38] Cf. Franzelin, "De Traditione," pp. 612-613. Perrone, "De Locis Theologicis," Part iii., nn. 95, 240.

[39] "We submit to the Church not blindly, but with our eyes open, and *solely on the ground that our reason, freely exercised, is convinced* that she is authorized by God to speak to us in His name; or rather that it is He, the indwelling Holy Ghost, that speaks to us in her voice and through her as organ."—Brownson's Works, vol. vii., p. 512.

[40] Cf. John, v. 36-47; xii. 37-44; xv. 22, 24; xvi. 8, 9; i. 11; iii. 11; vii. 5; x. 25.   [41] Jules Simon.

[42] God's word is the highest and most conclusive proof possible of the truth of what it asserts. "No demonstration," says Chillingworth, "can be greater than this—*God hath said so ; therefore it is true.*"—"Religion of Protestants," p. 463.

[43] Hurter, "Theologia Generalis," vol. i., n. 654. Reason in the case of dogmas of faith has at most only a *negative* authority. If they contra-

dict reason, it has the right to say they are false and incredible, and that it cannot accept them; but if they are merely above the plane of reason, then reason has neither the right nor competency to say whether they are true or false. It can conclude nothing against a doctrine of faith on the ground that it is unable to see its truth. ⁴⁴ Hurter, *ibid.*

⁴⁵ "If," says Dr. Brownson, "the Church is the representative of God's authority on earth, then, since subjection to God abridges no man's natural liberty, there is and can be no incompatibility between the authority asserted by Catholics for the Church in faith and morals and the most perfect moral and mental freedom."—Vol. vii. 589.

⁴⁶ *The Christian Register*, a weekly organ of the Unitarians, once spoke of Dr. Brownson as a man "of commanding intellect, great intelligence, and fearlessness of thought," who, "as a dialectician has no equal"; who "has analyzed and thoroughly possessed himself of more systems of philosophy than other reputed scholars have even looked at." "He has been," continues the *Register*, "no superficial student among the greatest masters of thought, and his mind is hardly inferior to the ablest of them, in subtilty, in force of argumentation, and in extreme ingenuity." It has no hesitation in ranking him "with the great masters of thought."—Cf. Works, vol. vii., pp. 230, 256.

⁴⁷ Works, vol. vii., pp. 278-280. This was written nearly nine years after his conversion. Fourteen years later, referring to the same subject, he wrote: "We have had some experience of those interior struggles [of Protestants regarding the natural and supernatural], and *many a tragedy has been enacted in our own soul*, but it is with difficulty we recall them; *in the peace and serenity* of Catholic faith and hope *they have almost faded from the memory*; and yet the period of our life since we became a Catholic has been with us the period of our *freest* and *most active and energetic* thought."—Works, vol. iii., pp. 310-311.

⁴⁸ Rev. Thomas A. Finlay, S. J., "An Address."—*Irish Ecclesiastical Record*, April, 1883, pp. 221, 222.

⁴⁹ Speaking of his first formal act of Catholic faith Dr. Brownson says: "In submitting to her [the Catholic Church] I yielded to the highest reason; and my submission was intelligent, not an act discarding reason, but an act of reason itself in the full possession and free exercise of its highest powers. No act of belief is or can be more reasonable; and, in performing it, I kept faithfully the resolution I made on leaving Presbyterianism, that henceforth I would be true to my own reason, and maintain the rights and dignity of my own manhood. No man can accuse me of not having done it. I never performed a more reasonable act, a more manly act, or one more in accordance with the rights and dignity of human nature, though not done save by Divine Grace moving and assisting thereto, than when I knelt to the Bishop of Boston, and asked him to hear my confession and reconcile me to the Church, or when I read my abjuration and publicly professed the Catholic faith."—"The Convert," pp. 310-311 (Works, vol. v., p. 182.) And in the preface to this volume he writes: "I consider submission to the teaching of the Church the *noblest exercise I can make of my reason and free will.*"—p. x.

"It was one of the happiest moments of our life," writes the late Father

NOTES TO CHAPTER IV.

Hecker, "when we discovered for the first time that it was not required of us either to abandon our reason or drown it in a false excitement of feeling to be a religious man. That to become a Catholic, so far from being contrary to reason, was *a supreme act of reason.*"—"Questions of the Soul," p. 286.

[50] "The Grounds of Faith, " p. 58. See also Franzelin, "De Traditione," pp. 603, 696, 706. Perrone, "De Fide," nn. 68, 256; Hettinger, *op. cit.*, pp. 177-178.

[51] Cf. Cardinal Newman, "Grammar of Assent," p. 181, and "Discourses to Mixed Congregations," p. 228.

[52] The Protestant, who thinks, has reason to doubt, and on his theory is bound to inquire. The Catholic, resting, as he does, for his faith, on the *infallible* authority of the Church, cannot reasonably doubt, or consistently inquire. Cf. Cardinal Newman, "Discourses to Mixed Congregations," pp. 229-231.

[53] Cf. Leo XIII., Encyclical Letter, "*Æterni Patris,*" 4th Aug. 1899; Perrone, "De Locis Theol.;" part iii., n. 274 *et seq.*

[54] Works, vol. iii., 393.   [55] *Ibid.*

[56] This is a list principally of English converts. The compiler states that his purpose is to give only prominent names, for "a list embracing all members of society" would make "a volume which, for dimensions, would have favorably compared with the 'Post Office Directory.'" After observing "that there is hardly a single English noble family that has not given one or more of its members to the Roman Catholic Church," he goes on to classify the converts as follows: 'The Nobility and Gentry,' 1559; 'The Public Service,' 34; 'Architects,' 13; 'The Arts and Sciences,' 29; 'The Army,' 141; 'The Navy,' 30; 'The Medical Profession,' 49; 'The Legal Profession,' 73; 'Literature,' 38; 'Publishers,' 7; 'Relations of Clergymen,' 269; 'Clergymen,' 80; 'Oxford University,' 295; 'Cambridge,' 151; other universities and colleges, 20.

Speaking of this list *The Christian Globe* (Protestant) observed that it "gives one a startling view of the rapid advancement which Roman Catholicism had made of late years *in certain quarters.*" Dr. Foster, a Methodist Episcopal Bishop, frankly admitted, not long ago, that "there is no mission field in the world where she [the Catholic Church] had not more converts *than all combined Protestantism.*" Cf. Marshall's "Christian Missions."   [57] Works, vol. iii., p. 188.

[58] John xxi. 15-17; Luke xxii. 32.

[59] Cf. Franzelin, "De Traditione," p. 683; Mazzella, "De Virt. Inf.," n. 656.

[60] "Liberty of Thought," Rev. Thomas A. Finlay, S. J., in *The Irish Ecclesiastical Record,* April, 1883, pp. 222-225.

[61] "Certainly the Church does not condemn the labors of those who wish to know the truth, since God has placed in human nature the desire of laying hold of the true; *nor does she condemn the effort of sound and right reason by which the mind is cultivated, nature is searched, and her more hidden secrets brought to light.*"—Pius IX., Letter to the Bishops of Austria, 1856. Cf. also Letter to the Archbishops of Munich, Dec. 11, 1862. "So far is the Church," says the Vatican Council, "from opposing the cultivation of human arts and sciences, that it, in many ways, helps and

promotes it. It neither ignores nor despises the benefits which flow from them into the life of man; it rather confesses that, inasmuch as they proceed from God, the Lord of Sciences, so, if rightly handled, by the help of His Grace, they lead to God. Nor does the Church forbid that such sciences *should use their own principles and their own method within their own sphere ;* but while recognizing this just liberty, it carefully watches that they do not adopt errors repugnant to the Divine Doctrine, or, stepping over their boundaries, invade and disturb the domain of faith."— "Constit. Dogmatica de Fide Catholica," cap. iv. Cf. also Leo XIII., Encyclical Letter, *Æterni Patris*, 4 Aug. 1879.

⁶² Apologia, p. 277 (2d ed. 253.)   ⁶³ Luke x. 16.

⁶⁴ Vol. iii., p. 344. "As Infallibility," he elsewhere observes, "by its very nature, can teach only what is true; and as there are and can be no rights that are not founded on truth, how does Infallibility conflict with the rights of reason, or conscience, or liberty, or civil allegiance? Instead of being the enemy it is the guardian and protector of all rights because the guardian and expounder of the divine law, natural and revealed, from which alone all rights are derived."

⁶⁵ The Convert," chap. xix., pp. 313-314 (Works, vol. v., pp. 184-185.)

⁶⁶ Vol. iii., p. 311.

⁶⁷ Brownson's Works, vol. ix., p. 550. Dr. Draper ("Conflict between Science and Revealed Religion," pp. 359-361) gives a number of instances which he calls "stern witnesses bearing emphatic and unimpeachable testimony against the ecclesiastical claim to infallibility." The reader will see, on reference to the Doctor's pages, that the instances he gives are "stern witnesses" to the fact that he knew very little about the Catholic dogma of Infallibility.

⁶⁸ "Constitutio Dogmatica de Fide Catholica, cap. iv. Cf. also Franzelin, "De Traditione," pp. 126 (note), 600-691, 714-718; Mazzella, "De Virtutibus Infusis," nn. 1058-1074; Denzinger, "Enchiridion," n. 398.

⁶⁹ "Now reason itself teaches that the truths of revelation and those of nature cannot really be opposed to one another, and that whatever is at variance with them must *necessarily be false.*" Leo XIII., Encyclical Letter, June 20, 1888.

⁷⁰ Encyclical Letter, June 20, 1888.

⁷¹ "Like a friendly star, faith points out to him the harbor of truth, so that he can have no fear of going out of his course."—Leo XIII., Encyclical Letter, Aug. 4, 1879.

⁷² Infallibility, as Mr. Mallock justly remarks, is a support, "and those who cling to it can venture fearlessly, as explorers, into currents of speculation that would sweep away altogether men who did but trust to their own powers of swimming."—Is Life Worth Living?" chap. xii., p. 310.

⁷³ Cf. Brownson's Works, vol. ix., 497 *et seq.*

⁷⁴ Cf. Harter, "Theol. Gen.," vol. i., n. 665; Mazzella, "De Virt. Inf.," n. 1053 *et seq.*; Perrone, "De Locis Theol.," part iii., n. 248 *et seq.*

⁷⁵ "Constit. Dogmat. de Fide Catholica," cap. iv.

⁷⁶ November 9, 1846.

⁷⁷ Works, vol. i., p. 326; vol. ix., pp. 578-579; vol. viii., 32.

⁷⁸ John viii. 32.

CHAPTER V.

HOW DO CATHOLICS MEET THE OBJECTIONS TO INFALLIBILITY?

Objection: Infallibility, you claim, covers the domain of morals as well as that of faith, the domain of duty as well as of truth. Now, " what are the departments and functions of human life which do not and cannot fall within the domain of morals ?" " About seventy-five per cent. of all we do belongs to the department of conduct," and " conduct and morals, we may suppose, are nearly co-extensive." " Three-fourths, then, of life are thus handed over " to Infallibility's dominion. And "who will guarantee to us the other fourth?" Again, is not "duty a power which rises with us in the morning and goes to rest with us at night "? Is it not " co-extensive with the action of our intelligence "? Is it not " the shadow which cleaves to us, go where we will, and which only leaves us when we leave the light of life "? Now, Infallibility claims the entire province of duty. Nothing, then, lies beyond its grasp but, at most, " the dregs and tatters of human life." Such being the case, how can one believe in and submit to its authority without forfeiting " his moral freedom "? [1]

Answer: This objection illustrates the importance of the distinction noted above. [2] Mr. Gladstone here confounds moral *doctrine* with moral *conduct*, moral *truth* with moral *action*, moral *principle* with moral *practice;* and thus, by a "monstrous widening of the sphere of Infallibility," he makes it cover the conduct as well as the doctrine, the action as well as the truth, and the practice as well as the principle, "as if the Pope pursued every man through his life, pronouncing *ex-cathedra* judgments on all his acts." Archbishop Ullathorne, from whom I am quoting, continues: "He [Mr. Gladstone] confounds judgment upon moral doctrine with judgment upon moral acts, and by this confusion of ideas contrives to bring all human life under the prerogative of Infallibility. No wonder that after this monstrous widening of the sphere of Infallibility he is enabled to hurl so many figures of rhetoric against, *not* the Pope's Infallibility, *but his own invention.*"[3] Anybody will see, on consulting the acts of the Council, that Infallibility, in the case of morals, is expressly restricted to "*doctrine* regarding morals (*doctrina de moribus*)."[4]

Objection: The dogma of Infallibility gives the Pope supreme and absolute power over the faith of Catholics. On the one hand, it empowers him to determine what they are to believe and not to believe, what they are to do and not to do in matters of faith and morals; and on the other hand it binds them to accept unreservedly and in all cases his judgment without right of question or appeal. "The effect of it," says Mr. Gladstone, "described *with literal rigor*, was to place the entire Christian religion in the breast of the Pope, and to suspend it on his will. . . . The will (then) and arbitrament of one man will for the future decide, through half the Christian world, what religion is to be. . . . He has only to use the words, 'I, *ex cathedra*, declare,' and all that may follow, *be they what they may*, must now and hereafter be absolutely accepted, by every Roman Catholic who takes the Vatican for his teacher, with what in their theological language they call a divine faith, as must any article of the Apostles' Creed."[5]

Now, what if the Pope should, by virtue of his Infallibility, call upon Catholics to believe doctrines which deny or disregard the legitimate rights of others? What if he should use his Infallibility against those who do not believe in him, or do not happen to think as he does on any question of interest to him? What if he should claim for Infallibility authority over the various branches of science, or in matters purely political, and use it to the detriment of civilization, governments, and states? There is nothing whatever to prevent him from using his Infallibility in this way; for, remember, "the Pope himself, by himself, is judge without appeal"[6] of when, and how, and for what purpose he may exercise his Infallibility; "He is supreme and only final judge" in the case, "with no legislature to correct his errors, with no authoritative rules to guide his proceedings, with no power on earth to question the force or intercept the effect of his decisions."[7] The case is perfectly clear: the dogma of Infallibility is a standing menace to both private and public rights.

Answer: Among the many objections raised to the dogma of Infallibility, there is, perhaps, no one that influences the minds of non-Catholics so powerfully as this; and yet a moment's calm reflection is sufficient to show that it simply involves a contradiction in terms. For while it presupposes the doctrine of Infallibility, and professes to be directed against that doctrine, *as* defined by the Vatican Council and explained and understood in Catholic teaching, it goes on to argue as if there were no such thing at all, or as if Infallibility may, at any moment, become fallible. It is based, as is evident, not on facts, but on the fear and assumption that the Pope may abuse his Infallibility; that there is nothing to prevent him from doing so, and nothing to protect the public from an arbitrary, capricious, and, it may be, dangerous and positively hurtful use of it. In assuming such a possibility, the objector completely overlooks the meaning and purpose of Infallibility; for, granting for the moment that his fears are reasonable, and that the state of things which they picture to his imagination is possible, what, then, we ask, is the meaning? what the purpose, of Infallibility? Infallibility, as already explained, implies a supernatural, divine assistance—an overruling divine providence which, according to promise, is ever present and never fails to protect the Pope from even the possibility of error in his *ex-cathedra* acts. Is not this overshadowing protection of God's Holy Spirit an all-sufficient guarantee that the Pope will never and can never abuse his Infallibility, or exercise it arbitrarily or capriciously, much less to the injury of public or private right? Does it not preclude all possibility of any such abuse?

In Catholic teaching the assistance of Infallibility is an unfailing divine guarantee (*a*) that the Pope will teach unerringly the truths of Christian faith and the principles of Christian morals; (*b*) that he will never teach, as a truth of faith or a principle of morals, any doctrine or principle not really contained in the deposit of Revelation; and (c) that he will never use its authority in matters that have no connection with and are in no sense necessary for the exposition or defence of faith and morals, or for any purpose whatever save to witness, guard, propose, define, and defend the teaching of Revelation. What, therefore, the objection assumes as possible, is excluded as impossible by the very nature of Infallibility, inasmuch as God, who gives that assistance, directs, controls, and limits its use according to infinite wisdom, justice, and truth.

The question, then, reduces itself to this: Did Christ our Lord promise to His Church and to the Pope, its Visible Head, the abiding assistance of Infallibility? If he did, and this is to be determined by the arguments given in Chapter III., then, unless we can suppose that our Divine Lord may prove unfaithful to His promises, and that His *word*, notwithstanding what He said to the contrary, *may pass away*, or that the Holy Spirit failed in His trust, there is, manifestly, neither force nor reason in the objection. It springs from a perfectly groundless and unreasonable fear, and can frighten and disturb those only who misunderstand or who, for the moment, forget the meaning of the Catholic dogma. Against a fallible Pope the objection would have weight; but against an infallible Pope it is an absurdity pure and simple.

To all such questions, then, as "Why may not the Pope use his Infallibility to make other than revealed truths dogmas of Catholic faith, or to define *ex cathedra* other doctrines and facts than those which bear upon faith and morals?" "Why may he not, in the name of Infallibility, impose what he pleases on the belief of Catholics?" "Why may he not make 'somebody's private opinion of to-day a matter of faith for all the to-morrows of the future?'"⁸ "Why may he not any day 'invent a new tenet and declare it a part of the Gospel, or deny, and order others to deny, an ancient and universally received Christian doctrine?'"⁹ "Why may he not, in the name of Infallibility, trample on the rights of conscience, and invade the civil domain?" "Why may he not make *ex-cathedra* demands on the obedience of Catholics at variance with their duties as citizens, and to the injury of the state?" To these and all like questions our answer is simple and perfectly satisfactory: No, the Pope cannot do any such thing, *because he is infallible*—because the divine assistance which overshadows him stands in the way and renders all such acts on his part utterly impossible.¹⁰

Objection: There can be no addition made to "*the faith once declared to the Saints.*"¹¹ That is sufficient for all men and for all time. Consequently, no doctrine not contained in that sacred deposit can ever be made obligatory on the Christian belief of any one. Now, the doctrine of Infallibility is a new doctrine; it was not defined until the year 1870; before that date it was not an article of faith, but since it is. The dogma of Infallibility, therefore, is an addition to "*that which hath been believed everywhere, always, and by all men.*" And, then, if it be true that this doctrine was added to the Catholic faith in 1870, how, in the face of such a fact, can it be true that Catholic faith never changes? And what becomes of "the proud boast of *semper eadem?*"[12]

Answer: Catholic theologians[13] agree in teaching:

1. That the Christian Revelation, or the object of Christian faith, was made through and completed in the Apostles; that since their death no new revelation intended for universal belief has been made; and that no such revelation is to be expected.

2. That neither the Church nor the Pope has power to add to, or to take from, or to alter in one jot or tittle, the contents of this Apostolic Revelation or deposit of faith;[14] that the office of the Church and of the Pope, in regard to it, is simply that of Witness, Guardian, and Interpreter; and that the *sole* purpose of Infallibility, as expressly stated by the Vatican Council,[15] is to enable them to discharge this trust faithfully and effectively.

3. That every truth, every proposition of this deposit of Revelation is and has ever been *implicitly* of Catholic faith; but that only those portions of it which have been authenticated by the infallible authority of the Church and by her proposed for the belief of all the faithful, are *explicitly* of Catholic faith.[16]

4. That Catholics never have, never will, and never can be called upon to believe as an article or dogma of faith a proposition, teaching, or truth not contained in that Apostolic deposit; for it is beyond question that *only* what it contains can be the object of Catholic faith.[17]

5. That an infallible or *ex-cathedra* definition of faith, whether of a General Council or of the Pope alone, is not an addition to "*the faith once delivered*

to the saints," but merely a formal, authoritative, and definite declaration of what that faith is on the point in question; that in such cases neither the Council nor the Pope has ever claimed, or professed to do any more than to propose for the *explicit* faith of all what is contained in the Revelation made to the Apostles, and, consequently, what was already necessarily of *implicit* faith.[18] So have definitions of faith ever been understood in the Church; and such their history proves them to be. Indeed, this is, in many cases, expressly stated in the preamble or introduction to the definition.[19]

With these principles in mind, we come to the point of the objection. It is true that the doctrine of Infallibility was not formally defined until July 18, 1870; but that by no means proves it to be a new doctrine. The doctrine of the Divinity of Christ was not defined until the Council of Nice, A. D. 325; nor the doctrine of One Person in Christ until the Council of Ephesus, A. D. 431; nor the doctrine of the immortality of the soul until the fifth Lateran Council, A. D. 1512–1517; nor the doctrine of a *personal* God until the Vatican Council, A. D. 1869–1870. Were all these doctrines, therefore, new at the respective dates mentioned? When the Church, says Mr. Mallock, "formulates in these days something that has not been formulated before, *she is no more enunciating a new truth than was Newton when he enunciated the truth of gravitation.*"[20] The objection clearly overlooks the fact that the Church, as a rule, never formally and explicitly defines a doctrine until it is contradicted or denied, or has become obscured in men's minds, and faith in it is endangered.

"The Church," says Cardinal Manning, "teaches and transmits the whole divine tradition of natural and supernatural truth, *but defines only those parts of the deposit which have been obscured or denied.*"[21] To those who ask why such or such a doctrine was not before declared a dogma of faith, "our answer," says Cardinal Newman," "is that, commonly, truths of the Apostolic *depositum* are not made dogmas or articles of faith till they have been *publicly denied.*" And, speaking of the history of the doctrinal definitions of the Church, this same eminent authority says: "These definitions, which are but the expression of portions of the one dogma which has ever been received by the Church, are the work of time; they have grown to their present shape and number in the course of eighteen centuries, under the exigency of successive events, such as heresies and the like; and they may of course receive still further additions as time goes on."[23] Moreover, it confounds the truth or doctrine with the formal and authoritative definition of it. All that is new about the doctrine of Infallibility is its definition; the doctrine itself is as old as Christianity, and has ever been believed and acted upon as a truth of its teaching. "Before the definition of the Vatican Council," writes Cardinal Manning, "the Infallibility of the Roman Pontiff was a doctrine revealed by God, delivered by the universal and constant tradition of the Church, recognized in Œcumenical Councils, presupposed in the acts of the Pontiffs in all ages, taught by all the saints, defended by every religious order and by every theological school except one, *and in that one disputed only by a minority in number, and during one period of its history;*

believed, at least implicitly, by all the faithful, and therefore attested by the passive Infallibility of the Church in all ages and lands, with the partial and transient limitations already expressed."[24]

Protestant writers bear a similar testimony to the traditional belief of the Church in Papal Infallibility. "In the Catholic Church," says a contributor in the *Union Review* (May, 1875), "it was always an article of faith that our Lord, by the assistance of His Holy Spirit, preserved the whole Church, in her collective capacity, from falling into error in her dogmatic teaching. *But it was also a point of belief, which may be traced up to the Apostolic age,* that in the administration of this teaching authority, *the See of Peter held a supreme office;* that it was the centre of ecclesiastical operations, if we may use such a term; *that apart from it there would be no genuine orthodoxy, no true Catholicity;* and that in all the controversies which from time to time divided the Christian world, *the most crucial test of truth was the adherence to any dogma by the See of Peter.*"[25]

Then, as regards the statement that before the definition of the Vatican Council (A. D. 1870) the doctrine of Papal Infallibility was not an article of faith. Here, for the sake of clearness, I must introduce a simple but important distinction the neglect of which leads to much misunderstanding and confusion of thought. The distinction is that made by theologians between *Divine* and *Catholic* faith, and explained as follows: Divine faith is belief in whatever God has supernaturally revealed; Catholic faith is belief in what God has supernaturally revealed and the

Church, in the exercise of her infallible authority, has proposed *as such* to the faithful. To be of Divine faith all that is necessary is that the doctrine or truth in question be divinely revealed; while to be of Catholic faith it is necessary that the doctrine be not only divinely revealed, but also that it be proposed as revealed for the belief of all the faithful by the infallible authority of the Church or Pope. Then, and then only, it is called an article or dogma of Catholic faith. "It can hardly be necessary," writes Cardinal Manning,[19] "to add that, in order to constitute an article of [Catholic] faith two conditions are necessary: the one intrinsic, the other extrinsic; the former, that the doctrine to be defined be contained in the divine revelation; the latter that it be proposed to us by the Church as revealed." "For any doctrine," says the "Faith of Catholics,"[20] "to be of Catholic faith *two things are necessary*: first, that it be revealed; second, that it be proposed by the Church. Of which two conditions, *if either be wanting, such a doctrine is not of Catholic faith.*" From which it follows that while every truth of Catholic faith is necessarily of Divine faith, every truth of Divine faith is not of Catholic faith, because the Church has not proposed specifically and in detail all the truths contained in Revelation."

Now the doctrine of Papal Infallibility was a doctrine of *Divine* faith ever since the days of the Apostles, because it was a part of the revelation made through them; but before the definition of the Vatican Council it was not an article of *Catholic* faith; because before that event it was not definitely proposed by the Church as obligatory on Catholic belief."[?] The doctrine, then, though an addition to *Catholic*[?] faith is not an addition to "*the faith once delivered to the Saints.*"

The celebrated canon of St. Vincent of Lerins—quod *ubique*, quod *semper*, quod *ab omnibus*, creditum est—referred to in the objection, is frequently quoted as a condemnation of the dogmas of the Immaculate Conception and of Papal Infallibility; but it is nothing of the kind. What St. Vincent says is, that "what has been believed everywhere, always, and by all men," is of Catholic faith; and that is perfectly true. But he does not say, as the objection would have it, that *only* that is to be believed which has been held everywhere, always, and by all men. That is, the canon is true in its obvious, *affirmative*, sense, but not in a *negative* or exclusive sense."[?]

Catholic faith does not and never did profess to exclude all change or progress. There can be no change in it by addition (from without) or subtraction, of corruption or decay; but there may be change by way of development from within, or natural growth, such as takes place in the boy growing into manhood. "Growth in its creed," says Cardinal Newman,"[?] "is a law of its life." "The developments and additions in dogmatic statements which have occurred between the Apostolic and the present age," says His Eminence in another place,"[?] "are but a result and an evidence of spiritual life." But this change does not in the case of Catholic faith, any more than in the case of the boy, destroy its identity or rob it of "the proud boast of *semper eadem*."[?] There may, then, be "progress" in matters of faith, not indeed of the faith in the faithful, but of the faithful in the faith—a progress in the knowledge of the faith. Truths of Revelation which at one time may be known *as such* only obscurely or doubtfully, may, at a later period, be known more fully, clearly, and for certain, because more fully declared in the teaching of the Church, or because they are definitely authenticated by her infallible authority. Thus, a doctrine at one time doubted and even denied by many, and believed only implicitly, may afterwards become the object of explicit faith—a dogma of Catholic faith. "In this," writes Cardinal Hergenröther,[15] "all theologians agree, that much for a long time lay more obscurely hid in the consciousness of the Church, which was afterwards more clearly enunciated and brought to the fuller apprehension of all, and thus became the subject of the *fides explicita.*" And again, after quoting the saying of the great Pope Gregory, that "the more the world draws near to its end, the more lavishly will the stores of eternal science be opened unto us," this same eminent authority goes on to observe: "Particular dogmas must, in the course of ages, undergo no change, no mutilation, no disfigurement, but receive a more precise expression, a more suitable formulization, *a development setting forth all the consequences involved in them;* they must, according to Vincent Lerins, receive *evidentiam, lucem, distinctionem*—evidence, light, discrimination; but they must preserve also what they intrinsically possess: *plenitudinem, integritatem, proprietatem*—their fulness, their integrity, their peculiarity. *By means of a natural process of development, a religious truth can come out at one time, or in one place, more definite, more clear, more universal, than at other times, or in other places."* [**]

Objection: Then Catholics may be called upon any day to believe, of necessary faith, what the day before was not of obligation.

Answer: Yes, Catholics may, in the future, as in the past, be called upon to believe *explicitly* what previously they were bound to believe only *implicitly;* but this does not imply any change in their faith other than that of progress in the knowledge of it. Neither does it imply any power on the part of the Church or Pope to make arbitrary demands on their faith or to add to their creed whatever their good pleasure may prompt." For bear in mind that we are obliged to give the assent of Catholic faith only to what "the Church, either by a solemn judgment or by her ordinary and universal *magisterium*, proposes for our belief, *as having been divinely revealed;*" [**] and that in Infallibility we have an unfailing divine pledge that neither the Church nor the Pope can ever teach us *as divinely revealed* truth what is not *de facto* so. While, then, as loyal Catholics, we are always ready to believe of necessary faith whatever the Church or the Pope, in the exercise of their supreme teaching authority, may propose as such, we are, at the same time, perfectly certain that we shall never and can never be called upon to believe as an article of faith what is false or what God has not revealed and wished us to believe. Herein consists the great blessing of Infallibility, and the great security and advantage of Catholics in matters of religion.

Objection: Is not the Pope, like other men, subject to the weaknesses of human nature and liable to sin? Have there not been Popes of questionable character—men, in some cases, of bad, wicked lives? How can we be reasonably asked to believe such men infallible?

Answer: This objection is based on a false assumption; it supposes that Infallibility consists in, or, at least, has a necessary connection with, or dependence on personal virtue and sinlessness of life; but this is not the fact. The prerogative of Infallibility neither means, nor implies, nor demands, in its possessor sanctity of life, much less immunity from sin. It is wholly independent both of the virtues and of the vices of the person who possesses and exercises it, and consists exclusively, as we have seen, in the assistance of the Holy Spirit of Truth promised to those who, by God's own appointment, are the guardians and teachers of His Law." Greater gifts than that of Infallibility have been communicated to and exercised by men of sinful, wicked lives. Was not Balaam a sinful, wicked man? And does not the Bible tell us that at the very time he was sinning, and sinning grievously, he was not only infallible, but, more, possessed the gift of prophecy?" Was not Caiphas, the High Priest, a weak, sinful, and very wicked man? And again, we have it on the authority of the Bible that, while actually contriving the death of our Saviour, he was inspired with the gift of prophecy *because he was High Priest.*" These examples prove that there is nothing impossible or repugnant in a man being at the same time a wicked man and an inspired prophet. And if a sinful, wicked man may possess the greater gift of inspiration or of prophecy, why may he not also possess the lesser gift of

Infallibility? God inspired a wicked Balaam and a Caiphas to prophesy infallibly. Why may He not assist a wicked Pope to teach infallibly?

Again, is there not a broad distinction between the personal worthiness or unworthiness of a man and his official position and acts? And may not a man fulfil his official duties in a most efficient and creditable manner, even though his private life may be blemished and his personal virtue very questionable? The Scribes and Pharisees, we know, were not remarkable for the goodness of their lives; and yet they "sat in the chair of Moses." " *And because they did*, what they taught was true and had to be followed. The sins and ill-deeds of Popes, then, are no objection to their Infallibility, and those who use them as such only display their ignorance or malice, or both."

Objection: The Popes are not always men of remarkable wisdom or of great learning. Some of them, in fact, were, comparatively speaking, possessed of little learning and apparently less wisdom. How, then, justify the claim of such Popes to Infallibility?

Answer: No doubt this objection would be difficult to meet if the Pope's claim to Infallibility were based on his learning, or wisdom, or sagacity; but this is not the case. The prerogative of Infallibility does not consist in the *learning* or *wisdom* of men, but in the *power* of God." Nor is the Pope's claim to it based on the possession of these qualities in a superior degree, but solely on the promises of Christ. The following extract from a pastoral letter of the German bishops (August 31, 1870) clearly sets forth Catholic teaching on this point. The bishops are speaking specially of infallible decisions of General Councils; but as the Pope's Infallibility is the same as that of a General Council, their words are equally applicable to his *ex-cathedra* judgments. "These decisions," says the pastoral, "according to the unanimous and undoubted tradition of the Church, have always been held to be preserved from error *by a supernatural and divine assistance.* Hence the faithful in all times have submitted themselves to these decisions *as the infallible expressions of the Holy Ghost Himself*, and, with undoubting faith, have held them to be true. They have done so, *not as persons might suppose*, because the bishops were men of mature and extended experience; *not* because many of them were versed in all sciences, *not* because they had come together from all parts of the world, and therefore, in a certain sense, brought together the human knowledge of the whole earth; *not*, lastly, because through a long life they had studied and taught the word of God, and hence were trustworthy witnesses of its meaning. All this, indeed, gives to their declarations a very high—indeed, perhaps, the highest possible—degree of mere human trustworthiness. *Still this is not a sufficient ground to rest supernatural faith.* For this act, in its last resort, rests not on the testimony of men, even when they are the most worthy of confidence, and even if the whole human race, by the voice of its best and most noble representatives, should bear witness to it; but such an act always rests wholly and alone on the truth of God Himself. When, therefore, the children of the Church receive with faith the decrees of a General Council, they do it with a conviction that

God the Eternal, and alone of Himself Infallible Truth, coöperates with it in a supernatural manner, and preserves it from error." " As, then, the Pope may be infallible, though not a saint, so, too, he may be infallible, though not conspicuous either for learning or for wisdom."

"The fact is," continues Mr. Proctor, in the article already referred to, "that the doctrine of Papal Infallibility as it is *really* taught by the Catholic Church is almost a corollary of the doctrine of Bible inspiration. According to the latter doctrine, in its only reasonable form, men like Moses, David, Solomon, Ezra, Isaiah, and the like, in no sense to be regarded as perfect, either in wisdom or in conduct, were inspired as respects certain matters which they addressed to men in regard to religion. The former doctrine, *in the only form ever adopted by the Catholic Church*, asserts that the Popes, though in no sense to be regarded as perfect either in wisdom or in conduct, *have always been, and always will be, so far guided or restrained (as the case may be) that if or when they addressed the whole Church ex-cathedra on matters relating to morals or doctrine, their teaching will be true.* In conduct a Pope may be imperfect or even wicked; in regard to science, art, or literature, he may be ignorant or unwise; in theological matters even dealt with by a priest or a doctor of the Church, a Pope may make serious mistakes; but no Pope, let his personal qualifications be what they may (let him be as overbearing as Moses, as unscrupulous as David, as selfish as Solomon, as ignorant as Mathew, as contentious as Paul), *will ever address to the whole Church ex-cathedra false teaching as to morals or as to doctrine."*

Objection: But have not Popes contradicted Popes? And is not the fact of such a contradiction sufficient to condemn your doctrine of Infallibility? Moreover, have not Popes actually fallen into heresy and become heterodox?

Answer: Bear in mind what has been already stated, that not every case of contradiction between Pope and Pope militates against the dogma of Infallibility, but only a contradiction in *ex-cathedra* definitions or judgments." Now we freely admit that if, in the whole history of the Papacy, from the day of Pentecost to the present moment, *one solitary case* can be cited where an *ex-cathedra* act of one Pope contradicted an *ex-cathedra* act of another, or of a General Council, such a fact would be absolutely fatal to the doctrine of Infallibility. But that case does not exist and cannot be produced. The enemies of Infallibility have searched history through and through; lynx-eyed, they have scrutinized the acts of Popes and councils for eighteen hundred years, but without success. One single case would have been sufficient for their purpose, but that one single case they have failed to discover." Here is a fact that certainly affords a strong presumption of the truth of the Catholic claim that the Popes have been guarded and assisted by the supernatural and special providence of Infallibility; for how, otherwise, account for the wonderful harmony in the *ex-cathedra* teaching of the Popes from St. Peter to Leo XIII.?

As to the charge of heresy or heterodoxy, I have only to repeat what I have just said on the charge of contradiction. Produce one single, indisputable case of a Pope in an *ex-cathedra* definition or condemnation falling into heresy, and our position becomes utterly untenable.

Objection: But what about the cases of Liberius and Honorius? Are they not such cases as you call for ? And does not the latter, especially, finally and certainly dispose of the doctrine of Papal Infallibility?

Answer: It is worthy of note that formerly both the number of Popes charged with heresy and the number of distinct charges preferred against some of them was far greater than it is now."[*] The progress of historical studies (which, by the way, we have been so often told means the gradual overthrow of everything Papal) has gone on reducing the numbers until at present the more respectable of our opponents rely entirely on the two cases cited. What, then, have we to say to these remaining cases?

The former case, as stated by the Anglican, Dr. Littledale, is this: "Pope Liberius subscribed an Arian creed, and anathematized St. Athanasius as a heretic."[48]

1. In answer I observe: that it is by no means certain that Liberius subscribed any Arian creed; and, supposing that he did, there is no certainty as to what creed that was.

The history of the case shows that there may be question of any one of three different creeds, or rather formulas of faith. Two of these formulas, the first and the third, were on the face of them orthodox, and heterodox only inasmuch as they did not expressly exclude the Arian heresy; the other, the second, was certainly heterodox and Arian.

Now, if the Pope subscribed the first or the third, as Protestants generally maintain, it yet remains to be proved that he did so in the heterodox rather than in the orthodox sense; and in proof of this there is not one particle of evidence. The presumption in the case is altogether the other way; for it is unquestionable that his exile was due to the fact that he would not accept the heresy."

And if he subscribed the second formula, again it would be necessary to prove that he did so not simply as a *believer*, but as the *Teacher of the Universal Church expressly intending to make the heresy* an article of Catholic faith;" for otherwise it would not be an *ex-cathedra* act, nor, consequently, an objection to the doctrine of Infallibility. But, again, there is no evidence whatever to prove that Liberius acted in the latter capacity rather than in the former; while again the presumption is in favor of the former. For, admittedly, if he subscribed the formula, he did so in order to escape from exile and death; and to gain this end it does not seem that it was at all necessary that he should not only accept the heresy himself, but impose it on the belief of the Church."

2. But my thesis does not in the least require that I should question, much less disprove, the statement contained in the objection. For we may allow that Liberius subscribed an Arian creed, and in an Arian sense; and that he did so not simply as a *believer*, but as the supreme *Teacher* of the Church, and yet in no way compromise the doctrine of Infallibility. For it is a notorious fact, denied by no one, that the Pope was not free at the time, and that if he did subscribe the heretical creed, as charged, he did so under

coercion and from fear of death. His act, consequently, had no binding force; for, as Bossuet has observed, "every act extorted by violence is null by every title, and protests against itself." The mere fact, then, that he was not free in his action is of itself fatal to the objection; for no act, not perfectly free, can be an *ex-cathedra* act; and no act but an *ex-cathedra* act can be an objection to the dogma of Infallibility.

"It is astonishing to me," writes Cardinal Newman," "how any one can fancy that Liberius, in subscribing the Arian confession, promulgated it *ex cathedra*, considering he was not his own master when he signed, and it was not his drawing up. Who would say that it would be a judgment of the Queen's Bench or a judicial act of any kind? if ribbon-men in Ireland seized one of her Majesty's judges, hurried him into the wilds of Connemara, and there made him, under terror of his life, sign a document in the very teeth of an award which he had lately made in court on a question of -property. . . . Liberius's subscription can only claim a Nag's Head's sort of Infallibility."

Father Ryder characterizes, as "a purely gratuitous assertion," the statement "that Liberius anathematized St. Athanasius as a heretic." " Any way, such a fact would not in the least affect the dogma of Infallibility.

But the case of Pope Honorius is the one which, in the opinion of the opponents of Infallibility generally, is absolutely fatal to that dogma. Dr. Littledale states the case thus: "Pope Honorius was unanimously condemned by the Sixth General Council as a heretic for having publicly sided with the Monothelite heresy, and officially taught it in dogmatic Pontifical letters; .... and a successor of his, Leo II., wrote to assure the Spanish bishops that Honorius and his accomplices in heresy were certainly damned." "

Answer: This is, in truth, the only case of difficulty in regard to the doctrine of Papal Infallibility; but the difficulty, as we shall presently see, is only apparent. The history of the case, briefly stated, is this: At the time in question there was a controversy going on as to whether Christ had *two wills and two operations* or only one. The Monothelites, as the name implies, taught that though He had two natures, He had only one will. The orthodox party, on the other hand, held that He had two wills as absolutely distinct, one from the other, as His two natures. During the controversy, Sergius, the Patriarch of Constantinople, and a leader of the Monothelites, wrote to Honorius, representing to him that the interests of religion demanded that he should intervene and impose silence on both parties. Honorius acceded to his request, and wrote him two letters to that effect; and on account of these letters he was condemned by the Sixth General Council, A. D. 681. The contention, then, is that in these letters Honorius taught the doctrine of one will, or the Monothelite heresy.

A full discussion of this case involves an examination of three questions: 1. Was Honorius condemned by the Sixth General Council as a heretic? 2. Did his letters contain heresy? 3. Were they *ex-cathedra* utterances.

The third is the only question that calls for an answer in these pages; and the answer is, Certainly no; they were not *ex-cathedra* utterances, and for the following reasons: 1. They *define* nothing; the Pope *expressly declares*⁶⁴ more than once that he had no intention of defining anything. 2. There is nothing in the letters to show that the Pope demanded the assent of the universal Church to their teaching; he did not even have them published. In fact, it was only after his death that the world heard of them for the first time. Two, then, at least, of the essential conditions of an *ex-cathedra* utterance are wanting to these letters;⁶⁵ and that being so, no matter what their teaching may be, they can be no objection to Infallibility. "If," says Cardinal Newman,⁶⁶ "the Pope is infallible only when he speaks *ex cathedra*, as the Vatican Council has defined, and if the conditions required by the Council for an *ex-cathedra* utterance are considered, it follows that whatever Honorius said in answer to Sergius, and whatever he held, *his words were not ex cathedra, and therefore did not proceed from his Infallibility.*" In the opinion of the Cardinal the action of the Council in condemning him presents no difficulty whatever; for, taken in the most unfavorable light, it means nothing more than that he *personally* was a heretic; which, as we have seen,⁶⁷ may be the case without prejudice to the Catholic dogma. "The condemnation of Honorius by the Council," says His Eminence, "*in no sense compromises the doctrine of Papal Infallibility.* At the most, it only decides that Honorius, in his own person, was a heretic, *which is incompatible with no Catholic doc-*

trine."⁶⁶ "Whatever Honorius wrote," says *The Month*,⁶⁷ "in the two private letters to Sergius, on which the whole charge is based, he certainly *defined* nothing. *No historical fact could be plainer or clearer.* His first letter may be summed as saying that neither of the opposite doctrines should be preached, as the point has not yet been properly examined, and has never been settled. In the second he *formally declares that he does not intend to define in the matter at all.* And thus the objection, *as an objection against the dogma of Papal Infallibility, is settled briefly and unanswerably,* leaving the attack on the character of the Pope to be dealt with *as an altogether distinct question.*" The Pope, then, did not "officially teach in *dogmatic* Pontifical letters" Monothelitism.

Having disposed of the case as an objection to Infallibility, a few words on the other points raised above will not be out of place. A host of writers maintain that the doctrine of the Letters is perfectly orthodox, though many admit that the wording is open to misinterpretation. They, therefore, contend that Honorius was condemned, *not because he had fallen into heresy and had taught it*, but because he favored it by imposing silence on the orthodox party and omitting to define the truth when it was his duty to do so. That is, in other words, he was condemned, not for teaching heresy, but for culpably neglecting to suppress it. This, they maintain, was clearly the view of Pope Leo II., who confirmed the acts of the Council. In a letter to the Spanish bishops this Pope states that Honorius was condemned, "*because he did not extinguish the flame of heretical dogma, as it be-*

came his Apostolic authority, in the commencement, but rather fed it by his negligence." ⁶⁰ That is, in other words, Honorius was censured for a *moral* fault—a neglect of duty, not for a *doctrinal* error. His crime was not that he *taught* error, but that he *omitted* to teach the truth—a circumstance which not only is no objection ⁶¹ to Infallibility, but does not even militate against his personal orthodoxy. "Pope Honorius," writes Cardinal Hergenröther,⁶² "may be reproached with having *encouraged error indirectly by not proceeding against it with timely* vigor, but it cannot be said that he *defined* error, *which would alone tell against the dogma.* . . . A Pope is not infallible in proceedings such as those of Honorius, who contributed unintentionally to the increase of heresy by not issuing decisions against it. *His letters contain no decision, neither do they contain any false doctrine.* No decision of his ever was or could be condemned as false; otherwise the Sixth Council would have contradicted itself, *for it recognized that the Holy See had at all time the privilege of teaching truth.* He was condemned for having rendered himself morally responsible for the spread of heresy by having neglected to publish decisions against it; *and in this sense alone was his condemnation confirmed by Leo II."* And in his work, " Anti-Janus," ⁶³ he says: "We must set by the side of the Council's sentence *the letter of confirmation of Pope Leo II.;* and however we may explain the Pontiff's words, *more we cannot extract from them* than that the anathema punished a *forgetfulness* of duty rather than a moral complicity in the Monothelite errors. *This has been the view hitherto taken by the most distinguished theologians*, and among others by many doctors of the Sorbonne, to wit, *that Honorius was not a heretic, but only a favorer of heresy.*" "I will here affirm," writes Cardinal Manning,⁶⁴ "that the following points in the case of Honorius *can be abundantly proved from documents:*⁶⁵ (1) That Honorius *defined* no doctrine whatsoever; (2) that he forbade the making of any new definition; (3) that his fault was *precisely* in this *omission* of Apostolic authority, for which he was justly censured; (4) that his two epistles *are entirely orthodox;* though, in the use of language, he wrote as was usual before the condemnation of Monothelitism, and not as it became necessary afterwards. It is an anachronism and an injustice to censure his language used before that condemnation, as it might be just to censure it after the condemnation had been made." Finally, Cardinal Hergenröther,⁶⁶ summing up the result of the whole controversy on the case, which he says claims an "almost immeasurable literature," writes: "The defenders of the Pope may, in fact, consider it a great triumph for their cause that, *in despite of all the array of learning and critical acumen* brought to bear against their opinion, they have not yet been refuted; still less has the adverse sentiment been raised to the fulness of evidence; nay, that deeper historical inquiries serve ever to establish their belief on a more solid basis." ⁶⁷

In reference to the second part of Dr. Littledale's statement, Fr. Ryder says:⁶⁸ "No Pope ever wrote to the Spanish bishops, or to any one else, to the effect that Honorius was 'damned.' Gregory II. (so the Doctor had it in the first editions of 'Plain Reasons') had never any occasion to touch upon the Honorian matter, but Leo II., in his letter to the Spanish bishops, in which he gives an account of the procedure of the Sixth Council, refers to Honorius as, amongst others, '*æterna damnatione mulctati*,' which simply means, involved in a final anathema. See the expression in the Professio in the 'Liber Diurnus,' '*Nexu perpetuæ anathematis.*' The Church has never allowed herself to define any one's eternal damnation, and still less supposed herself empowered to inflict it."

Objection: But what about the celebrated case of Galileo? This, certainly, is "a leading case in point," and one that unquestionably involves a "break-down of Infallibility." Did not the Congregation of the Index publish on March 5, 1616, "a decree condemning as 'false, unscriptural, and destructive of Catholic truth,' the opinion that the earth moves round the sun?" And was not Paul V., though the fact "is disputed amongst Roman theologians," "personally responsible for the decree," inasmuch as he "undoubtedly set the Index at work, and entirely agreed with its finding?" Did not the Congregation of the Inquisition (1633) compel Galileo "to retract and abjure" his views? And did not Pope Urban VIII., on June 30th of the same year, order "the publication of the sentence, thereby, *according to Roman ecclesiastical law*, making Galileo's compulsory denial of the earth's motion a theological doctrine—*binding* on all Christians everywhere?" [69]

Answer: In the mind of the impartial inquirer this objection will give rise to two questions: one regarding the facts of the case, the other the bearing of those facts on the dogma of Infallibility. The former: Did the Pope approve and confirm with his Apostolic authority the decisions of the Roman Congregation in the case of Galileo? The latter, assuming that he did: Does this act on the part of the Pope involve a "break-down of Infallibility"? Or does it place Catholics "in the dilemma of having to reject either the earth's movement or the Pope's Infallibility as defined by the Vatican Council?" On the first point I will merely remark that there is no proof that the Pope ever formally approved and confirmed the decrees in question; they do not, directly or indirectly, mention the Pope's name or contain a single word to show that they were issued by his orders or had received his approval and confirmation. And if they were merely the decisions and decrees of the Congregations," clearly they are no objection to Papal Infallibility; for "the extremest advocate of the authority of the Roman Congregations has never claimed for their decrees, *as such*, the character of a Papal *ex-cathedra* judgment." [11]

But the question whether or not the Pope did approve and confirm these decrees does not in the least affect the dogma of Infallibility. For we must not forget that a mere Papal confirmation would not raise them to the dignity of infallible utterances,[12] and infallible utterances *they should be* to prove a "break-down of Infallibility." Here Mr. Proctor, who, be it remembered, was an eminent scientist, and *no believer* in Papal Infallibility, will speak for me. After assuring his readers that he "*specially studied and weighed during eight years*" the whole subject, this impartial writer observes: "Not quite as absurd," though quite as *incorrect*, is the idea that Papal Infallibility is disproved by the decision (*supposing for the moment it received the Papal sanction*) against Galileo. . . . The Catholic doctrine on the subject [of Papal Infallibility] is perfectly definite; and *it is absolutely certain* that the decision in regard to Galileo's teaching, shown now to have been unsound, *does not in the slightest degree affect* the doctrine of Infallibility, either of the Pope or of the Church . . . . The decision was neither *ex cathedra* nor addressed to the whole Church; *in not one single point* does the case illustrate this doctrine of Papal Infallibility as defined by the Vatican Council." [14] This, I think, sufficiently disposes of the "leading case." [15]

Objection: But, after all, of what practical value is Infallibility? To aid effectually the faith of the believer, the latter should himself be infallible. For how can I believe any doctrine unless I can say infallibly that said doctrine has been taught infallibly? Well, this is the prerogative of the Pope alone; "and so it is plain that there is no real safeguard against error in having an infallible *teacher* unless his disciples be also infallible *hearers*." [16] Catholics, therefore, with Infallibility are no better off or more secure in their position than Protestants without it.

Answer: To make an act of faith in any doctrine all that is necessary is that I should know for certain that the doctrine has been taught infallibly; and to attain to such certainty I need not be infallible. The difficulty here arises from confounding Infallibility with certitude—two very different things. [17]

CONCLUSION.

Dear Reader: You have now before you what Infallibility really means in the faith of Catholics; and is it not a reasonable, a beautiful, and a comforting dogma? one worthy of God, of His Wisdom, and Goodness, and eminently suited to the needs of man —of his reason, conscience, and soul? Is it not almost a self-evident necessity of religion? Where interests the most vital are at stake, where it is a question of truth or error, of salvation or damnation, what can be more reasonable, natural, and needful to fickle, erring man than an infallible Teacher of God's holy and saving law? Would it not be a strange thing if God, having given us the truth, had left it without such a Teacher and Guardian?

You have also before you the reasons why Catholics believe in Infallibility; and are they not many, forcible, and convincing? Are they not all that any unprejudiced mind could reasonably demand? Look into your own rooted beliefs—your religious beliefs. Are the reasons on which they rest more numerous, more forcible, more convincing? Is reason clearer? Is revelation? Take any one of the doctrines of Christianity in which you believe—the Trinity, the Incarnation, the Atonement, Everlasting Punishment, or the Inspiration of the Bible—and commit to paper the reasons for your faith in it. Place them side by side with the arguments for Infallibility. Weigh well and dispassionately the matter; and does the balance incline to your belief as against Infallibility? *Just make the experiment and see.*

THE OBJECTIONS TO INFALLIBILITY? 239

Thirdly, you have before you the most popular and forcible objections to Infallibility, and the answers to them. Are they not fairly stated and satisfactorily answered? Does any insurmountable difficulty remain?

Lastly, taking into account the exposition of the dogma, the reasons for believing it, and the answers to the objections advanced against it—what more, I ask, do you need but the *grace* of faith? Well, that comes not of argument but of God alone.

"Faith is the *gift* of God, and not a mere act of our own which we are free to exert when we will. It is quite distinct from an exercise of reason, though it follows upon it. I may feel the force of the argument for the divine origin of the Church; I may see that I ought to believe; and yet I may be unable to believe. This is no imaginary case; there is many a man who has ground enough to believe, who wishes to believe, but who cannot believe. It is always indeed his own fault, for God gives grace to all who ask for it, and use it, but still such is the fact, that *conviction is not faith*. Take the parallel case of obedience; many a man knows he ought to obey God, and does not and cannot,—through his own fault, indeed, but still he cannot; for through grace alone can he obey. Now, faith is not a mere *conviction in reason*, it is a firm assent, it is a clear certainty greater than any other certainty; and this is wrought in the mind by the grace of God, *and by it alone*. As then men may be convinced, and not act according to their conviction, so may they be convinced, and not believe according to their conviction. They may confess that the argument is against them, that they have nothing to say for themselves, and that to believe is to be happy; and yet, after all, they avow they cannot believe, they do not know why, but they cannot; they acquiesce in unbelief, and they turn away from God and His Church. Their reason is convinced, and their doubts are *moral* ones, arising in their root from a fault of the will. In a word, *the arguments for religion do not compel any one to believe, just as the arguments for good conduct do not compel any one to obey.* Obedience is the consequence of willing to obey, and faith is the consequence of willing to believe; we may see what is right, whether in matters of faith or obedience, of ourselves, but we cannot *will* what is right without the grace of God. Here is the difference between other exercises of reason and the arguments for the truth of religion. It requires no act of faith to assent to the truth that two and two make four; we cannot help assenting to it; and hence there is no merit in assenting to it; but there is merit in believing that the Church is from God; for though there are abundant reasons to prove it to us, yet we can, without an absurdity, quarrel with the conclusion; we may complain that it is not clearer, we may suspend our assent, we may doubt about it, if we will, and *grace alone* can turn a bad will into a good one." "

Faith, then, is a grace from above. Now, perhaps, God is offering you this great grace at this very moment. Perhaps it may be the first impulses of this grace that directed your attention to this little book and its subject. Perhaps this grace is at present pointing you to Infallibility as to a column of light in the dark wilderness of human opinions. Stop! Think!

And take care that you "receive not the grace of God *in vain*." " If grace calls you now, and you heed not its voice, it may go away, never to return.

"God has not chosen every one to salvation: it is a rare gift to be a Catholic; it may be offered to us once in our lives and never again; and, if we have not seized on the 'accepted time,' nor know ' in our day the things which are for our peace,' oh, the misery for us! What shall we be able to say when death comes, and we are not converted, and it is directly and immediately our own doing that we are not?

"'Wisdom preacheth abroad, she uttereth her voice in the streets: How long, ye little ones, love ye childishness, and fools covet what is hurtful to them, and the unwise hate knowledge? Turn ye at My reproof; behold I will bring forth to you My spirit, and I will show My words unto you. Because I have called, and ye refused, I stretched out My hand and there was none who regarded, and ye despised all My counsel and neglected My chidings; I also will laugh in your destruction, and will mock when that shall come to you which you feared; when a sudden storm shall rush on you and destruction shall thicken as a tempest, when tribulation and straitness shall come upon you. Then shall they call on Me and I will not hear; they shall rise betimes, but they shall not find Me; for that they hated discipline and took not on them the fear of the Lord, nor acquiesced in My counsel, but made light of My reproof, therefore shall they eat the fruit of their own way, and be filled with their own devices.'

"Oh, the misery for us, as many of us as shall be

in that number! Oh, the awful thought for all eternity! Oh, the remorseful sting, 'I was called, I might have answered, and I did not!' And oh, the blessedness, if we can look back on the time of trial, when friends implored and enemies scoffed, and say: The misery for me which would have been had I not followed on, had I hung back when Christ called me! Oh, the utter confusion of mind, the wreck of faith and opinion, the blackness and the void, the dreary scepticism, the hopelessness which would have been my lot, the pledge of the outer darkness to come, had I been afraid to follow Him! I have lost friends, I have lost the world, but I have gained Him who gives in Himself houses and brethren and sisters and mothers and children and lands a hundredfold; I have lost the perishable and gained the Infinite; I have lost time and I have gained eternity. 'O Lord, my God, I am Thy servant, and the son of Thine handmaid; Thou hast broken my bonds. I will sacrifice to Thee the sacrifice of praise, and I will call on the Name of the Lord.' " [99]

NOTES TO CHAPTER V.

¹ Mr. Gladstone, "Vatican Decrees," pp. 17, 11. Cf. also Schulte in Fessler, "True and False Infallibility," p. 48.
² Page 18.
³ Mr. Gladstone's "Expostulation Unravelled," pp. 53-54.
⁴ Vatican Council, "Constit. Dogmat. Prima de Ecclesia Christi," cap. iv. Mr. Gladstone falls into a similar error in treating of the obedience due to the Pope's supreme but fallible authority, not only in matters of faith and morals, but also in what appertains to the discipline and government of the Church. Here, again, confounding the *duty* of obedience with the *practice* of obedience, he extends to the latter what the Council teaches of the former only. (See 'Vatican Decrees,' pp. 18-20.) "Three times," says Cardinal Newman, "does he make the Pope say, that no one can *disobey* him without risking his salvation; whereas what the Pope does say is, that no one can *disbelieve* in the *duty* of obedience and unity without such risk." *Letter*, etc., p. 51. Cf. also Archbishop Ullathorne, "Mr. Gladstone's Expostulation Unravelled," pp. 59-60, 63. To disobey the Pope's mandate is one thing; to deny, or disbelieve in, the duty of obedience to the Pope's authority is another, and very different thing. In Catholic teaching the latter act would, *of itself*, place its author outside the pale of the Church; the former would not, though in some cases it may subject its author to the penalty of excommunication. The agent in the one case, would be guilty of the sin of heresy; in the other, of the sin of simple disobedience merely. Mr. Gladstone's mistaken view of the Church's teaching in this matter constitutes the basis of "*his most vehement and declamatory accusations.*"
⁵ "Vaticanism," pp. 46, 49-50. Cf. also Dr. Littledale "Plain Reasons," pp. 15-16.
⁶ "Vaticanism," p. 51.
⁷ "Vatican Decrees," pp. 20-21.
⁸ "Vaticanism," p. 51.
⁹ "Plain Reasons, etc," p. 16.
¹⁰ Cf. Cardinal Hergenröther, "Catholic Church and Christian State," vol. i., pp. 82, 83, 113-120, 201. Hettinger, "The Supremacy of the Apostolic See," pp. 108, 121, 163. Cardinal Newman, "Apologia," pp. 271, 277-278 (2d ed. 246, 253-254).
¹¹ St. Jude, chap. i. 3.
¹² "Vatican Decrees," p. 2.
¹³ Cf. Franzelin, "De Trad.," thesis xxii.; Mazzella "De Virt. Inf.," nn. 489, 507. God has in the past, and may in the future make private revelations—revelations intended for individuals, but here there is question of a revelation intended for all,—a catholic revelation.

¹⁴ Cf. Franzelin, "De Trad.," p. 272; Cardinal Manning, "The Grounds of Faith," Lecture iii., p. 45. "To the Apostles," writes Cardinal Newman, "the *whole* of revelation was given, by the Church it is transmitted; no simply *new* truth has been given to us since St. John's death; the *one* office of the Church is to guard 'that noble deposit' of truth, as St. Paul speaks to Timothy, which the Apostles bequeathed to her in its fulness and integrity."—Letter to the Duke of Norfolk, p. 131.

¹⁵ "Constit. Dogmat. Prima de Ecclesia Christi," cap. iv.

¹⁶ Cf. Franzelin, "De Trad.," pp. 121, 289; Perrone, "De Fide," nn. 125, 144. We believe a truth *explicitly* when, having that truth clearly and in express terms before our minds, we make an act of faith in it. We believe a truth *implicitly* when we make an act of faith, not directly and formally in the truth itself, but in some other truth or principle containing it. Thus he, who says, 'I believe that there is a God,' or, 'I believe that the Son of God became man,' or again, 'I believe that the Church is God's representative on earth to teach men the truths of salvation,' believes *explicitly*, and makes acts of *explicit* faith in the existence of God, in the Incarnation, and in the Divine Mission of the Church. While he who says, 'I believe all that God has revealed,' or 'I believe all that the Church proposes for my belief,' believes *implicitly* and makes acts of *implicit* faith, in the one case, in every truth of Revelation, and in the other, in every revealed truth proposed by the Church for the belief of all, and that even though he does not know specifically the truths in either case. So too he who makes an *explicit* act of faith in a universal proposition, or in a complex proposition, believes implicitly all particular propositions contained in the one and all the constituent parts of the other.— Cf. Franzelin, pp. 279 (note), and 313; Mazzella, "De Virt. Inf.," n. 366.

¹⁷ Cf. Franzelin, "De Trad.," p. 274; Mazzella, "De Virt. Inf.," n. 507, Prop. xix.; Perrone, "De Fide," n. 113; Hurter, "Theol. Gen.," vol. i., nn. 663 a, 664.—"We are all agreed," writes Cardinal Manning, "that the *only* subject-matter of faith is the original revelation of God."—"Grounds of Faith," Lecture iii., pp. 44-45. And in a sermon delivered previous to the Council he says, in reply to those who were then hard at work to convince the world that the Council was about to define doctrines that were not *revealed*. "I do not know what they may be [the doctrines the Council may define], *but of this I am sure*, that the General Council will not, *because it cannot*, define any doctrine which has not been *revealed*. . . . *The revelation of God is the only object of our faith*."—"Sermons on Ecclesiastical Subjects," vol. iii., p. 119.

¹⁸ Cf. Franzelin, "De Trad.," p. 273; Mazzella, "De Virt. Inf., n. 513; Perrone, "De Fide," n. 117; "Faith of Catholics," vol. i., Introduction viii.-ix., xxxv-xxxvi. "All belief dogmatically (infallibly) defined *must form a part of revelation*, and must consequently be contained in the divine word whether written or unwritten; for, if the word of the Church is the immediate and living rule of our faith, she herself has, in the word of God, her supreme and fundamental rule. The Church, by dogmatical (*ex-cathedra*) decisions, does not then create the truth; she makes neither the dogma nor the revelation of it; she merely proclaims its existence with infallible authority. The dogma which authority proclaims to-day,

NOTES TO CHAPTER V. 245

was yesterday; before the decision it existed in its substance; after the decision, it appeared with its formula, and is of obligation. The part of the Church, in dogmatic (infallible or *ex-cathedra*) definitions may, then, be defined, *the legitimate and infallible declaration of a revealed truth."—*Father Felix, quoted by Father Russo in "The True Religion," pp. 100-101.

The office and powers of the Church in regard to Revelation are well illustrated by the office and powers of the Supreme Court in regard to our Constitution. The Supreme Court is not above the Constitution, neither is the Church (or Pope) above Revelation. The Supreme Court cannot go beyond the Constitution; neither can the Church go beyond Revelation. The Supreme Court cannot import a new clause into the Constitution; neither can the Church add a new truth to Revelation. The decision of the Supreme Court is not a new law, neither is the definition of the Church a new doctrine. The Supreme Court can only interpret the Constitution; the Church can do no more in the case of Revelation. The decision of the Supreme Court is theoretically irreversible; that of the Church is really so. Neither allows the right of appeal; both are final, with this difference, however, that while one, by a legal fiction, is formally infallible, the other, by the assistance of the Holy Spirit of Truth, is so in truth and in fact.

[19] Cf. Introduction to Definition of Infallibility, Vatican Council, Dogma Const. on the Church, cap. iv., and to the Definition of the Immaculate Conception B. V. M., Bull "Ineffabilis Deus," Dec, 8. 1854.

[20] "Is Life Worth Living?" chap. xi., p. 287.

[21] "The Vatican Council and its Definitions," p. 48.

[22] "Via Media," vol. i., note p. 241. *Definitions may be said to be that one only boon which heresy has conferred on the Church."—*"English Religion," by A. M., p. 31.

[23] "Anglican Difficulties," Lecture xii., p. 345.

[24] "The Vatican Council and its Definitions," pp. 133-134, ("Petri Privilegium," part iii.) Cf. also Hergenröther, "Catholic Church and Christian State," vol. i., pp. 91-118; Hettinger, "The Supremacy of the Apostolic See," chaps. xix-xxi.; Knox, "When Does the Church Speak Infallibly?" pp. 31-48. The Cardinal gives ample proof of this statement in his "Petri Privilegium," part ii., chap. iii., and part iii., chap. v.

[25] In Allnatt's "Which is the True Church?" p. 32. "The Popes, for many centuries, have acted as though they were infallible." "Cyclopædia of Biblical, Theological, and Ecclesiastical Literature," prepared by the Rev. John McClintock, DD., and James Strong, S. F. D., vol. iv., p. 570. Hence Cardinal Manning observes that, though the word " Infallibility " was not invented in early years, "the thing existed *in its most energetic reality."—*"The True Story of the Vatican Council," p. 58.

Dr. Döllinger, speaking as a *historian* and addressing a company of *savants* at Munich in 1845, said: "Gentlemen, the question is this: It is true that the Infallibility of the Pope is not a dogma defined by the Church; yet any who should maintain the contrary *would put himself in opposition to the conscience of the whole Church, in the present as in the past."—*Quoted by Mr. A. F. Marshall in an article entitled "Mr. Gladstone and Dr. Döllinger," in the Liverpool *Catholic Times,* September, 1890.

²⁶ "Petri Privilegium," part ii., p. 62.

²⁷ Vol. i., p. 1. See also Franzelin, "De Trad.," pp. 275-276, 308, 708-709. Mazzella, "De Virt.," nn. 281, 364, 366, 460, 465; Schrader, "De Theologia Generatim Commentarius," p. 108; Perrone, "Prælectiones Theologicæ de Fide," nn. 14, 190, 257; Hurter, "Theol. Gen.," vol. n. 663; Veronius, "De Regula Fidei Catholicæ," cap. i., sect. 1, 2; Humphrey, "The Divine Teacher," pp. 27-28.

²⁸ Cf. Perrone, "De Fide," nn. 120, 257; Hurter, "Theol. Gen.," vol. i. n. 663a.

²⁹ Had Mr. Gladstone known of this distinction he would not have accused Cardinal Manning of contradicting a formal declaration made by the Irish Bishops at the beginning of the century. What the Cardinal stated was, "That the Infallibility of the Pope was a doctrine of *Divine* faith before the Council of the Vatican was held." What the Bishops severally declared (1810) was that "it was not an article of *Catholic* faith, neither am I thereby required to believe or profess, that the Pope is infallible." Between the statement and the declaration Mr. Gladstone sees a "diametrical contradiction." From the explanation given in the text the reader will see at a glance that between the two there is no contrariety whatever, much less contradiction. This is a simple matter, but it is sufficient to show how necessary it is, even for persons of Mr. Gladstone's intellectual attainments, to study carefully Catholic theology before venturing to write on it. Cf. Vatican Decrees, p. 15; "Vaticanism," pp. 18-19; 22-23. What has been said in the text satisfactorily explains also the case of "painful alteration," quoted in "Vaticanism," Appendix D., p. 62. Cf. also Dr. Littledale, "Plain Reasons," pp. 199-200.

³⁰ Catholic faith is here taken to mean what theologians ordinarily mean by the expression, namely, *explicit* Catholic faith. For, as a truth of revelation, it was since the day of Pentecost of *implicit* Catholic faith (See above, p. 214). Of course if one, previous to its definition, were convinced, beyond all reasonable doubt, that it was a truth of Revelation, he was certainly bound to believe it *explicitly*, not however by *Catholic*, but by *Divine*, faith. This remark applies to any truth of Revelation hitherto not proposed by the Church. Cf. Franzelin, "De Trad.," pp. 276-277, 709; Mazzella, "De Virt Inf.," nn. 404, 489-491; Hurter, "Theol. Gen.," vol. i., n. 663; Perrone, "De Fide.," n. 125; Hettinger, "The Supremacy of the Apostolic See," p. 106.

³¹ Cf. Franzelin, thesis xxiv.; Mazzella, n. 542 *et seq.*; Hettinger, pp. 107-108; Hergenröther, "Catholic Church and Christian State," vol. i., p. 91.

³² Letter, etc., p. 156.

³³ Essays on Miracles," p. 171.

³⁴ "There is," says Cardinal Newman, "the same difference between the modern and primitive teaching and action of the Catholic Church as between the boy and the man. Such difference as little interferes with the identity of the modern and primitive teaching as with the identity of the man and boy."—"Via Media," vol. i. p. 82 (note).

³⁵ Anti-Janus, p. 253.

³⁶ *Ibid.*, p. 251. Cf. also pp. 251-252, and Franzelin, "De Trad.," thesis xxiii., xxiv.; Mazzella "De Virt.," n. 515 *et seq*; Perrone, "De Fide," n,

117. Hettinger, "The Supremacy of the Apostolic See," chaps. xix., xx., xxi., pp. 104-110. Catholicism, says Mr. Mallock, will be found on examination to be "the logical development of our natural moral sense, developed, indeed, and still developing, under a special and supernatural care—*but essentially the same thing;* with the same negations, the same assertions, the same positive truths, and the same impenetrable mysteries; and with nothing new added to them, but help, and certainty, and guidance."—"Is Life Worth Living ?" chap. xi., p. 302.

³⁷ "This growth or development in the Church's teaching proceeds on fixed laws under the safeguard of her infallibility, *which secures* her from whatever is abnormal or unhealthy."—Cardinal Newman, "Via Media," vol. i., (note) p. 82. Cf. also "Anglican Difficulties," Lecture xii., p. 344. Replying to Dr. Littledale's statement that, because the Pope can infallibly define what Catholics are to believe, therefore "No Roman Catholic can any longer tell what his religion may be at any future time," Father Ryder observes: "A Roman Catholic knows that 'at any future time' he will hold every one of the articles of faith he holds at present with the possible addition of certain others, which, as they grow out of the twilight of doubt into the light of certainty beneath the articulation of the Church, will present themselves as the natural complement and explication of those he already possesses."—"Catholic Controversy," p. 134.

³⁷* Vatican Council, "Const. Dogmat. de Fide Catholica," cap. iii.

³⁸ See above, pp. 4, 5.

³⁹ Numbers xxii. 38.   ⁴⁰ John xi., 49, 51.

⁴¹ Math. xxiii., 2, 3. Our Divine Lord Himself, says Mr. Allnatt, "warned his followers to distinguish between the *official acts* and the *personal unworthiness* of any of His ministers, when He said: "The Scribes and Pharisees *sit in the chair of Moses;* all things, *therefore,* whatsoever they bid you observe [teach or command *ex-cathedra*] *observe and do,* but *do ye not after their works,* for they *say* [teach truly in their official capacity], but *do not* " (*i. e.,* do not practice what they themselves teach and enjoin). Math. xxiii., 2, 3.—"Which is the True Church ?" p. 79.

⁴² "One hears," wrote the late distinguished scientist, R. A. Proctor, "an ignorant but most zealous Protestant talk such nonsense as this: 'How can the Pope be infallible when such a Pope was notoriously unwise, and such another a man of evil life?' It would be just as reasonable to say, How can we believe David to have been inspired when we find that he behaved not only villanously, but most foolishly, in regard to Uriah the Hittite and his wife ?"—"Knowledge," vol. ix., p. 273.

⁴³ 1 Cor. ii., 4, 5, 13.

⁴⁴ Quoted by Cardinal Manning, "Petri Privilegium," appendix viii. See also above, p. 25, note 23.

⁴⁵ "Infallibility," says Dr. Brownson somewhere, "in no way depends on the Pope's personal attainments or endowments, on his learning, wisdom, or sanctity; it rests on the promise and assistance of God, who can choose the foolish things of this world to confound the wise, the weak things to bring to naught the mighty, and make even the wicked the instruments of His will, and the organs of His word."

⁴⁶ "Again and again," says Dr. Draper, "Popes have contradicted each

other." ("The Conflict, etc.," p. 359.) Doctor, have they contradicted each other in *ex-cathedra* utterances? If not, you have said nothing to the point in your indictment of Papal Infallibility. The Doctor goes on to instance a number of "well-known errors" into which he says the Papacy has fallen; and then, with an air of trumph, asks, "How is it possible to coördinate the infallibility of the Papacy," with such errors? Now not one of the Doctor's fatal "errors" conflicts with the doctrine of Papal Infallibility. Anybody who understands the doctrine will see this at a glance. Pity our author did not properly inform himself before writing.

⁴⁷ "This claim [to infallibility] is one, as we shall see when we understand its nature, that *no study of ecclesiastical* history, no study of comparative mythology, *can invalidate now, or even promise to invalidate.*" —W. H. Mallock, "Is Life Worth Living?" chap. xii., pp. 313-314.

⁴⁷* In Cardinal Bellarmine's day, as many as forty Popes were charged with heresy or error in teaching. See his "De Summo Pontifice," lib. iv., caps. viii-xiv. ⁴⁸ "Plain Reasons," p. 175.

⁴⁹ Of course to sign either of these formulas under the circumstances, implied moral guilt; but a *moral* fault is not a *doctrinal* error. And of the latter only there is question here.

⁵⁰ See above, pp. 12, 17, 20.

⁵¹ "When once in the possession of his See, and surrounded by his orthodox supporters, he appears to have resumed his *old position of resolute orthodoxy.*"—Smith & Wace, "Dictionary of Christian Biography," vol. iii., p. 723.

⁵² "Historical Sketches," vol. ii., p. 340. Cf. also Cardinal Hergenröther, "The Catholic Church and Christian State," vol. i., p. 83. This case is fully discussed by Professor Gilmartin of Maynooth College, in the *Irish Ecclesiastical Record*, April, May, June, 1888. Cf. also Hergenröther, "Anti-Janus," pp. 74-75; Ryder, "Catholic Controversy," pp. 27-28; and Rivington's "Dependence," chap. iv., and an article by the same author in the *Dublin Review*, July, 1891, pp. 139-141. By consulting these authors, especially the articles in the *Record*, the reader will see what credit is due to the following statement of another professional controversialist: "The heresy of Liberius is notorious *and not even questioned.*" —Collette, "The Papacy," p. 43.

⁵³ The writer of the article on "Athanasius" in the "Dictionary of Christian Biography (Smith & Wace), a standard Protestant work, admits that the letter, in which Liberius is made to say that he had put Athanasius out of his communion for refusing to come to Rome when summoned, "*is justly regarded as a forgery.*"—Vol. i. p. 192.

⁵⁴ "Plain Reasons," p. 175. It is worthy of note that in three editions of the Doctor's book published previous to Father Ryder's "Reply" it was Gregory II. (not Leo II.) who wrote to the Spanish Bishops. The Doctor made the correction, but, with his usual frankness, said nothing about the blunder. Seeing that this work is circulated by the *Society for Promoting Christian Knowledge*, I think it well to place before the reader the following estimate of it, with some references which will tell him where he will find the Doctor's statements examined in detail.

"What are we to think of Dr. Littledale's 'Plain Reasons'? The

NOTES TO CHAPTER V. 249

author has sent to the *Guardian* newspaper, between the years 1880 and 1885, no less than *eighteen* letters containing retractions and corrections of mistakes which had been pointed out to him by persons whom he could not, I presume, afford to ignore, I say this because his book is full of arguments refuted over and over again, indeed, to quote a phrase from his own organ of opinion—*The Church Times*—used with respect to a religious opponent of that journal, ' *When he has been exposed and refuted he never confesses and apologises, but waits till he thinks the refutation is forgotten, and then brings up the discredited statement as fresh as ever.*' Says Dr. Lee, Vicar of All Saints', Lambeth,' Every edition of Littledale's book receives fresh corrections, *while in several cases the corrections are equally inaccurate with the statements presumed to be corrected.*' To the edition of "Plain Reasons," issued in 1881, are prefixed no less than twenty-nine pages of closely printed ' additions and corrections,' —mainly the latter, in all 13,340 words of *errata;* pretty well, one would think, for a book of 200 pages. Now mark, these are not merely additions to the work, but corrections of gross mistakes, *which mistakes the author has not acknowledged in many instances, but has quietly passed them over,* for the manifest reason that to acknowledge them would be to give up his position and his charges against the Catholic and Roman Church—in fact would destroy his case. Dr. Lee has tabulated these corrections thus:

Regarding historical facts	51
Regarding dogmatic facts	43
Regarding *inaccurate* quotations from writers on history and Canon law	29
Regarding historical and theological quotations half made, *often with remarkable omissions and qualifications*	30
Regarding quotations from the Fathers, which, when sought out, *are found to bear an entirely different meaning from that which* Dr. Littledale *put upon them*	24
Confusing the *personal opinion* of Catholics with the defined doctrine of the Church	17
Assuming that current opinions of theologians are without doubt defined dogmas	7
Total	201

Dr. Lee adds, ' Several of the above-referred-to *corrigenda* and subadded notes contain several other retractions, further detailed explanations, and careful explainings away of *grave* mistakes.' "—"The Character of Dr. Littledale as a Controversialist," by Owen C. H. King: Burns & Oates, London. See also "Catholic Controversy: A Reply to Dr. Littledale's ' Plain Reasons,' " by H. J. D. Ryder: Burns & Oates, London. "Truthfulness and Ritualism," by Orby Shipley, M. A.: Burns & Oates, London. "Dishonest Criticism," by James Jones, S. J : John Hodges, London. "Controversy on the Constitutions of the Jesuits, between Dr. Littledale and Dr. Drummond": Manitoba *Free Press* Print, Winnipeg. Mr. Shipley exposed with such effect the untruthfulness and unfairness of Dr. Littledale's pamphlet entitled "Why Ritualists Do Not Become Roman Catholics," that the *English Church Union*, under whose auspices it was published, was compelled to withdraw it from circulation.

[54*] "We," says the Pope, "must not wrest what they say into Church

dogmas." "We leave the matter to grammarians." "We must not *define* either one or two operations." "We must not *defining* pronounce one or two operations." Cf. Ryder, "Catholic Controversy," foot-note, p. 29.

⁵⁵ See above, pp. 16, 17, 20.   ⁵⁶ Letter, etc., p. 121.
⁵⁷ See above, p. 12, and note 55, p. 27.   ⁵⁸ Letter, etc., p. 123.
⁵⁹ October, 1889, pp. 285-286.
⁶⁰ In Hettinger's "The Supremacy of the Apostolic See," p. 96.
⁶¹ See above, pp. 17, 18.
⁶² Catholic Church and Christian State," vol. i., p. 83.   ⁶³ Page 81.
⁶⁴ "Petri Privilegium," part iii, appendix vi. Cf. also part ii., note, p. 92, and 150. The Cardinal elsewhere ("The True Story of the Vatican Council," p. 205) observes that Pius IX. would have been guilty of the same crime had he under the circumstances not defined in the Vatican Council the doctrine of Infallibility.

⁶⁵ All the documents relating to the case are given in Bouix, "De Rom. Pont," part 2, sect. 5.
⁶⁶ "Anti-Janus," p. 82.
⁶⁷ The reader, who desires to go more fully into this case, may consult "The True Faith of Our Forefathers," pp. 106-118; Bottalla, "Pope Honorius Before the Tribunal of Reason and History"; Ward, "The Condemnation of Pope Honorius"; Hettinger, *op. cit.*, chap. xvii., pp. 83-97; Perrone, "De Romani Pontificis Infallibilitate," cap. vi.; Franzelin, "De Verbo Incarnato," Thesis xl., Schol.; Mazzella, "De Ecclesia," n. 1089 *et seq.*   ⁶⁸ "Catholic Controversy," p. 30.
⁶⁹ Dr. Littledale's "Plain Reasons," etc., pp. 181-182.
⁷⁰ This is the opinion of the author of the article on Galileo in the Encyclopedia Britannica.
⁷¹ Father Ryder, "Catholic Controversy," p. 35.
⁷²See above, p. 23.
⁷³ As the objection referred to above, note 42.
⁷⁴ "Knowledge," vol. ix., p. 274.
⁷⁵ Dr. Littledale adds in a foot-note, "In 1822 Pius VII. ratified a decree of the Inquisition, licensing all Copernican treatises on astronomy; while in 1835 the works of Copernicus, Kepler, and Galileo were taken off the Index; *which amounts to a Papal admission* that Paul V. and Urban VIII. *erred in their definition of heresy*, and so were fallible teachers." Nonsense! Cf. "The Pope and the Bible," Richard F. Clarke, S. J., pp. 15-17. "It is little short of ridiculous," writes Cardinal Hergenröther, "to speak of the Index, which is merely a list of forbidden writings, as infallible decisions."—"Catholic Church and Christian State," vol. i., p. 81. The historical and scientific aspect of this case is well treated in *The Catholic World*, January, February, 1869, October, 1887. Cf. also Wegg-Prosser, "Galileo and his Judges."

⁷⁶ Dr. Littledale, *op cit.*, p. 185. Cf. also Mr. Gladstone, "Vaticanism," pp. 52-54.   ⁷⁷ Cf. Perrone, "De Locis Theologicis," part iii., n. 76.
⁷⁸ Cardinal Newman, "Discourses to Mixed Congregations," disc. xi., pp. 224-225. Cf. also Discs. x. (p. 211), and ix.
⁷⁹ II. Cor. vi. 1.
⁸⁰ Cardinal Newman, *op. cit.*, disc. xi., pp. 235-237.

APPENDIX A.

THE HAPPINESS OF CONVERTS.

"All thy children shall be taught of the Lord, and great shall be the peace of thy children."— Isaias liv. 13.

CONVERTS to the Catholic Church realize more fully and more vividly, perhaps, than anybody else, the blessed happiness of the certainty, security, and peace that come of Infallibility. Words seem to fail them in the endeavor to express the feeling of satisfaction, contentment, repose, and joy that all at once takes possession of them on entering the Church.

Here are a few testimonies on the point:

Mrs. Elizabeth Bayley Seton, foundress of the Sisters of Charity in America, was, before her conversion, "*oppressed with doubts and fears.*" After that event she wrote of "*the completion of her happiness*" in the following terms:

"On the 14th of March (1805) I was admitted to the true Church of Jesus Christ, with a mind grateful and satisfied as that of a poor shipwrecked mariner on being restored to his home. . . . I seemed then to be admitted to a new life and to the *peace which passeth all understanding;* and with David I now say, *Thou hast saved my soul from death, my eyes from tears, and my feet from falling;* and certainly most earnestly desire to *walk before Him in the land of the living,* esteeming my privilege so great, and what He has done for me so far beyond my most lively hopes, that I *can scarce realize my own happiness.*"

Herman Cohen, a distinguished musician, speaks of the happiness which he experienced after making his submission to the Church, in these terms:

"I feel a sweet *tranquillity*, a perfect *peace, the rest of a child in its mother's bosom.*"

Monsignor Doane, the son of a Protestant Episcopal Bishop, writes of his happiness as a Catholic thus:

"I thank God that I can say, 'It was a true report that I heard in mine own land' of the glory and blessedness of the Catholic Church. 'Mine eyes have even seen it, and behold the half was not told me; it exceeded the fame which I had heard.' Nay, when I remember the many doubts and misgivings which I felt when I was a Protestant, and the many fears with which I shrank from joining myself to a system which I had long believed to be corrupt and horrible, and when I compare these feelings with the *certainty*, and *peace*, and *blessedness* which I have found since I had the grace to make the venture, it seems to me as if the change which I have made can be compared only to the *happy death of the just*, from which in years gone by they perhaps shrunk with dread, and hardly dared to look forward to it, but to which they forever look back as to their new birth into a blessed state beyond all that the heart of man can conceive. Oh, that every one of my dear friends who are still trembling on the brink of that which seems to me so dark a river would take courage by our example and risk all upon the faith of the words of Christ. *And for myself I need ask nothing else, nor is there anything others need ask for me, beyond the grace of perseverance, that, having been sought out by the grace of my Lord and Saviour, and brought into the Church of His Mercy, contrary to my own deserts, I may endure unto the end*, and through the blood of my Lord and Saviour may lay hold of eternal life. Amen." [1]

---

[1] These testimonies are taken from "Conquests of Our Holy Faith," by James J. Tracy.

The late Father Hecker, founder of the community of the Paulist Fathers, wrote of how he felt, after finally making up his mind to enter the Church, in these words:

"I feel very cheerful and at ease since I have consented to join the Catholic Church. *Never* have I felt the *quietness*, the *immovableness*, and the *permanent rest* that I do now. *It is inexpressible.*"— Diary, June 13, 1844. Cf. *The Catholic World*, December, 1890.

His happiness, after making his first confession,[1] is almost unbounded. His diary reads as follows:

"August 2—*Penance! joy! unbounded love!* Sweet Jesus, Thy love is infinite! *Blessed faith! Sweet love!* I possess

---

[1] Though perhaps somewhat foreign to the subject, I am tempted to give to the reader a singularly beautiful passage on Confession from the pen of Cardinal Newman:

"How many are the souls in distress, anxiety, or loneliness, whose one need is to find a being to whom they can pour out their feelings unheard by the world! Tell them out they must; they cannot tell them out to those whom they see every hour. They want to tell them and not to tell them; and they want to tell them out, yet be as if they be not told; they wish to tell them to one who is strong enough to bear them, yet not too strong to despise them; they wish to tell them to one who can at once advise and can sympathize with them; they wish to relieve themselves of a load, to gain a solace, to receive the assurance that there is one who thinks of them, and one to whom in thought they can recur, to whom they can betake themselves, if necessary, from time to time, while they are in the world. How many a Protestant's heart would leap at the news of such a benefit, putting aside all distinct ideas of a sacramental ordinance, or of a grant of pardon and the conveyance of grace! *If there is a heavenly idea in the Catholic Church, looking at it simply as an idea, surely, it is next after the Blessed Sacrament, Confession is such. And such is it ever found in fact—the very act of kneeling, the low and contrite voice, the sign of the Cross hanging, so to say, over the head bowed low, and the words of peace and blessing. Oh, what a soothing charm is there, which the world can neither give nor take away! Oh! what piercing, heart-subduing tranquillity, provoking tears of joy, is poured almost substantially and physically upon the soul, the oil of gladness,* as Scripture calls it, *when the penitent at length rises, his God reconciled to him, his sins rolled away forever! This is Confession as it is in fact.*"—"Present Position of Catholics in England," Lecture viii., pp. 351-352.

an internal glory, a glowing flame of love! Let my whole life be an act of penance! . . . . *O ancient faith, how dear, how good is God in giving us sinners to thee! Blessed is the grace of God that leadeth sinners to thee! Oh! how thou hast comforted the soul!* It would turn from thee, but thou strengthenest it. The cup was bitter, but *infinitely more sweet is the joy thou givest.* My soul is clothed in brightness; its youth is restored. *Oh, blessed, ever blessed, unfathomable, divine faith!* O faith of Apostles, martyrs, confessors, and saints!"— Cf. *The Catholic World,* January, 1891.

This is how Dr. Brownson speaks of the change that comes over the convert:

"It is not easy to conceive the sense of *freedom* and *relief* one experiences in passing from Rationalism or any other form of Protestantism to Catholicity. The convert to the Church is the prisoner liberated from the Bastile; a weight is thrown from his shoulders, the manacles fall from his hands, and the fetters from his feet; he feels as light and as free as the air, and he would chirp and sing as the bird. This world changes its hue to his eyes; and he runs and leaps under the blue sky of a boundless universe. His thought, his mind, his very soul, is lighted up, and revels in the freedom of universal truth. He feels that he has something whereon he can stand, that he has no longer to bear up the Church, but that the Church can bear him up. He is conscious of an unfailing support, and no longer fears that he is in danger every step he takes of having his footing give way and of falling through. *His heart bounds with a sense of unlimited freedom, and with a joy unspeakable.* He experiences in his soul and through all his frame the truth of Our Lord's words to the Jews, 'If *the Son make you free, you shall be free indeed.*' "—" Works," vol. viii., pp. 379-380.

Speaking of himself before his conversion, he says: " *We had wandered in darkness, stumbling from error to error, with downcast look and saddened heart, craving for freedom and finding only bondage.*"—" Works," vol. xiv., p. 343. He tells us that he tried almost every form of Protestantism, and could find peace in none of them. At length, after "*twenty-five years of intense mental activity, and an incessant struggle for light and a religion on which I could rely,*" he became a Catholic, and at last his great soul "*found peace and repose.*"—"The Convert," chap. xix.

Nearly twenty-seven years after, he thus beautifully describes the happiness and joy he then experienced:

"*Nothing could exceed the joy* we felt as the truth flashed more and more clearly on us, and we saw that there was deliverance for us from the error and sin, the doubt and uncertainty, we suffered from for more than forty years of a wearisome life. We were the wanderer returning home, the lost child returning to lay his head once more on his mother's bosom. Every step that brought us nearer to her was a new joy. *And when we found ourselves in her embrace our joy was unspeakable.* We could not recall anything we had lost, or count anything we might yet have to endure; we could only sing the *Magnificat*, and we have done nothing since but sing in our heart the *Te Deum.*"—"Works," vol. xix., pp. 556–557.

Writing a few months after his death, his son, replying to those who predicted that his great, bold, and fearless mind could never work in subjection to the Catholic Church, testifies that "*for thirty years no thought had ever entered his mind which could by any possibility be construed into a doubt of any doctrine of that Church, or a hesitation to obey her authority.*" Again: "Though there was much to *try* him, and to *shake* him, if he could be shaken, *there never entered his mind one doubt, one suspicion of the truth of Catholicity.*" "As advancing years," continues the son, "brought profounder knowledge of the truth, and clearer and deeper insight into the errors and vagaries of Protestantism and modern scientific infidelity, *his love for the Church grew more and more fervent, and he blessed the Almighty daily more and more for the infinite goodness shown him in rescuing him from his wanderings in the mazes of doubt and unbelief, and for bringing him to the clear light of truth in the bosom of the Infallible Church.*"— Preface to "Convert," pp. v., viii.

In the "Valedictory" with which he closed the "Review" in 1876, thirty-two years after his conversion, and a short time before his death, he wrote:

"*I have, and I desire, no home out of the Catholic Church, with which I am more than satisfied, and which I love as the dearest, tenderest, and most affectionate mother. My only ambition is to live and die in her communion.*"—"Works," vol. xx., p. 438.

"Whither, then, shall I turn but to thee, *O glorious Roman Church,*" exclaims Mr. Allies, "to whom God has given, in its fulness, the double gift of ruling and of teaching? . . . . Too late have I found thee, who shouldst have fostered my childhood, and set thy gentle and awful seal on my youth; who shouldst have brought me up in the serene regions of truth, apart from doubt and the long agony of uncertain years. . . . O, too long sought, and too late found; yet be it given to me to pass under thy protection the short remains of this troubled life, to wander no more from the fold, but to find the chair of the Chief Shepherd to be indeed 'the shadow of a Great Rock in a weary land!' "—"The See of St. Peter," preface.

The longer the convert's experience of Catholicity is, the greater becomes his sense of certainty, serenity, and peace. Twenty-three years after his reception into the Church, the poet Aubrey De Vere writes:

"In the Church I have found an *ever-deepening* peace, a freedom *ever widening*, a genuine and a fruitful method for theological thought, and a truth *which brightens more and more into the perfect day.*"— *The Catholic World*, February, 1875, p. 577.

"*I feel*," wrote Cardinal Manning, shortly after he became a Catholic —" *I feel as if I had no desire unfulfilled, but to persevere in what God has given me for His Son's sake.*"—Letter to I. R. Hope-Scott, Q. C., April 7, 1851.

Cardinal Newman [3] describes his passing from Anglicanism to Catholicism as "*like coming into port after a rough sea.*" Nineteen years after the event he writes:

"From the time that I became a Catholic, of course I have no further history of my religious opinions to narrate. In saying this, I do not mean to say that my mind has been idle, or that I have given up thinking [4] on theological subjects; but that I have had no changes to record, *and have had no anxiety of heart whatever. I have been in perfect peace and contentment. I never had one doubt.*"—"Apologia," p. 264 (2d ed. 238).

---

[3] "Of this most remarkable man I must pause to speak a word. In my opinion, his secession from the Church of England has never yet been estimated among us at anything like the full amount of its calamitous importance. . . . The ecclesiastical historian will perhaps hereafter judge that this secession was a much greater event even than the partial secession of John Wesley, the only case of personal loss suffered by the Church of England, since the Reformation, which can be at all compared with it in magnitude."—Mr. Gladstone, "Vaticanism," pp. 5-6.

[4] Dr. Brownson speaks of the years of his life after he became a Catholic as "the period of our freest and most active and most energetic thought." —Works, vol. iii., p. 311. The testimony of these two great minds does not quite harmonize with Dr. Littledale's explanation of the intellectual peace of converts to the Catholic faith. According to his view of the matter, when converts speak of their freedom from religious doubt after entering the Church, they "really mean nothing more than that *they have given up thinking.*"

17

Eleven years later he speaks more fully and emphatically on the point:

"From the day I became a Catholic to this day, now close upon thirty years, I have never had a *moment's misgiving* that the communion of Rome is that Church which the Apostle set up at Pentecost—which alone has 'the adoption of the sons, and the glory, and the covenants, and the revealed law, and the service of God, and the promises,' and in which the Anglican communion, whatever its merits and demerits, whatever the great excellence of individuals in it has, as such, no part. *Never have I for a moment hesitated* in my conviction, since 1845, that it was my clear duty to join the Catholic Church, as I did then join it, which in my own conscience I felt to be divine. Persons and places, incidents and circumstances of life, which belong to my first forty-four years, are deeply lodged in my memory and my affections; moreover, I have had more to try and afflict me in various ways as a Catholic than as an Anglican; *but never for a moment have I wished myself back; never have I ceased to thank my Maker for His mercy in enabling me to make the great change, and never has He let me feel forsaken by Him, or in distress, or any kind of religious trouble.*"—Postscript to his "Letter to the Duke of Norfolk," etc., pp. 149-150.

For many years after their reception into the Church, reports were persistently circulated and published about the last two eminent converts, to the effect that they were dissatisfied with the step they had taken, and were thinking of returning to Anglicanism. They repeatedly denied the truth of such reports. In one of his published letters on the subject, Cardinal Manning says:

"From the hour I saw the full light of Catholic faith, *no shade of doubt has ever passed over my reason or my conscience.* I could as soon believe that a part is equal to the whole as that Protestantism, in any shape, from Lutheran-

THE HAPPINESS OF CONVERTS. 259

ism to Anglicanism, is the Revelation of the day of Pentecost."— Letter to Archbishop Lynch, of Toronto, February 24, 1886.

And Cardinal Newman writes indignantly:

"I have not had one moment's wavering of trust in the Catholic Church ever since I was received into her fold. I hold, and ever have held, that her Sovereign Pontiff is the centre of unity and the Vicar of Christ; and I ever have had, and have still, an *unclouded* faith in her creed in all its articles; a *supreme* satisfaction in her worship, discipline, and teaching; and an *eager longing, and a hope against hope*, that the many dear friends whom I have left in Protestantism *may be partakers of my happiness*. . . .

"*Return to the Church of England! No!* 'The net is broken, and we are delivered.' I should be a consummate fool (to use a mild term) if in my old age I left 'the land flowing with milk and honey' for the city of confusion and the house of bondage."—Letter to the Editor of the *Globe*, June 28, 1862.

Elsewhere the Cardinal speaks of the world's thoughts about converts thus:

"The truth is that the world, *knowing nothing of the blessings of the Catholic faith*, and prophesying nothing but ill concerning it, fancies that a convert, after the first fervor is over, feels nothing but disappointment, weariness, and offence in his new religion, and is secretly desirous of retracing his steps. . . . That there can be *peace* and *joy*, and *knowledge*, and *freedom*, and *spiritual strength* in the Church is a thought far beyond the world's imagination; for it regards her simply as a frightful conspiracy against the happiness of man, seducing her victims by specious professions, and, when they are once hers, caring nothing for the misery which breaks upon them, so that by any means she may detain them in bondage. Accordingly, it conceives we are in perpetual warfare with our own reason, fierce objections are ever rising within us, and we forcibly repressing them. . . . The world disbelieves our doctrines itself, and cannot understand our own believing them. It considers them so strange that it is quite sure, though we will not confess it, that we are haunted day and night by doubts, and tormented with the apprehension of yielding to them. I really do think it is the world's judgment that one principal part of a confessor's work is the putting down such misgivings in his penitents. It fancies that the reason is ever rebelling, like the flesh; that doubt, like concupiscence, is elicited by every sight and sound, and that temptation insinuates itself in every page of letter-press, and through the very voice of a Protestant polemic. . .

"*But, my dear brethren, if these are your thoughts, you are simply in error. Trust me, rather than the world, when I tell you that it is no difficult thing for a Catholic to believe; and that, unless he grievously mismanages himself, the difficult thing is for him to doubt. He has received a gift which makes faith easy; it is not without an effort, a miserable effort, that any one who has received that gift unlearns to believe. He does violence to his mind, not in exercising, but in withholding his faith.*"—"Discourses to Mixed Congregations," Disc. xi., pp. 221-222. Cf. also Disc. ix., pp. 186-187.

In the following "exquisitely beautiful words" the illustrious Cardinal addresses the Church and appeals to those who are without her fold:

"*Oh, long sought after, tardily found, desire of the eyes, joy of the heart, the truth after many shadows, the fulness after many foretastes, the home after many storms, come to her, poor wanderers, for she it is, and she alone, who can unfold the meaning of your being and the secret of your destiny. . . . Oh, my brethren, turn away from the Catholic Church, and to whom will you go? It is your only chance of peace and assurance in this turbulent, changing world. There is nothing between it and scepticism when men exercise their reason freely.*" [b]—"Mixed Congregations," Disc. xiii., pp. 281-282. Cf. also Disc. x., pp. 212-213.

---

[b] After giving long and careful consideration to the question of a *via media*, he elsewhere observes: "I came to the conclusion that there was no medium, in true philosophy, between *Atheism* and *Catholicity*, and that a

And, addressing his brethren in the faith on the signal grace which God has bestowed on them, His Eminence says:—

"O my dear brethren, what joy and what thankfulness should be ours, that God has brought us into the Church of His Son! What gift is equal to it in the whole world in its preciousness and in its rarity! In this country in particular, where heresy ranges far and wide, where uncultivated nature has so undisputed a field all her own, where grace is given to great numbers only to be profaned and quenched, where baptisms only remain in their impress and character, and faith is ridiculed for its firmness, for us to find ourselves here *in the region of light, in the home of peace, in the presence of saints*, to find ourselves where we can use every faculty of the mind and affection of the heart in its perfection because in its appointed place and office, to find ourselves in possession of *certainty, consistency, stability*, on the highest and holiest subjects of human thought, to have hope here and heaven hereafter, to be on the Mount with Christ, while the poor world is *guessing and quarrelling* at its foot, who among us shall not wonder at his own blessedness! who shall not be awestruck at the inscrutable grace of God which has brought himself, not others, where he stands? As the Apostle says, 'Through our Lord Jesus Christ let us have by faith access into this grace wherein we stand, and glory in the hope of the glory of the Sons of God. And hope confoundeth not; because the love of God is poured out into our hearts by the Holy Ghost who is given us.' And, as St. John says, still more exactly to our purpose, 'Ye have an unction from the Holy One;' Your eyes are anointed by Him who put clay on the eyes of the blind man; 'from Him you have an unction, and ye know,' not conjecture, or suppose, or opine, bnt 'know,' see, 'all things.' 'So let the unction which you have received of Him abide in you. Nor need ye that any one teach you, but as His unction teaches you all things,

---

perfectly consistent mind, under those circumstances in which it finds itself here below, *must embrace either the one or the other*."—"Apologia," p. 231 (2d ed. 198).

and is true and no lie, and hath taught you, so *abide* in Him.' You can abide in nothing else; opinions change, conclusions are feeble, inquiries run their course, reason stops short, *but faith alone reaches to the end, faith only endures*. Faith and prayer alone will endure *in that last dark hour*, when Satan urges all his powers and resources against the sinking soul. What will it avail us then to have devised some subtle argument, or to have led some brilliant attack, or to have mapped out the field of history, or to have numbered and sorted the weapons of controversy, and to have the homage of friends and the respect of the world for our successes,—what will it avail to have had a position, to have followed out a work, to have reanimated an idea, to have made a cause to triumph, if after all *we have not the light of faith to guide us on from this world to the next!* Oh, how fain shall we be in that day to exchange our place with the humblest, and dullest, and most ignorant of the sons of men, rather than to stand before the judgment-seat in the lot of him *who hast received great gifts from God, and used them for self and for man, who has shut his eyes, who has trifled with the truth, who has repressed his misgivings, who has been led on by God's grace, but stopped short of its scope, who has neared the land of promise, yet not gone forward to take possession of it!*"—*Op. cit.*, disc. ix., pp. 189-191.

"You are then what you are, not from any excellence or merit of your own, but by the grace of God who has chosen you to believe. You might have been as the barbarian of Africa, or the free-thinker of Europe, with grace sufficient to condemn you, because it had not furthered your salvation. You might have had strong inspirations of grace and have resisted them, and then additional grace might not have been given to overcome your resistance. God gives not the same measure of grace to all. Has He not visited you with over-abundant grace? and was it not necessary for your hard hearts to receive more than other people? *Praise and bless Him continually for the benefit; do not forget, as time goes on, that it is of grace; do not pride yourselves upon it; pray* ever not to lose it; and do your best to make others partake of it."—*Op. cit.*, disc. x., pp. 211-212.

"*Diverse doctrines resound, various heresies arise. Fly to the tabernacle of God—namely, the Catholic Church; there you will be protected from the contradiction of tongues.*"—St. Augustine.

APPENDIX B.

SOME FACTS RELATING TO THE VATICAN COUNCIL.

THE following extracts are from the leading articles and special correspondence of the chief English newspapers at the time of the opening of the Council:

"In historic importance, in traditional dignity, in the splendor of the associations that gather round its name, no assembly in the world, past or present, can pretend to compare with the great Parliament of the Latin Church. The unbroken continuity of the history of that Church, its undeniable and uninterrupted descent from the Church founded by the Apostles, renders this Council .... the immediate successor and representative, in a sense in which no other council can rival its claims, of the Council of Nicæa, if not of the Council of Jerusalem. Nor is its actual power and consequence unworthy of its traditional heritage. . . . It is the representative assembly, the omnipotent legislature of a compact and coherent body of Christians, whose number approaches more nearly to two than to one hundred millions."—The *Standard*, December 10, 1869.

After referring to the attempts made by the enemies of the Pope and of the Church to hinder the assembling of the Council, the special correspondent of the same journal (December 11th) wrote:

"Nevertheless, all has been in vain; and the dispassionate observer is compelled to confess that the spectacle of so many hundreds of Bishops, coming from the farthest quarters of the earth at the beck of an old man, powerless in all but in spiritual thunderbolts, is one that, occurring in the nineteenth century, and especially at this period of it, is calculated to strike the believing with a pious admiration, and even the incredulous, like ourselves, with irrepressible astonishment."

"It must be admitted that, weak as is the temporal power of the Pope, no other prince could have assembled such a body as met to-day in the Council-hall of St. Peter's, and no other could have provided them with such a magnificent temple. From the remotest quarters of the globe—from a land that was but just heard of when the Council of Trent sat, from a land that was then wholly unknown—from Palestine and Syria, the cradles of Chr'stianity; from Persia, from China, from India, from Africa, from the Western Isles, as well as from the countries washed by the Mediterranean, men of various tongues and diverse origin, men of great learning and of great age, have come together to this famous city, in obedience—voluntary and spiritual obedience—to the Pastor who claims to be the Successor of Peter and the Vicegerent of God upon earth."—The *Daily News*, December 14, 1869.

"Seven hundred bishops, more or less, representing all Christendom, were seen gathered round one altar and one throne, partaking of the same Divine Mystery, and rendering homage, by turns, to the same spiritual authority and power. As they put on their mitres or took them off, and as they came to the steps of the altar or the foot of the Common Spiritual Father, it was impossible not to feel the unity and the power of the Church which they represented."—The *Times*, December 16, 1869.[1]

"Profound intelligence .... gleamed in everything that the Vatican Council had done."— Dr. Draper, "History of the Conflict between Religion and Science," p. 353.

The first step in reference to the Council was taken on the 6th of December, 1864. On that date Pius IX., after maturely considering the matter himself, communicated in strict secrecy, to all the cardi-

---

[1] Taken from Mr. Allnatt's "Which Is the True Church?" p. 81.

nals then in Rome, his intention to convoke the Council. He directed them to weigh well the subject, each by himself, and to send in to him in writing and separately their views. Twenty-one opinions were handed in, and all but two were in favor of the project. In March, 1865, he appointed a Commission of Cardinals to meet and confer together on the same subject, and to examine and report on the written opinions just referred to. This body advised for the convocation of the Council. In April of the same year, a circular letter was, by order of the Pope, sent to thirty-six bishops of all nations, selected for their knowledge in theology and canon law, and for their experience in the government of the Church. The bishops were requested to state in detail the matters which in their opinion, ought be brought before the Council. On the 17th of November the Papal Nuncios at Paris, Vienna, Madrid, Munich, and Brussels were officially notified of the Pope's intention to summon the Council, and requested to give their opinions on the advisability of the step. They were further requested to send on to Rome the names of two theologians or canonists of special reputation in the countries to which they were accredited. On the recommendation of the Commission of Cardinals, the Pope appointed a special commission to prepare the work for the Council. This consisted of five Cardinals, eight Bishops, and a secretary, to which were afterwards added more than a hundred consulting theologians summoned to Rome from different parts of Italy, from France, Belgium, Germany, England, Spain, and the United States. This Commission of Direction, as it was called, was divided into five sections: 1. On Doctrine; 2. On Discipline; 3. On Religious Orders; 4. On Foreign Missions and the Eastern Churches; and, 5, On Politico-Ecclesiastical, or Mixed Questions. The Commission on Doctrine, with twenty-four consultors, sat for twenty-seven months, and held fifty-six sessions, in which time it drew up three, and only three, *schemata*, or draft-decrees: one on Catholic Faith against Materialism, Rationalism, and Pantheism; another on the Church of Christ; and the third on Christian Marriage. After the opening of the Council it met only once. On the 26th of June, 1867, the Pope, in a public audience, announced to more than five hundred Bishops, then assembled in Rome to celebrate the eighteenth centenary of the martyrdom of SS. Peter and Paul, that he had decided on convoking the Council.

On the 1st of July the Bishops presented their answer in the form of an address, to which were appended 503 signatures. "With the utmost joy, then," they say, "is our mind filled at learning from your sacred mouth that you have resolved, amid the many dangers of the present time, to convoke 'that greatest remedy for the greatest perils of Christianity,' as your glorious predecessor, Paul the Third, called it, —an Œcumenical Council." The Pope caused to be distributed to the Bishops papers containing seventeen questions on the matters which he thought advisable to bring before the Council.

On the feast of SS. Peter and Paul, June 29, 1868, the bull convoking the Council was issued, and the 8th of December, 1869, was named as the date of assembling. The Council opened on the appointed day with 719 Fathers, which number increased later on to 764. It was the most representative ecclesiastical council ever held. Some thirty nations were represented in it. The officials were appointed by the Pope, and consisted of five Cardinals to preside over the discussions, two custodians, a secretary and sub-secretary, seven notaries, eight tellers of votes, seventeen masters of ceremonies, ten assigners of places, and twenty-three shorthand writers[2] (eight Italian, four French, four German, two English, two Irish, one Scotch, and two American). There were two kinds of sessions of the full Council: one public, at which the work of the Council would be put through its final stage of confirmation and promulgation; the other private, in which the discussion of the subject-matter was carried on. Of the former there were, altogether, four; of the latter, eighty-nine. The Pope presided at the former; at the latter he was represented by a cardinal. He himself never appeared at the sessions. Latin was the language of the Council.

Though the right of proposing the subjects which were to engage the attention of the Council belonged to the Pope, yet he formally announced beforehand that "if any among the fathers of the Council have anything to propose which they believe will tend to the general benefit, they shall freely propose it." This privilege was subject to the following restrictions: (1) The proposal should be put in writing and submitted to a Commission on Postulates. This was appointed by the Pope, and consisted of twelve Cardinals, two Patriarchs, ten Archbishops, and two

---

[2] No official had a vote.

THE VATICAN COUNCIL. 269

Bishops. On it were represented Italy, Germany, Belgium, France, Spain, England, Ireland, South America, Mexico, United States, and the East. The United States were represented by Archbishop Spalding, Baltimore; England, by Archbishop, now Cardinal, Manning, and Ireland by Cardinal Cullen; (2) The proposal must regard the welfare of the whole Church, not of this or that diocese; (3) It must be accompanied by the reasons why its author or authors deem it useful and opportune; and (4) It must not conflict with the constant belief of the Church, or her inviolable traditions.³

On the 20th of December the Council proceeded to elect by private vote Commissions or Committees: 1, On Faith; 2, On Discipline; and, 3, On Religious Orders. The Commission on Faith was far the most important. Seven hundred and twenty-one votes were cast, each Father voting for twenty-four, the number of members composing the Commission. One Patriarch, thirteen Archbishops, nine Bishops, and one Vicar-Apostolic were elected, with a Cardinal appointed by the Pope to preside over their deliberations. Of the elected members, four were Italian, two German, one Austrian, one Hungarian, one Polish, one Belgian, one Swiss, one Dutch, two French, two Spanish, one English (Cardinal Manning), one Irish (Archbishop Leahy, Cashel), two South American, two North American (Archbishops Spalding, Baltimore; and Alemany, San Francisco), and two Asiatic. It has been repeatedly stated⁴ that those who

---
³ Constitution *Multiplices Inter*, November 27, 1869.
⁴ "From the opening of the Council, the Infallibilists showed themselves so uncompromising that they refused to give to the minority even one single representative in the important commission on dogmatical sub-

were opposed to the definition of Infallibility were not allowed a single representative on this commission. This is contrary to fact. The late Cardinal Simor, then Archbishop Primate of Hungary (who signed the counter-petition on Infallibility, thus: "John Simor, etc., intimately persuaded of the pernicious results to Catholicity in Hungary of making the definition which is asked for by some"), actually received the fifth largest number of votes. The Commissions on Discipline and on Religious Orders, each composed of twenty-four members, were chosen in the same manner. On the former the United States were represented by Archbishop McCloskey, of New York, and Bishop Heiss, of La Crosse; England, by Bishop Ullathorne, of Birmingham; and Ireland, by "John of Tuam"; and on the latter, Bishop Ryan of Buffalo, Bishop Clifford of Clifton, and Bishop Derry of Clonfert represented the same three countries.

The mode of procedure, regulated by the Constitution *Multiplices Inter*, was as follows: the *schemata*, or draft-decrees, prepared by the Commission of Direction, were printed and distributed to the Fathers. Ten days at least were given them to study the subject before it came up for discussion. In this they had the aid of consulting theologians of their own choice. The *schemata* were entirely the work of the theologians and canonists of the Commission of Direction. They had no authority from the Pope; and this the Pope stated at the outset. So the Fathers of the Council were perfectly free to examine, discuss, ac-

---

jects."—"Cyclopædia of Biblical, Theological, and Ecclesiastical Literature," prepared by the Rev. John McClintock, D.D., and James Strong, S. T. D., vol. iv., p. 574. Cf. also "Encyclopædia Britannica," "Vatican Council."

cept, reject, or amend them as they thought fit. The Pope never interfered in the deliberations of the Council; he was not even present at any stage of them. He was present only in the public sessions, where what had been discussed and settled came up for final vote, confirmation, and promulgation. The Fathers who wished to speak were required to send in their names to the President beforehand. The President named the day for the discussion of the *schema*, and on that date he proposed it in a General Congregation of the whole Council. The principle was first discussed, and then the various parts. Every member was free to speak, and the discussion lasted so long as there remained any one who wished to take part in it. The whole debate was taken down in shorthand, and then written out in full and referred to one or other of the Commissions elected by the Council. The Commission carefully examined the *schema* in the light of the speeches made. What was found pertinent was admitted, either to modify or to reform it. It was then reprinted, distributed to the Fathers, and reported by the Commission to the Council. In its amended form the *schema* was again discussed, and, if further amendments were found necessary, the same process was repeated until its different parts were accepted by a majority of the Council. When the discussion was concluded, a formal vote was taken on the whole *schema*. This vote was given in three forms: 1, *Placet*, or Aye; 2, *Non placet*, or No; 3, *Placet juxta modum*, or Aye with modification. Those who voted *Placet juxta modum* were required to send in their amendments in writing. The Commission once more examined the subject, accepted or rejected the amendments, and reported back to the Council, giving the reasons for their action. This concluded the consultive action of the Council. The solemn enactment in public session followed. On the 20th of February this mode of procedure was, on the petition of forty-three bishops, amended by the Constitution *Apostolicis Litteris*. Henceforth, the Fathers were required to send in writing, before the discussion on any *schema* opened, the observations they had to make on it. These were examined by the Commission, and the *schema*, amended or recast, was then proposed for discussion. Secondly, the Council got the power of *closure*, so that, on the petition of ten Fathers, the President could at any stage of a debate put it to the vote of the Members, whether they wished the debate prolonged or closed. A simple majority decided the question. This power was used only *once*.

The world at large would have it, that the chief object [*] the Pope had in view in convoking the Council, was to define his own Infallibility; and yet, strange to say, the subject had absolutely *no place* in the programme prepared for and submitted to the Council. Of the Cardinals consulted in the first instance, only two mentioned the subject. It "was hardly so much as named," says Cardinal Manning,[°] "in the midst of an *interminable* list of subjects" suggested in the answers of the thirty-six Bishops consulted.

[*] "One of the chief objects for which the Vatican Council was called in 1869 was to . . . . enroll the doctrine of Papal Infallibility among the formal Church doctrines."—"Cyclopædia of Biblical, Theological, and Ecclesiastical Literature," vol. iv., p. 570.

[°] "The True Story of the Vatican Council," p. 28.

There was not one word about it in the paper containing seventeen questions which the Pope had distributed to the five hundred Bishops assembled in Rome in June, 1867. The preparatory Commission on Doctrine discussed the subject, and reported that, though "the Infallibility of the Roman Pontiff *can* be defined as an article of faith," yet the judgment of the Commission is that this subject ought not to be proposed by the Apostolic See except at the petition of the Bishops." The subject, accordingly, did not appear in the official programme, or *schemata*.[7] "But the newspapers and governments of Europe were so certain that the Definition was intended, and so anxious that it should be prevented, that they forced the subject on the attention of the Bishops far more effectually than the Pope could himself have done. The elaborate arguments and vehement invectives of the press, the threats, combinations, and intrigues of statesmen,[8] turned what would otherwise be a luxury of faith into a stern necessity. Not to define the Infallibility now would be to deny it."[9] The result was that on the 28th of January, 1870, a petition, bearing the names of 410 Bishops, was presented to the Commission on Postulates, asking that the subject should be introduced to

[7] More than that: when the petitions for and against the Definition were afterwards presented, the published records of the Council show that, actually, the representatives of the Pope, Cardinal de Angelis, Chief President of the deliberative sessions of the Council, and Cardinal Bilio, President of the Commission on Faith, more than once expressed themselves in favor of postponing, in accordance with the desire of the Opposition, the Definition; and when it became evident that the majority would not consent to this, Cardinal Bilio, we learn, used every effort to restrict the scope of the Definition. He was successful with the Commission, but not with the Council.

[8] Cf. Cardinal Manning, "The True Story of the Vatican Council," pp. 67-71.

[9] *The Month*, February, 1891, p. 206.

the Council for discussion and definition.[10] On the following day a counter-petition bearing 136 signatures was presented. The Commission decided to allow the introduction of the subject, and accordingly a Chapter on Infallibility was added to the *schema* on the Church. The *schema*, which consisted of an introduction and four chapters, was distributed to the Fathers on the 6th of March. Eighteen days were given them to prepare and make in writing whatever commentaries they thought fit. One hundred and forty-nine papers, representing the views of above 200 Fathers, were handed in to the Commission on Faith. These were carefully examined, analyzed, and printed in a volume of 242 pages, 4to. A copy was given to each of the Fathers. The Commission made its report to the Council on the 13th of May, and on the following day the general discussion on the principle and tenor of the amended text opened. It was continued *through fourteen entire sessions of four hours each,* and was brought to a close on the 3d of June. Sixty-four had spoken, of which nearly one-half belonged to what was called the Opposition. The

---

[10] After referring to the opposition in question, the petition went on to say: "If then the Council of the Vatican, being thus challenged, were to be silent, and omit to give testimony to the Catholic doctrine on this point, then Catholics would, in fact, begin to doubt the true doctrine, and the lovers of novelty would triumphantly assert that the Council had been silenced by the arguments brought forward by them." In a notice of the "Acta et Decreta Sacrosancti Œcumenici Concilii Vaticani," recently published, a writer in the *Dublin Review* observes that the volume contains documents which prove beyond all doubt that "the Definition of the Pope's Infallibility is due neither to Pius IX., nor to the Jesuits, nor to any other religious order, but simply to the majority of the Bishops, who, *urged by the incessant attacks of a certain party on the Pope, the Council, and the Pope's Infallibility, as hitherto practically assumed in the Church,* thought it to be their indispensable duty to bring the Catholic truth into relief."—*Dublin Review,* January, 1891, pp. 232-233.

majority of the speeches were on the question of Infallibility; the average duration of the speeches was above three-quarters of an hour. This was the *one* case in which the *closure* was moved, and the circumstances were the following: Long before it was moved, all the arguments on the principle of the *schema* were exhausted." There was nothing, then, but repetition and waste of time, which became hard to bear. Five special discussions, one on each portion of the *schema*, were yet to follow, and every member of the Council had a right to take part in each of these five discussions. So a petition to close the general discussion, signed by 147 Fathers, among whom were many of the Opposition, was presented to the President. Three days' grace were given, and then the *closure* was moved and carried by an overwhelming majority.

The special discussions followed: that on the fourth Chapter—that is, on Infallibility—began on the 15th of June, with 572 fathers present, and occupied *twelve* days, closing by mutual consent on the 4th of July. During the interval fifty-seven spoke. The whole Chapter, with ninety-six amendments, was then referred to the Commission on Faith. This made its report on the 11th of July, and the chapter was passed by a large majority. On the 13th of July a formal vote was taken on the whole *schema*. There were present 601 fathers, all that remained in Rome,"

---

[11] "I can conscientiously declare," writes Cardinal Manning, "that long before the general discussion was closed, all general arguments were exhausted. The special discussion of details also had been to such an extent anticipated that nothing new was heard for days."—"The Vatican Council and Its Definitions," p. 87.

[12] Fifteen had died during the sitting of the Council, and nearly a hundred others had asked and obtained leave to return to their dioceses.

with the exception of about a dozen, who were too ill to attend. The result of the vote was as follows: *Placets*, or *Ayes*, 451; *Non placets*, or *Noes*, 88; and *Placets juxta modum*, or *Ayes with modification*, 62.[13] The *schema*, with 163 amendments, was sent back to the Commission; this reëxamined the whole matter, and made its report on the 16th of July. The whole draft was then reprinted and distributed, and once more put to the vote, and passed. On the evening of the 17th fifty-seven of the Opposition signed a last protest against the Definition, and declared their intention to leave Rome at once. The reason of their action they explained in these words: "Our faithful love and reverence do not allow us, in a matter so closely concerning the person of Your Holiness, to say openly in the face of our Father, *Non placet*. . . . Meanwhile, we profess inviolate faith and obedience towards the Church of God and towards Your Holiness."[14] On the 18th the public session was held. There were present 535 Fathers. The decree was read aloud from the *Ambo*, and every Father was called upon to give a final vote. The vote in public session could be only *Placet* or *Non placet*—Aye or No. Each Bishop, as his name was called, took off his mitre, rose from his seat, and voted. The result was 533[15] *Placets* and 2 *Non placets*. The Pope, hav-

---

[13] The majority of those 62 were for strengthening the Definition by adding, in opposition to Gallicanism, the clause, "and therefore such definitions of the Roman Pontiff are irreformable *of themselves*, and *not from the consent of the Church.*"

[14] The author of the article on the Vatican Council in the "Encyclopædia Brittanica," without one particle of evidence for the truth of the statement, tells his readers that "their flight was prompted by *fears for their personal safety.*"

[15] The majority included 49 of the 62 who voted *Placet juxta modum* on

ing received the numbers from the tellers, published them to the Council, and immediately confirmed the decree. No sooner had he done this than the two Bishops who voted *Non placet* threw themselves on their knees, and made a profession of faith in the dogma. Every one of the fifty-seven who signed the protest of July 17th sent in his adhesion to the Definition.

Throughout, the opposition was not to the doctrine but to the expediency of *defining* it at that time; this the Opposition, while believing in the doctrine, thought unnecessary, unwise, and unseasonable. "A grave injustice," says Cardinal Manning, "has been done to the bishops who opposed the definition. . . . They were treated (by the world outside) as if they denied the truth of the doctrine itself! Their opposition was not to the doctrine, but to the *defining* of it, and not even absolutely to the defining of it, but to the defining of it *at this time*. . . . Not five bishops in the Council could be justly thought to have opposed the truth of the doctrine. *This is the testimony of one who heard the whole discussion, and never heard an explicit denial of its truth.*" [16] The question then discussed was not the truth of the doctrine, but the *opportuneness* of defining it.

---

the 13th. The minority contained one of that number, one also signed the protest of the 17th, and the remaining 11 did not vote, some being absent through sickness.

[16] Cardinal Manning, "The True Story of the Vatican Council," p. 100. Cf. also Archbishop Ullathorne, "Mr. Gladstone's Expostulation Unravelled, p. 51; Cardinal Newman, "Letter," etc., p. 18. "*I have always,*" wrote the Archbishop of Cologne, a prominent member of the Opposition, "*given my assent to the truth.*"—Pastoral, September 10, 1870. The illustrious Dupanloup, who was considered the literary and oratorical leader of the Opposition, wrote to the Pope on February 18, 1871: "I wrote and spoke against nothing but the *opportuneness* of the Definition. As to the *doctrine* itself, *I have always professed it.* In fact, the petition presented against defining the doctrine contains an explicit admission of its

"Once for all," says Cardinal Manning, "let it be said in this place that the question whether the Infallibility of the Head of the Church be a true doctrine or not was never discussed in the Council, nor even proposed to it. The only question was whether it was expedient, prudent, seasonable, and timely, regard being had to the condition of the world, of the nations of Europe, of the Christians in separation from the Church, to put this truth in the form of a *Definition.*" [17]

So much for the facts of the case. Now for a little fiction:

"On the appointed day the Council opened. Its objects were to translate the *Syllabus* into practice, *to establish the dogma of Papal Infallibility,* and define the relations of religion to science. Every preparation had been made that the points determined on should be carried. The bishops were *informed* that they were coming to Rome, *not to deliberate,* but to *sanction* decrees *previously made by an infallible Pope. No* idea was entertained of any such thing as *free discussion.*[18] The minutes of the meeting were not permitted to be inspected; the prelates of the Opposition were *hardly* allowed to speak. On January 22, 1870, a petition requesting that the Infallibility of the Pope should be defined was presented; an opposition petition of the minority was offered. *Hereupon the deliberations of the minority were forbidden,* and their publications prohibited. And though the *Curia*

---

truth. The signers, says Dr. Littledale, in the "Encyclopædia Brittanica," "*admitted that Papal decrees ex cathedra on faith and morals are irreversible.*"

[17] "The True Story of the Vatican Council," p. 101. The above facts are taken chiefly from this and another volume, "The Vatican Council and Its Definitions" ("Petri Privilegium," part iii.), by the same author, and from two articles in *The Month*, February and March, 1801. These articles are based on the work already mentioned and lately published, "Acta et Decreta Sacrosancti Œcumenici Concilii Vaticani."

[18] The writer in the "Encyclopædia Brittanica" says that there was not even a "*shadow of freedom*" about the deliberations of the Council.

had provided a compact majority, it was found expedient to issue an order that to carry any proposition it was not necessary that the vote should be near unanimity; a simple majority sufficed. The remonstrances of the minority were altogether unheeded."—"History of the Conflict between Religion and Science," by John William Draper, M. D., LL.D., pp. 334–335.

This work has had a large circulation, and is considered by thousands a standard authority.

Wonder has been expressed at the subsequent action of those Bishops who opposed the Definition of Infallibility. They have been denounced as inconsistent, because when the definition was actually made they submitted to it. Is, I ask, the action of legislators who proclaim their obedience to a law, the passage of which they stoutly opposed, considered inconsistent? The Bishops in question, as we have seen, did not disbelieve in the doctrine; they only opposed the formal definition of it at the time. Their action, then, in submitting amounted to this: They now believed, as a *defined* dogma, what they previously held as an *undefined* doctrine.

But even if they did not previously hold the doctrine, still their action can be vindicated from the charge of inconsistency. It is said that an American Prelate, a stanch member of the Opposition, made the following defence: On his arrival home the public was very anxious to know what his position in reference to the dogma was. A reporter called on him and asked if he had accepted the Definition; and on being answered in the affirmative, he asked how he justified such a course of action. The Prelate replied that his justification was very simple. "I have always," said he, "believed in the Infallibility of a

General Council. A General Council has solemnly defined the doctrine of the Pope's Infallibility. Therefore, my principles, even when in opposition, oblige me to accept and assent to the Definition; that is all." His justification was complete; his consistency unimpeachable.

Perhaps the best explanation and justification of the action of the Bishops in question is contained in the following extract made from the *Pastoral* of one who carried his opposition to the very end. The words were written from Rome in the month of June, when the contest over the Definition was at its height.

"It is one. of the glories of the Catholic Church never to make a truth the formal object of the obligatory belief of the faithful without a profound and complete examination, in which each Bishop, as official witness and judge of the faith, raises a free voice to express before God and the Church whatsoever he finds in the depths of his conscience. And from this rigorous examination, this discussion, which turns to the light every aspect of the doctrine one by one, there results a certitude higher than any human certitude. Nevertheless, all that is but a preparation for the final work; *the Divine element has not yet come in.* After all the reasons have been heard, all the testimonies collected, after the Council has deliberated in all maturity and freedom, *then the Church, by the mouth of her Chief, pronounces and defines.* At that moment every other voice must be hushed. The Church teaches: *God has spoken.*"

Disastrous consequences were loudly predicted as the result of the Definition. "We were told the definition of the Infallibility would alienate the fairest provinces of the Catholic Church, divide the Church into parties, drive the scientific and independent into separation, and set the reason of mankind against the superstitions of Rome. We were told of learned professors, theological faculties, entire universities, multitudes of laity, hundreds of clergy, the flower of the Episcopate, who were prepared to protest as a body, and to secede. There was to be a secession in France, in Germany, in Austria, in Hungary. The 'Old Catholics' of England would never hear of this new dogma, and with difficulty could be made to hold their peace."[19] What were the actual results? *Parturient montes!*

---

[19] Cardinal Manning, "The Vatican Council and Its Definitions," pp. 158-159. ("Petri Privilegium," part iii.). "Thousands amongst the clergy," wrote Dr. Döllinger, "hundreds of thousands amongst the laity, think as I do, and hold it impossible to accept the new article of faith."—Declaration of March 28, 1871. "To declare the Pope infallible," alarmingly wrote the *Augsburg Gazette* (June 15, 1868), in solemn warning to all whom it may concern, "is *to announce the destruction of the world*"!!!

APPENDIX C.

PONTIFICAL DECREES AND THE OBEDIENCE DUE TO THEM.

AUTHORITATIVE decrees of the Pope, or of the Pontifical Congregations, are of three different kinds, namely,—doctrinal, disciplinary, and prudential. The *doctrinal* decree prescribes what is to be held as true and pertaining to faith or morals, or what is to be rejected as false or in some way prejudicial to the purity of the one or the integrity of the other; the *disciplinary* decree prescribes what is to be done as right and what is to be avoided as wrong; and the *prudential* decree merely imposes silence in the interests of peace and good will, without either approving or disapproving of the controverted doctrine. The disciplinary and prudential decrees emanate from the legislative authority of the Church, and are directly and immediately addressed to the will, and demand merely external obedience and respectful silence; the doctrinal decree emanates from the teaching authority of the Church, and is directly and immediately addressed to the intellect, and demands, in addition, interior assent—obedience of thought.[1] But as doctrinal decrees are of different kinds, so, too, is the interior assent which they demand.

---

[1] Cf. Franzelin, "De Trad.," pp. 127, 131, 141 (note); Mazzella, "De Virtutibus Infusis," n. 449; Cardinal Newman, "Apologia," pp. 275, 281-284 (2d ed. 250, 257-260); Knox, "When Does the Church Speak Infallibly?" pp. 104-105; Clarke, "The Pope and the Bible," pp. 16-17.

Doctrinal decrees, as we have seen,[2] may be fallible or infallible. Infallible decrees also are of two classes; one class deals exclusively with truths of Revelation, and with errors directly opposed to dogmas of faith. The truths are set forth or defined as *revealed*, and the errors are condemned as *heretical*. The other class deals with *unrevealed* truths connected with or bearing on truths of Revelation, and with errors condemned or censured by the Church for any reason whatever short of *direct* heresy. Then, theologians distinguish three kinds of interior assent; the first is called the assent of *divine* faith; the second the assent of *ecclesiastical* faith, or, as some have it, *mediately*[3] divine faith; and the third simply *religious* assent.

The object of the first kind of assent must be a *divinely revealed* truth; and, therefore, it is due and can be given only to infallible or *ex-cathedra* decrees of the first class just mentioned. The object of the second kind of assent must be a truth proposed or defined by the *infallible* authority of the Church, or Pope; and, therefore, this assent is due and can be given only to infallible or *ex-cathedra* decrees of the second class mentioned. While the *religious* assent can be given, and, ordinarily, is due to fallible doctrinal decrees.

The *motive* or reason of assent in the first instance is *solely* the authority of God revealing the truth; in the second the *infallible* authority of the Church; and in the third the ordinary fallible but still divinely constituted teaching authority of the Church.

---
[2] See above, pp. 15-16.
[3] So called because it is given on the infallible authority of the Church, in which, as a *revealed* truth, we believe by (immediate) divine faith.

The assent in the first and second cases excludes all deliberate doubt and all deliberate fear of error or its possibility; it must be absolutely undoubting, unconditional, supreme, infallible, and irrevocable. In the third case, though not required to be supreme or absolute, the assent may be undoubting; and though not infallible, it is as a rule true. It is virtually given subject to revision, suspension, or recall, as circumstances may require; and its firmness depends on the greater or less authority of the teacher and the greater or less presumption of the consent of the supreme, infallible authority. To refuse such assent where demanded would, unless in a very rare case, be a violation of duty and sinful, because the authority that commands it is sacred and divinely constituted.[4] If, however, a theologian, or a philosopher, or a man of science had *really grave reasons* to doubt the decision, or to believe it wrong in a particular case, such a one would be justified in giving merely a conditional assent, or even suspending assent altogether until the infallible authority had spoken.[5]

---

[4] To refuse assent in the first case would be *heresy*; to do so in the second case, strictly speaking, would not be heresy, because heresy is the direct denial of a truth *divinely* revealed and proposed *as such* by the Church for our belief. But such an act would be proximate to heresy (*hæresi proximus*), inasmuch as it would indirectly imply the denial of the infallibility of the Church—a divinely revealed truth binding on our faith.

[5] Cf. Franzelin, "De Trad.," pp. 127-152; Hurter, "Theol. Gen.," vol. i. nn. 680-682; Mazzella, "De Virt. Inf.," nn. 454-456; Lehmkuhl, "Theol. Moralis," vol. i., n. 304; Bishop Hedley, *Dublin Review*, October, 1887.

INDEX.

A CATHOLIC'S reasons for believing in the dogma of infallibility, 31-32.
Alford, Dean, 143.
Allies, Mr. T. W., 111, 146, 151, 256.
Ambrose, St., 104, 149, 150.
An *ex-cathedra* utterance, what it means, 16, 28, 29, 30; it alone is infallible, 16; conditions necessary to, 16, 21; conditions explained, 17-21; what precisely in an *ex-cathedra* utterance is infallible, 21-22.
Arguments for infallibility. (1), the importance of salvation, 33-34; (2), the Goodness and Love of God, 34-35; (3), the Wisdom of God, 35-39; (4), the Justice of God, 39-40; (5), the characteristics of saving faith, 41-50; (6), the rights of reason and conscience, 50-57; (7), a contrast: with and without infallibility, 62-77; (8), scriptural evidence, 88-97, 136-140.
Arnold, Matthew, 64, 78.
Assent of faith, the essential qualities of, 41, 51, 284; different kinds of assent, 283.
Assistance of infallibility, the nature and extent of, 5, 6, 7, 8.
Aubrey DeVere, 256.
Augsburg Gazette, 281.
Augustine, St., 129, 150, 153, 263.

B ASIL, St., 149.
Bellarmine, Cardinal, 29, 248.
Benedict XIV., 27.
Bengel, 148, 149.
Beza, 48, 82.
Bible, The, not a sufficient or a safe rule of faith, 57-61, 141.
Bloomfield, 143, 147.
Bossuet, 10, 60, 82, 113, 114, 123, 128, 133, 229.
Britannica, Encyclopedia, 250, 270, 276.
Brownson, Dr., 78, 81, 159-162, 166, 174, 182, 192, 193, 199, 200, 201, 203, 204, 205, 207, 247, 254, 255, 256, 257.

C ATHOLIC faith, what is necessary to a dogma of, 10, 218, 243; growth of Catholic dogma, 219-221; Catholic and Divine faith, how they differ, 217, 218; definitions of faith, when formulated, 215-216; Catholic faith not tyrannical, 175-177; Catholic faith most reasonable, 177, 178.
Calvin, 48.
Challenge to the Scientist, 193-194.
Challenge to the Historian, 226.
Chillingworth, 204.
Christianity, what it means in present discussion, viii.
Chrysostom, St., 104, 126, 130, 149, 152.
Church, scriptural evidence of

286 INDEX.

its divine institution, 84–88, 141; is infallible, 88–97; not a spiritual despotism, 155–162, 203; submission to, not intellectual bondage, 175–176; submits her claims to the judgment of reason, 144, 165–168; what she denies to reason, 167–169; the Church and the Supreme Court of the U. S., a comparison, 245.
Churchman, The, 83.
Cohen, Herman, 252.
Collette, Mr. C. H., 248.
Commentary, The Speaker's, 143.
Conclusion, an appeal to the Reader, 238.
Confession, 253.
Conscience and infallibility rule in different spheres, 19; direct conflict between them impossible, ibid.
Converts to Rome, list of, 181, 206; testimonies of, 174, 175, 181, 182, 192, 193, 205, 206, 251–263.
Conybeare, Mr. W. J., 73.
Cyclopedia of Biblical, Theological and Ecclesiastical Literature, 245, 270, 272.
Cyprian, St., 94, 149.
Cyril of Alexandria, St., 104.

DAILY News, The (London), 264.
Decrees, Pontifical, three kinds of, 282; the obedience due to, ibid.
Decrees of the Roman congregations, 23, 236, 250.
Denzinger's Enchiridion, 27, 204.
De Sales, St. Francis, 72, 82, 103, 104, 107, 108, 118, 133, 144, 146, 151.
De Wette, 68, 75.
Dictionary of Christian Biography, 248.
Divine and Catholic faith, difference between, 217–218.

Doane, Monsignor, 252.
Dogmatic Facts, 29.
Döllinger, Dr., 105, 138, 148, 245, 281.
Draper, Dr., 1, 2, 3, 25, 207, 247, 265, 278, 279.
Dublin Review, 248, 274, 284.
Dupanloup, Bishop, 277.

EDINBURGH Review, 74, 75.
Encyclopedia Britannica, 250, 270, 276.
Emerson, R. W., 73.

FACTS, dogmatic, 29.
Faith defined, 41, 50, 51; what is essential to, 41, 51, 284; sole motive of, 51, 177–178; different meanings of; 78; definitions of faith, when formulated, 215–216; Divine and Catholic faith, how they differ, 217–218; explicit and implicit faith, 214, 221, 244, 246; what is necessary to a dogma of Catholic faith, 10, 218, 243; growth of Catholic dogma, 219–221; faith is most reasonable, 165–167, 177–178; the demands it makes on reason, 52, 173; what it denies to reason, 167–169; Catholic faith not tyrannical, 175–177; faith helps to strengthen, develop, elevate and ennoble reason, 197–201; Catholic faith bestows peace of mind and conscience, 66–67, 251–263.
Fausset, Rev. A. R., 154.
Felix, Father, 244–245.
Fessler, Bishop, 8, 24, 28, 29, 30.
Finlay, Rev. Thomas A., 176–177, 185–189.
Foster, Bishop (M. E.), 206.
Fouard, Abbé, 149.
Franzelin, Cardinal, 21, 25, 26,

INDEX.

28, 29, 80, 204, 206, 207, 244, 246.
Fritzsche, 148.

GALILEO, the case of, 235.
Geffken, Prof., 1.
Gerard's *Institutes of Biblical Criticism,* 147.
German Bishops, Pastoral of, 224.
Gfrörer, 62, 63.
Gladstone, Mr., 2, 25, 29, 208, 209, 210, 246, 257.
Göther, Father, 25.
Gratry, Pére, 30.
Gregory the Great, St., 130, 150.
Gregory XI., 27.
Grotius, 80, 147, 151.
Guizot, 63.

HALLAM, 25, 144.
Happiness of Converts, 251-263.
Harpe, M. De la, 181.
Hecker, Father, 204, 205, 206, 253.
Helvetic Confessions, 80.
Hergenröther, Cardinal, 5, 6, 11, 18, 19, 20, 22, 25, 28, 139, 148, 220, 233, 234, 246, 250.
Hettinger, Dr., 15, 25, 27, 146, 206, 245, 247.
Historian, The, a challenge to, 226.
Hodge, Dr., 80.
Honorius, celebrated case of, 227, 229-235.
Hurter, Father, 26, 27, 28, 29, 80, 146, 204, 207, 244, 246.

INFALLIBILITY; the great importance of the question, v., vi., vii., 62-77; non-Catholic views of, 1, 2, 3, 25; true meaning of the word, 3; true meaning of the dogma, 4; origin and cause of infallibility, 4, 5, 25, 26; assistance of, 5, 6, 7, 8; not impeccability, 3, 5, 221-223; not inspiration, 5; how infallibility and inspiration differ, 5, 6, 7, 8; infallibility does not imply the gift of miracles, 8; the purpose of infallibility, 9; what it does *not* enable the Pope or the Church to do, 9, 10, 11; not a personal but an official prerogative, 11, 138; how far the jurisdiction of infallibility extends, 14, 15, 29; an *ex-cathedra* utterance alone is infallible, 16; the conditions essential to the exercise of infallibility, 16-21; infallibility and conscience, 19; decrees of Roman congregations as such not infallible, 23; how they may become so, *ibid;* the one act which can be made an objection to infallibility, *ibid;* infallibility is limited, 23-24; the Catholic's reasons for believing in infallibility, 31-32; the Church is infallible, 88-97; the Pope is infallible, 136-140; infallibility not a despotism, 155-162; infallibility and liberty of thought, 183-189; infallibility and free inquiry, 190; infallibility and intellectual development, 190-192; infallibility and science, 193-197, 206-207; infallibility a great help to the scientist, 196, 207; infallibility gives and guarantees intellectual liberty, 201-202; infallibility and conduct, 208; infallibility cannot be abused, 210-213; the dogma of infallibility not an addition to the faith, 213-219; wickedness of Popes no objection to infallibility, 3, 5, 221-223; ignorance or unwisdom of Popes no objection to infallibility, 5, 223-225; infallibility and the contradictions of Popes, 226; infalli-

bility and the heterodoxy of Popes, 12, 27, 226; the opposition in the Vatican Council was not to the doctrine, but to the opportuneness of defining it, 277–278.
Innocent III, 19.
Inspiration, what is necessary to, 5, 6; how it differs from infallibility, 6, 7, 8.
Institutes of Biblical Criticism, 147.
Intellectual liberty, in what it consists, 201; infallibility gives and guarantees it, 201–202.
Irenaeus, St., 142.
Irish Ecclesiastical Record, 81, 248.

JANUS, 2, 25.
Jerome, St., 130, 150, 153.

KEGAN, Paul, 81.
Kenrick, Archbishop F. P., 107, 132, 152.
Kent Stone, Mr. James, 102, 153.
King, Mr. Owen C. H., 248–249.
Kingsley, Mr. Charles, 2.
Knox, Father, 6, 17, 27, 245.

LANG, Mr. Samuel, 74.
Larremore, Mr. Wilbur, 73.
Lathrop, Mr. George Parsons, 181.
Lee, Dr. F. G., 249.
Leibnitz, 134–135,
Leo, the Great, St., 103, 121, 150.
Leo II., 232.
Leo XIII., 82, 196, 207.
Liberius, Pope, Case of, 227.
Liberty of Thought, what it means, 185; when allowable, 186–187; when not, 187–189; not a thing to boast of, 186–187; differs from intellectual liberty, 201–202.

MACAULAY, Lord, 65, 70.
Macmillan's Magazine, 2.
Mallock, Mr. W. H., 25, 66, 68, 72, 75, 76, 81, 82, 207, 215, 247, 248.
Manning, Cardinal, 6, 11, 17, 20, 25, 70, 78, 140, 143, 206, 216, 218, 234, 244, 245, 257, 258, 272, 275, 277, 278, 280, 281.
Marheineke, Symbolik, 65.
Marsh, Bishop, 147.
Marshall's *Christian Missions*, 79, 82.
Mazzella, Cardinal, 21, 26, 28, 29, 80, 146, 147, 204, 207, 244, 246.
McCarthy, Very Rev. Daniel, 107, 147.
Melancthon, 48.
Meyer, 147, 148.
Milman, Dean, 145.
Missions, Catholic, 66, 82; Protestant, 47, 66, 79, 80, 82.
Money, Canon, 73.
Month, The (London), 232, 273.

NEANDER, 145.
Nevin, Dr., 144.
Newman, Cardinal, 5, 7, 10, 15, 19, 20, 22, 28, 29, 42, 61, 66, 83, 204, 206, 216, 229, 231, 239, 240, 241, 242, 243, 244, 246, 247, 257, 258, 259, 260, 261, 262.
Norfolk, the Duke of, 83.

OBEDIENCE, The, due to the different kinds of Pontifical decrees, 282.
Objections to Catholic faith; it is tyrannical, 175; it is unreasonable, 175, 177–178; the Catholic has no voice in formulating his faith, 178, 179, 180; he is not free in his faith, 183; his faith is dependent on the will of the Pope, 221.

Objections to the Church; she is the enemy of reason, 162, 163, 165, 167, 170; her claims are irreconciliable with the rights of reason, 172; she dreads reason, 181, 182.

Objections to Infallibility; the dogma makes the Pope a despot, and the Church a despotism, 155–162; it extinguishes Liberty of Thought, 183, 189, 190; it bans free inquiry, 190; it is an obstacle to intellectual development, and tends to weaken, cripple, dwarf, and enslave the mind, 190, 191; it conflicts with Science, and is an impediment to its pursuit, 193, 195–197; it claims to itself the entire domain of conduct, 208; it gives the Pope supreme and absolute power over the faith of Catholics, 209; the Pope can use it as his caprice dictates in making dogmas of faith, 210, 247; the doctrine of infallibility is a new doctrine, 213; an addition to *the faith once delivered unto the Saints*, ibid; Popes are subject to sin, therefore cannot be infallible, 221–223, 247; Popes have been ignorant and unwise, therefore not infallible, 223–226, 247; Popes have contradicted Popes, a fact fatal to infallibility, 226; Popes have fallen into heresy, therefore not infallible, 226, 227; cases in point, 227; infallibility conflicted with Science in the case of Galileo, 235; infallibility, anyhow, no value to the believer, 237.

Objections to Papal Supremacy, 121–132.

PASTORAL of German Bishops, 224; of Swiss Bishops, 23–24, 25–26.

Perrone, Father, 5, 26, 27, 80, 204, 206, 207, 244, 246.

Pius IX., 11, 199, 203, 204, 206.

Pontifical Decrees, different kinds of, 282; the obedience due to, *ibid.*

Pope the, two characters of, 11, 12, 26; different offices which belong to him, 12; may be heterodox in his personal views, 12, 27, 231; infallible only as Supreme Teacher, 13, 27; his acts in any other capacity can be no objection to his infallibility, 13, 27; different classes of matters which fall under his jurisdiction, 73; the matters in which *alone* he is infallible, 14, 29; how far his infallible authority extends, 14, 15; his utterances on matters of faith and morals not always infallible, 15, 16, 23; Scriptural proof of the Pope's Supremacy, 97–120; Protestant testimony to, 132–135; testimony of the Fathers, 149–150; Scriptural objections to, 121–132; Scriptural proof of the Pope's infallibility, 136–140.

Proctor, Mr. R. A., 1, 225, 236, 247.

Puffendorf, 48.

Pusey, Dr., 1.

QUOD *ubique, quod semper, quod ab omnibus*, the meaning of, 219.

READER, an appeal to the, 238.

Reason, faith must respect its rights, 52, 53, 80, 170; Catholic faith acknowledges, respects and upholds them,

163-169, 170-171, 203-204; what these rights are, 163, 164, 172-173; the Church not the enemy of reason, 163-165; she submits her claims to reason and challenges its approval, 164, 165-168; what she denies to reason, 167-169; reason has only a negative authority in reference to dogmas of faith, 204-205; reason and faith cannot be in conflict, 194, 207.
Record, Irish Ecclesiastical, 81, 248.
Renan, M. Ernest, 145, 146.
Register, The Christian, 205.
Review, Dublin, 248, 274, 284; *Edinburgh*, 74, 75; *North British*, 66; *Quarterly The*, 78; *Union*, 217.
Rivington, Father Luke, 71.
Rossenmüller, 102, 147.
Ryder, Father, 229, 234, 247.
Ryle, Bishop (Episcopal), 70, 73.

SALMON, Dr., 25.
Schulte, Prof., 1, 2, 27, 28, 30.
Scientist, The, a challenge to, 193-199.
Seton, Mrs. Elizabeth Bayley, 251.
Smith, Dr., 27, 30.
Smith & Wace. *Dictionary of Christian Biography*, 248.
Standard, The (London), 264.
Sun, The (New York), 64, 65, 81, 83, 142.
Supremacy, Papal, proof of, 97-120, 132-135; Protestant testimony to, 144-146; testimony of the Fathers, 149-150; objections to, 121-132.
Supreme Court, The, of the U. S., and the Church, a comparison, 245.
Swiss Bishops, Pastoral of, 23-24, 25-26.

TAYLOR, Canon, 82.
Tertullian, 129.
The Daily News (London), 264.
The Churchman, 83.
The Faith of Catholics, 26, 218, 244.
The Month, (London), 232, 273.
The Standard, (London), 264.
The Sun, (New York), 64, 65, 81, 83, 142.
The Times, (London), 81, 265.
The True Faith of our Forefathers, 127, 146, 151, 154.
Thompson, Rev. I. S., 147.

ULLATHORNE, Archbishop, 27, 29, 209, 243.

VATICAN Council, the decrees of, quoted, 10, 16, 198, 206, 221; newspaper correspondence relating to, 264-265; short account of the steps taken for its convocation, 265-267; number of Fathers present, 268; officials, their number and nationalities, *ibid;* Commission on Postulates, number of members composing it and their nationalities, 268-269; Committee on Faith, election of, number of members and the nations represented, 269-270; Committees on Discipline and on Religious Orders, 270; *Schemata* to be discussed, how prepared, 270; rules governing the discussion of, 271-272; manner of voting, 271; the question of infallibility not included in the *Schemata* presented to the Council, 272-273; what led to its introduction, 273-274; time given to the debate on infallibility, and the number of speeches made, 274-275; voting on, 275-276; fifty-seven Fathers sign a protest and leave before final vote, 276; after definition all send in their adhesion to, 277; opposition not to the doctrine, but to the opportuneness of defining it, 277-278; strength of opposition, 274, 276; consistency of opposition in accepting the definition defended, 279-280; evil prophecies, 280-281.

Vaughan, Father, 101, 105.
Vicious Circle, The, 142.
Vizetelly, Mr., 74.

WETTE, de, 68, 75.
Whitby, 147.
Wiseman, Cardinal, 81, 106, 125, 142, 143, 148.

CHRISTIANITY
AND
INFALLIBILITY—
BOTH OR NEITHER.

By The Rev. DANIEL LYONS.

ONE VOLUME, 12MO.

COMMENTS.

"I think when the candid reader will have finished your book, he wi.l be compelled to admit the truth of your thesis: *that Christianity demands an authoritative, a living and infallible interpreter.*"
                                    CARDINAL GIBBONS.

"You certainly have taken up the question which must form the *key-stone* of the arch of religious truth. The world is to-day full of minds anxiously groping for religious certitude. You have shown them *where* and *how alone* it can be found. Your work evidences on every page extensive and careful study, *and I really do not know any popular manual in which this all-important subject is better handled.*"
   BISHOP KEANE, Rector of the Catholic University,
                                    Washington, D. C.

"Your book pleases me very much. The idea you have in view is eminently a practical one; and its development is clear, full, and replete with erudition. *It cannot fail to find acceptance and to do much good.*"
          A. SABETTI, S. J., Professor of Theology,
                                    Woodstock College, Md.

The Dublin Review.

"Cardinal Newman before entering the Church had come to the decision that there was no logical resting-place for a consistent mind between Atheism and Catholicity. Father Lyons has undertaken to establish in a popular treatise a similar conclusion, namely, given a supernatural revelation, *then a consistent believer is compelled either to accept with that revelation the Catholic Church as its infallible witness, guardian, and interpreter, or,* as St. Francis of Sales has said, *to commit himself without needle, compass, or rudder to the ocean of human opinions, where a miserable shipwreck awaits him.* The author has aimed at proving his point by explaining and defending the Catholic doctrine of Infallibility. *He has done his task well.* In clear and forcible language he has given a concise and logical summary of what Catholic theology has to say on this dogma, illustrating and supporting his explanations and arguments by an abundance of apt quotations from leading modern writers.

The work is divided into three parts. In the first, the writer explodes the inaccurate or grotesque notions of Infallibility current among non-Catholics by giving a clear and accurate explanation of what Catholics mean by the term. In the second part he develops the arguments for Infallibility, first, those for the *antecedent* necessity for an infallible authority, based upon our knowledge of the Goodness, Wisdom, and Justice of God, on the needs of the soul, and the requirements of Faith, Reason, and Conscience; and, secondly, those for the *de facto* existence of such an authority in the Catholic Church under its head, the Bishop of Rome. The third part, in which the chief objections against Infallibility are answered, is made to embrace *an excellent explanation of the relations of faith and reason.* Having drawn so sharply the limits of the object of Infallibility, it was almost necessary that a word should be added as to the obligation Catholics are under of obeying even the fallible decrees of an infallible authority. Accordingly we have in an appendix an accurate digest of the soundest theologians on this point. *The book is one that can be cordially recommended* to both clergy and laity for their own use, or for that of non-Catholic enquirers."

The Catholic Review, New York.

"The purpose of this work appears in the title. It is to prove that to attain certitude in a supernatural revelation of religious truths, a living, infallible witness, custodian and interpreter is an indispensable necessity. Therefore, all orthodox Christians must accept such an authority, if they wish to be logical and consistent. *Father Lyons seems to us abundantly to establish this thesis, which most assuredly contains the vital question of this and every age.* The book consists of 5 chapters and 3 appendices. Chap. I. explains in a clear, exhaustive manner the meaning of the dogma of Infallibility, and dissipates the erroneous views on the subject entertained and expressed by such men as Mr. Gladstone, Dr. Pusey, Dr. Littledale, Dr. Draper, the Provost of Trinity College, Dublin, Janus, and others. Mostly in the words of eminent theologians, like Newman, Manning, Franzelin, Mazzella Perrone, Hergenrother, Hettinger, and Hurter, the author's meaning of infallibility is given. He then states—*and with wonderful precision*—when the Pope is infallible, in what capacity, in what matters, and under what conditions. *A more satisfactory statement of the dogma it would be hard to find in the English language.* Chap. II., answering the question: "Why do Catholics believe in the dogma of Infallibility?" proves first the necessity of Infallibility. The arguments are drawn from the importance of salvation, the wisdom, justice, goodness of God, the characteristics of saving faith, the rights of reason and conscience. This part of the work may please most readers, although generally the fourth and fifth chapters, dealing as they do with objections, brings out the author's strongest points.

After considering the claims of the Bible, the author closes this admirable chapter with a striking contrast, which is somewhat in the nature of a summary, entitled "With and Without Infallibility." Chapter III. contains the Scriptural proof of the fact of Infallibility, and an examination of the Scriptural objections to Papal pretentions. Chapter IV. is taken up chiefly with the Rationalists' objections to the Church, Infallibility and Catholic faith. Infallibility makes the Church a despotism, it enslaves reason, bans free inquiry, proscribes free thought, stands in the way of intellectual development, opposes the progress of science, and is in conflict with its facts. These are some of the objections treated, all stated *with candor and fairness*, and discussed at length. Chapter V. considers the abuse of Infallibility and its dangers to civil, social and other rights. The author throws down the gage here, and issues a bold challenge: Point, he says, to a single demonstrated fact or truth of science which conflicts with the teaching of Infallibility and Catholics will give up the claim to it. To the historian he says:

In the history of 1800 years, and of more than 250 Popes, produce a single instance where an *ex-cathedra* utterance contradicted another, or where a Pope in an *ex-cathedra* utterance set forth heretical, or condemned true doctrine, and the whole edifice of Infallibility comes toppling to the ground. Then he discusses the cases of Liberius, Honorius and Galileo. *These chapters are magnificent.* The appendices contain much very interesting matter touching the Vatican Council, and the testimonies of eminent converts to the Catholic faith, and the peace of soul it brings. *It is not too much to say of this book that the English language contains no better one of its class on the subject.*"

The American Catholic Quarterly Review.

"The subject of this work forms one of—indeed, it is not too much to say that it forms—*the* crucial question of our age, and not only of our age, but of all ages. . . . . *We regard the volume as a very valuable addition to our Catholic literature. It ought to be in the possession of every intelligent Catholic layman.*"

The Monist, Chicago.

"Dr. Lyons' arguments are *well put and well reasoned out.* He sees clearly where the vulnerable point of the present condition of the Christian Churches lies—which the majority of Protestant theologians do not see."

The Month, London.

"Though much has been written on the subject of Infallibility, we are glad to *welcome* Father Lyons' new contribution to the subject. *It is a clear and able exposition of the dogma, and deserves to be widely known and recommended.* The chapters on the nature and necessity of Infallibility are especially good."

Catholic World.

"Father Lyons has written *one of the clearest and best expositions of the Catholic teaching on this subject that has yet appeared in English.* His method is excellent. In the first place he explains carefully what is meant by Infallibility, and patiently corrects the misconceptions which non-Catholics have concerning it. Then he proceeds to show why Catholics believe in the doctrine, *and he does this more fundamentally than most other writers.* 'How do Catholics meet the objection against Infallibility?' Here he sets forth the plain and candid answers which Catholics have for those who urge and make the most of the difficulties. These objections *are stated as fairly as* their authors could present them, and are satisfactorily met and refuted in every case."

The American Ecclesiastical Review.

"The author's method is thoroughly popular, and whilst he has admirably succeeded in avoiding that didactic and argumentative style which is apt to repel the ordinary reader of our day, he nevertheless leaves the distinct impression that his reasoning *is based on sound logic and strengthened by such authorities as would command the attention of every theological student.* . . . . The work is full of erudition, as is shown by the numerous notes, indicating a wide range of pertinent and careful reading. . . . . *The book is a solid and timely contribution to the theological literature of the day.*"

The Review of Reviews.

"An ably-written volume in defence of the dogma of Papal Infallibility."

The Tablet, London.

"This is a well-written defence of the Vatican dogma from the pen of a Catholic priest in the United States, and should be welcomed in England, where both the Catholic layman and the outside inquirer will find it useful as giving a clear explanation of what is contained and implied in the claim of Papal Infallibility. . . . . What, then, does Papal Infallibility mean? To have a clear and sufficiently full answer to this query, *written with theological exactness,* but without the technicalities of a science book, is, it will readily be admitted, a valuable addition to our Catholic literature. *And this is what we have in the volume* 'CHRISTIANITY AND INFALLIBILITY.' The chapters given to answering the objections, whether of Dr. Littledale or of less specious opponents, are full of interest and varied information, and the whole volume is replete with references to an amazing number of the more conspicuous modern writers, whether Catholic or Protestant."

The Ave Maria.

"*A notable and effective addition* to the religious literature of the day."

The Scotsman, Edinburgh.

"The argument is characterized by *great ability, and a strength of logic which is not to be easily resisted.* Current controversies in our own Churches show that it is being found necessary to hedge both Bible and Church standards round with what practically amounts to a claim of Infallibility on the part of the assembled clergy, and they thus give practical force to Mr. Lyons' contention on behalf of the more venerable and undisguised authority of the Catholic Church. That there is no abiding half-way house between that authority and perfectly free thought is a conclusion not to be easily avoided. . . . . We cannot enter here upon an examination of Mr. Lyons' reasoning. *It is exceedingly well done* from his point of view, and the book may be briefly characterized as *one of the best upon its own side of the question.*"

North British Daily Mail, Glasgow.

"It gives abundant evidence of wide reading, is comprehensive in the range of its argument, and shows no little acuteness and ability. *We do not know that anywhere else a better defence of this Papal dogma will be got.* Mr. Lyons starts with the consideration of the meaning of the dogma, and this is perhaps the most important chapter for Protestants in his book. He states with great clearness what the Pope's Infallibility is and what are its limitations. It is of the first moment in all controversy that the matter in dispute shall be distinctly apprehended on both sides. *And certainly the merit of distinctness here must be accorded to our author.* The line of argument followed to establish Infallibility is not new, but the old arguments are well put, and Mr. Lyons' way of putting them is worth looking at. Protestant controversialists must welcome an opponent who faces them so manfully as Mr. Lyons does."

The Catholic Times, Liverpool.

"*This is a most important work, and the most complete treatise on the subject* we have in the English language."

The Boston Pilot.

"An eloquent treatise on a subject on which the Catholic . . . . *cannot be too well informed*, for it is the one on which he is most frequently attacked."

North Western Chronicle, St. Paul.

"*No more useful* book can be put into the hands of an inquiring Protestant; and no more satisfactory treatise can a Catholic expend his time on for information on this difficult subject. The busy priest will find in it material ready to hand for many sermons. It is really a condensation of the best literature, old and new, on Infallibility, and that done up into clear English. It is remarkable for its erudition, not that dead matter collected from many sources, but learning assimilated and given out in a graceful manner. We congratulate Father Lyons on his excellent work."

Church Progress, St. Louis, Mo.

"Father Lyons' book is *one of the most valuable popular contributions to the subject of Infallibility that we have ever read.* His treatment is plain, simple and yet solid. It has the unique merit of dealing with a difficult question in a familiar and easy manner within the comprehension of the average reader. *We would like to see it in the hands of every Catholic in the country, and every Catholic who reads it should place it in the hands of his Protestant friends.*"

The Catholic Mirror.

"This book, with its striking title (is) meant *to set men thinking.*"

The National Press, Dublin.

"To the reader who has a liking for theological literature *we can heartily recommend the work;* its easy and graceful style will make him forget that he is studying a question of scientific theology; and to the student of theological science we can recommend it *as a luminous and accurate exposition* of one of the most important problems of his science."

The Appeal-Avalanche, Memphis.

"*One of the most valuable and interesting of religious textbooks.* . . . . It is a work of strong religious conviction *full of facts and logic.*"

Pueblo Chieftain.

"CHRISTIANITY AND INFALLIBILITY—BOTH OR NEITHER" is the title of *a remarkably well written* theological treatise. It is an explanation and discussion of the Catholic doctrine of Infallibility which cannot fail to *interest* and *instruct* the student of religious literature. Father Lyons, in an able manner, explains the dogma from a Catholic point of view, and after a careful perusal of his book that article of the Catholic faith, hitherto such a bugbear to non-Catholics, *is completely robbed of its supposed objectionable features.* THE CHIEFTAIN *cordially* recommends the work to all students of theology of every shade of religious doctrine."

The Catholic Herald, New York.

"The author's logic is excellent, and his fairness cannot be questioned. There is not a trace of special pleading; but the argument, all through, is manly, considerate and dispassionate."

Catholic Journal of the New South.

"This work does for one point of Catholic doctrine, *and that, after all, the most important one,* what Cardinal Gibbons' "FAITH OF OUR FATHERS" does for the whole range of Catholic dogma. . . . . There can be but little doubt that "CHRISTIANITY AND INFALLIBILITY" will soon take rank with the "FAITH OF OUR FATHERS" in securing converts to the Church, as well as in popular favor."

Georgetown College Journal.

"One who has since been received into the fold, speaking of Father Lyons' book, said to the writer of this notice: 'His arguments for Infallibility have a convergence and congruity that is simply irresistible. Admitting that there is a God, a divine providence, and you know that I admit that, how *reasonable* is Infallibility.' There was struck the key note of this little book. The dogma of Infallibility is a reasonable dogma, and Father Lyons has shown it to be such.

Small in volume, the work is exceedingly comprehensive in grasp. In the first place, what is meant by the dogma of Infallibility is explained with a lucidity that is no less admirable than is the mildness and gentleness with which he disabuses the non-Catholic of the erroneous views he has concerning it. Then, in two chapters, perhaps the best in the book, he tells why Catholics believe in the doctrine, exhibiting, as elsewhere, an erudition rarely met with. He then meets fully the objections urged against the dogma, and in the same gentle vein that runs through the book. There are three appendices, A, B and C, respectively, treating of 'The Happiness of Converts,' 'Some Facts Relating to the Vatican Council,' and 'Pontifical Decrees and the Obedience Due to Them.' These appendices are in reality short treatises giving the truth of what even some Catholics fall short of understanding.

In conclusion, it may be said that the book *well deserves* the hearty commendation and welcome it has received from our beloved Cardinal, from the Catholic press, and from the secular press. In fact, the praise has been so varied and general, that little, if anything new was left to be said by the *College Journal.*

NEW YORK AND LONDON: LONGMANS, GREEN, AND CO.

NADA THE LILY.

BY H. RIDER HAGGARD,
AUTHOR OF "SHE," "ALLAN QUATERMAIN," ETC.

**With 23 full-page Illustrations, by C. H. M. Kerr.
12mo, Cloth, Ornamental (Copyright), $1.00.**

"A thrilling book full . . . of almost incredible instances of personal daring and of wonderful revenge. . . . The many vigorous illustrations add much to the interest of a book that may safely be denominated as Mr. Haggard's most successful venture in the writing of fiction."—BOSTON BEACON.

"The story of 'Nada the Lily' is full of action and adventure; the plot is cleverly wrought and the fighting and adventure are described with spirit. Once begun it is, indeed, a story to be finished."—N. Y. TRIBUNE.

"The story is a magnificent effort of the imagination and quite the best of all that Mr. Haggard has done. There is no example of manufactured miracle in this story, for the story of the Ghost mountain, the Stone Witch, and the Wolves is nothing but the folk-lore of the African tribes, and in no respect similar to the wonders which the author introduced into the stories in which Allan Quatermain figures."—SPRINGFIELD REPUBLICAN.

"To my mind the realization of savage existence and the spirit of it have never been so honestly and accurately set forth. The Indians of Chateaubriand, and even of Cooper, are conventional compared with these blood-thirsty, loyal, and fatalistic Zulus. . . . The whole legend seems to me to be a curiously veracious reproduction of Zulu life and character."
—Mr. ANDREW LANG in the *New Review*.

"Rider Haggard's latest story . . . has a more permanent value than anything this prolific author has previously given to the public. He has preserved in this latest romance many of the curious tales, traditions, superstitions, and wonderful folk-lore of a nation now extinct, a people rapidly melting away before an advancing tide of civilization. The romance into which Mr. Haggard has woven valuable material is in his own inimitable style, and will delight those who love the weirdly improbable."—BOSTON TRAVELLER.

"No more complete picture of savage life has ever been presented to the world. . . . There are scenes in this book which seem destined to be preserved when the time itself and the people are quite forgotten. Such is the story of the Great 'Ingomboco,' when Chaka slays the false and lying wizards and witches. The discomfiture of the prophets of Baal is not more full of wonder and of terror. . . . This is, to our mind, the best book, the most sustained, the most powerful, the truest book, that Mr. Rider Haggard has yet produced."
—SATURDAY REVIEW.

SUCH IS LIFE.
A NOVEL.
BY MAY KENDALL,
AUTHOR OF "FROM A GARRET," "DREAMS TO SELL," ETC.

Cheaper Edition. Crown 8vo, $1.00.

"It is unusual. It has the constant charm of the unexpected and has in it both pathos, and humor. . . . The style is so choice, so refined, so full of all pervading beauty, that it is a special delight to fall upon such a book."—BOSTON TRAVELLER.

"A charmingly written story of a group of talented young people. . . . It is humorous and bright. . . . It is a bright, readable tale with a high moral tone, fit to have a place on any library table."—PUBLIC OPINION.

"A strong, individual piece of work like this is to be greeted with gratitude in days chiefly given over to literary inanities."—SPRINGFIELD DAILY REPUBLICAN.

"There is a charm, a freshness about this piece of fiction difficult to analyze, and at the same time to be perceived. . . . The book seems, indeed, like an abstract from life itself, so unexpected are its episodes and so reasonably unreasonable many of its conclusions. . . . A book which is to be commended for the delicacy and vigor of its art as well as for the wholesome quality of the morals it inculcates."—BOSTON BEACON.

LONGMANS, GREEN, & CO., 15 EAST 16th STREET, NEW YORK.

THE ONE GOOD GUEST.

A NOVEL.
By L. B. WALFORD,
AUTHOR OF "MR. SMITH," "THE BABY'S GRANDMOTHER," ETC., ETC.

12mo, Cloth, Ornamental, $1.00.

"It is a delightful picture of life at an English estate, which is presided over by a young 'Squire' and his young sister. Their experiences are cleverly told, and the complications which arise are amusing and interesting. There are many humorous touches, too, which add no slight strength to the story."—BOSTON TIMES.

"A charming little social comedy, permeated with a refinement of spontaneous humor and brilliant with touches of shrewd and searching satire."—BOSTON BEACON.

"The story is bright, amusing, full of interest and incident, and the characters are admirably drawn. Every reader will recognize a friend or acquaintance in some of the people here portrayed. Every one will wish he could have been a guest at Duckhill Manor, and will hope that the author has more stories to tell."—PUBLIC OPINION.

"A natural, amusing, kindly tale, told with great skill. The characters are delightfully human, the individuality well caught and preserved, the quaint humor lightens every page, and a simple delicacy and tenderness complete an excellent specimen of story telling."
—PROVIDENCE JOURNAL.

"For neat little excursions into English social life, and that of the best, commend us to the writer of 'The One Good Guest.'"—N. Y. TIMES.

"The story is bright, amusing, full of interest and incident, and the characters are admirably drawn. Every reader will recognize a friend or acquaintance in some of the people here portrayed. Every one will wish he could have been a guest at Duckhill Manor, and will hope that the author has more stories to tell."—PORTLAND OREGONIAN.

BEGGARS ALL.

A NOVEL.
By MISS L. DOUGALL.

Sixth Edition. 12mo, Cloth, Ornamental, $1.00.

"This is one of the strongest as well as most original romances of the year. . . . The plot is extraordinary. . . . The close of the story is powerful and natural. . . . A masterpiece of restrained and legitimate dramatic fiction."—LITERARY WORLD.

"To say that 'Beggars All' is a remarkable novel is to put the case mildly indeed, for it is one of the most original, discerning, and thoroughly philosophical presentations of character that has appeared in English for many a day. . . . Emphatically a novel that thoughtful people ought to read . . . the perusal of it will by many be reckoned among the intellectual experiences that are not easily forgotten."—BOSTON BEACON.

"A story of thrilling interest."—HOME JOURNAL.

"A very unusual quality of novel. It is written with ability; it tells a strong story with elaborate analysis of character and motive . . . it is of decided interest and worth reading."—COMMERCIAL ADVERTISER, N.Y.

"It is more than a story for mere summer reading, but deserves a permanent place among the best works of modern fiction. The author has struck a vein of originality purely her own. . . . It is tragic, pathetic, humorous by turns. . . . Miss Dougall has, in fact, scored a great success. Her book is artistic, realistic, intensely dramatic—in fact, one of the novels of the year."—BOSTON TRAVELLER.

"'Beggars All' is a noble work of art, but is also something more and something better. It is a book with a soul in it, and in a sense, therefore, it may be described as an inspired work. The inspiration of genius may or may not be lacking to it, but the inspiration of a pure and beautiful spirituality pervades it completely . . . the characters are truthfully and powerfully drawn, the situations finely imagined, and the story profoundly interesting."—CHICAGO TRIBUNE.

LONGMANS, GREEN, & CO., 15 EAST 16th STREET, NEW YORK.

WHEN WE WERE BOYS.
A NOVEL.
By WILLIAM O'BRIEN, M.P.
12mo, Cloth, $1.00.

"His book will be read with interest by two classes; first, by those who care only for a stirring narrative full of variety; second, by those who are interested in the long Irish struggle and desire to obtain a closer and fuller view of the theatre in which it is proceeding, and of the men and women of all classes who are actors in the drama."—N. Y. TRIBUNE.

"So good an Irish tale has not appeared before in many years."—N. Y. HERALD.

"Every character in it is so powerfully drawn and every incident so graphically described, that not only is the reader's interest not abated once he takes up the book, but grows deeper as he proceeds."—CATHOLIC STANDARD, Phila.

"The reader remains fascinated to the last page. It must be counted as one of the most distinctive and powerful of Irish stories. It will keep a place when the special temporary interest attending the circumstances of its appearance has ended, and the Irish problem of to-day has become part of the history of that unhappy country."—LITERARY WORLD, Boston.

"The book will be read by thousands, and do more than Speeches in Parliament or public meetings, or labored essays in reviews and magazines, to bring Ireland's real position home to the hearts of sympathetic men who have liberty."—CATHOLIC NEWS.

"In these pages we have the Irish question treated from within. . . . A fascinating . . . story, evidently drawn from life, and tinctured with the strong feeling of an actor in at least some of the scenes so pathetically pictured."—THE CRITIC.

"We do not overrate its political significance and influence when we predict that it will prove the greatest service the editor of *United Ireland* has thus far rendered to his struggling country.

"The book is one that will live. It is the novel of the hour, and the great political tractate of the hour as well. No man who wants to be abreast of the time can afford to overlook it. It is delightful reading, too. It abounds in dramatic incidents. It shows forth the lights and shadows of the Irish character, bringing all its contrasts of passion and tenderness, its simplicity and its guile."—THE CATHOLIC REVIEW.

HALF-HOURS WITH THE MILLIONAIRES.
Showing how much easier it is to make a million than to spend it.
EDITED BY B. B. WEST.
Crown 8vo, $1.50.

"A lively collection of humorous, good-natured satires on certain aspects of life, which, though aimed at London habits and usages, will fit anywhere. . . . The syndicate for doing good to impecunious persons is an idea. Why are there not several such combinations? . . . though satirical. It sets down nought in malice."—N. Y. ADVERTISER.

"A score of extremely droll sketches of imaginary philanthropy. . . . The book as a whole is amusing and not without some truths hidden in its agreeable persiflage. People who are not millionaires will enjoy it, but it is not certain that people who are millionaires will not enjoy it most of all—perhaps they will likewise derive a few very wholesome truths from its perusal."—BOSTON BEACON.

"A clever and amusing story, which makes no pretensions other than to be amusing. As a humorous book, 'Half Hours With the Millionaires' is a success."
—NASSAU LITERARY MAGAZINE.

"Is an interesting and amusing addition to the growing body of 'Half Hour' literature . . . these 'studies' in a line of research which few of his readers have opportunity of pursuing will be found not only entertaining but instructive."—HOME JOURNAL.

"A whimsically conceived and humorously written satire . . . on the wrong headedness of the pseudo-philanthropists, and the desperate and futile efforts that millionaires sometimes make to spend their money with happiness to themselves or profit to anyone else . . . a rather ingenious piece of work."—THE CRITIC.

LONGMANS, GREEN, & CO., 15 EAST 16th STREET, NEW YORK.

LONGMANS' SILVER LIBRARY.

A series of approved works in General Literature, well printed and uniformly bound.

Crown 8vo. Price, each volume, $1.25.

BAKER (SIR S. W.) EIGHT YEARS IN CEYLON. With 6 Illustrations.

BAKER (SIR S. W.) RIFLE AND HOUND IN CEYLON. With 6 Illustrations.

BARING-GOULD (S.) CURIOUS MYTHS OF THE MIDDLE AGES. With Illustrations.

CLODD (E.) STORY OF CREATION: A Plain Account of Evolution. With 77 Illustrations.

DOYLE (A. CONAN). MICAH CLARKE: A Tale of Monmouth's Rebellion.

GLEIG (REV. G. R.) LIFE OF THE DUKE OF WELLINGTON. With Portrait.

HOWITT (W.) VISITS TO REMARKABLE PLACES. With 80 Illustrations.

JEFFERIES (R.) FIELD AND HEDGEROW. Last Essays of. With Portrait.

JEFFERIES (R.) THE STORY OF MY HEART: My Autobiography. With Portrait.

JEFFERIES (R.) RED DEER. With 17 Illustrations by J. CHARLTON and H. TUNALY.

KNIGHT (E. F.) THE CRUISE OF THE "ALERTE:" The Narrative of a Search for Treasure on the Desert Island of Trinidad. With 2 Maps and 23 Illustrations.

LEES (J. A.) and CLUTTERBUCK (W. J.) B. C. 1887. A RAMBLE IN BRITISH COLUMBIA. With Map and 75 Illustrations.

MACAULAY'S (Lord) ESSAYS. LAYS OF ANCIENT ROME. In 1 Volume. With Portrait and Illustrations to the "Lays" by J. R. WEGUELIN.

MACLEOD (H. D.) THE ELEMENTS OF BANKING.

MARSHMAN (J. C.) MEMOIRS OF SIR HENRY HAVELOCK.

MERIVALE (DEAN). HISTORY OF THE ROMANS UNDER THE EMPIRE. 8 Volumes.

MILL (J. S.) PRINCIPLES OF POLITICAL ECONOMY.

MILL (J. S.) SYSTEM OF LOGIC.

PHILLIPPS-WOLLEY (C.) SNAP: A Legend of the Lone Mountain. With 13 Illustrations by H. G. WILLINK.

LONGMANS, GREEN, & CO.,
15 East 16th Street, New York.

LONGMANS' SILVER LIBRARY.

A series of approved works in General Literature, well printed and uniformly bound.

Crown 8vo. Price, each volume, $1.25.

NEWMAN (CARDINAL). APOLOGIA PRO VITA SUA.
NEWMAN (CARDINAL). CALLISTA : A Tale of the Third Century.
NEWMAN (CARDINAL). CRITICAL AND HISTORICAL ESSAYS. 2 Volumes.
NEWMAN (CARDINAL). DEVELOPMENT OF CHRISTIAN DOCTRINE (An Essay on the).
NEWMAN (CARDINAL). DIFFICULTIES FELT BY ANGLICANS IN CATHOLIC TEACHING CONSIDERED. 2 Volumes.
NEWMAN (CARDINAL). DISCUSSIONS AND ARGUMENTS ON VARIOUS SUBJECTS.
NEWMAN (CARDINAL). DISCOURSES ADDRESSED TO MIXED CONGREGATIONS.
NEWMAN (CARDINAL). GRAMMAR OF ASSENT.
NEWMAN (CARDINAL). HISTORICAL SKETCHES. 3 Volumes.
NEWMAN (CARDINAL). LOSS AND GAIN: The Story of a Convert.
NEWMAN (CARDINAL). PAROCHIAL AND PLAIN SERMONS. 8 Volumes.
NEWMAN (CARDINAL). SELECTION: Adapted to the Seasons of the Ecclesiastical Year, from the "Parochial and Plain Sermons."
NEWMAN (CARDINAL). SERMONS BEARING UPON SUBJECTS OF THE DAY. Edited by the Rev. W. J. COPELAND, B.D.
NEWMAN (CARDINAL). THE ARIANS OF THE FOURTH CENTURY.
NEWMAN (CARDINAL). THE IDEA OF A UNIVERSITY DEFINED AND ILLUSTRATED.
NEWMAN (CARDINAL). VERSES ON VARIOUS OCCASIONS.
NEWMAN (CARDINAL). THE PRESENT POSITION OF CATHOLICS IN ENGLAND.
NEWMAN (CARDINAL). THE VIA MEDIA OF THE ANGLICAN CHURCH. Illustrated in Lectures, etc.
NEWMAN (CARDINAL). TWO ESSAYS ON BIBLICAL AND ECCLESIASTICAL MIRACLES.
STANLEY (BISHOP). FAMILIAR HISTORY OF BIRDS. With 160 Illustrations.
WOOD (REV. J. G.) PETLAND REVISITED. With 33 Illustrations.
WOOD (REV. J. G.) STRANGE DWELLINGS. With 60 Illustrations.
WOOD (REV. J. G.) OUT OF DOORS. With 11 Illustrations.

LONGMANS, GREEN, & CO.,
15 East 16th Street, New York.

POLITICAL AMERICANISMS.

A Glossary of Terms and Phrases Current at Different Periods in American Politics. By CHARLES LEDYARD NORTON. 16mo, ornamental cloth cover, $1.00.

"It is impossible to look over the columns of a daily journal, especially during the progress of a spirited political campaign, without encountering numerous expressions and phrases, the meaning of which cannot be learned from any dictionary, but which, to one who is familiar with the current *argot* of the period, are often quite as vigorously expressive as the most picturesque slang of the streets. The vocabulary of the American politician has indeed become copious beyond what is generally believed, and the glossary presented herewith lays no claim to exhaustiveness. It includes, however, a number of phrases which can be found in no other compilation. . . ."—*Extract from Preface.*

"It will every year have additional value to the student of American political history."—PUBLIC OPINION.

"It will be found very useful in every library, and will answer many questions on the lips of men as well as boys, about the origin and significance of words that began as slang and by frequent use have been adopted into the language."—JOURNAL OF COMMERCE.

"A welcome addition to current books of reference and will certainly be esteemed highly by every student of American politics. . . Whilst Mr. Norton's compilation makes no claim to exhaustiveness, he is right in asserting that he has included a number of terms not to be found in any other volume. . . Altogether the best of its class and should achieve a decided success."
—BEACON.

"So fully does this book fill a vacant place in politico-historical literature that it is hard to understand why it has only just appeared. . . A book so complete that the reader must have a long and quick memory to discover what may be lacking. . . The volume is small, for the definitions are short; the work has been done so thoroughly in keeping with the true spirit of dictionary making that the reader will not be able to discover the author's own politics."
—N. Y. HERALD.

"Mr. Norton has done a good work in searching out and explaining a large number of expressions which, while they cannot be found in any dictionary, are a very important part of 'Newspaper English.'"—CHURCHMAN.

LONGMANS, GREEN, & CO.,
15 East Sixteenth St., New York.

WITH MY FRIENDS.
Tales Told in Partnership.
BY
BRANDER MATTHEWS.
With an Introductory Essay on the Art and Mystery of Collaboration.

12mo, cloth, colored top, $1.00.

Six tales written in partnership with H. C. Bunner, Mr. G. H. Jessop, Mr. W. H. Pollock, and Mr. "F. Anstey," with an Introductory Essay, reprinted from *Longmans' Magazine*.

"His collaborators in these clever stories . . . share with Mr. Matthews the facility, versatility and lightness of touch that enter so largely into the requirements of the short story. . . . 'The Documents in the Case,' already well known to many readers, is as good a specimen of original and witty story-telling as can be found."—CHRISTIAN UNION.

"Those who read 'With My Friends' out of mere curiosity to see 'how it is done' may fail to discover where the work fits together, but they will find the volume among the most entertaining of the many collections of short stories now presented to the public."—BOSTON TIMES.

"'With My Friends' is an aptly named series of short sketches. . . . 'The Documents in the Case,' though familiar to many readers, is so cleverly written that it will well repay a second or even a third reading."—HOME JOURNAL.

"Exhibits the art of story-making in partnership. They are very good tales."
—N. Y. FORUM.

"Perhaps the best thing in Mr. Matthews' book is his own introduction essay on 'The Art and Mystery of Collaboration.' It is both witty and instructive, and the examples of collaboration which follow are so well done that we think it would be virtually impossible to distinguish the respective work of the literary partners."
—N. Y. TRIBUNE.

"These stories all differ from one another, and Mr. Matthews is so successful in each and every one of his collaborations that it is hard to decide with which author the most pleasing result is obtained. . . . the volume is an ideal collection of its kind. It will amply repay all those who give it a careful and conscientious reading."
—BOSTON HERALD.

"All the tales have a liberal fund of humor and some of them are witty, while, of course, it is a fascinating problem to determine to which of the authors the different elements of attraction belong."—BOSTON BEACON.

"The stories of the book are meritorious in their way, but the true merit is that they are ingenious descriptions of occurrences from different standpoints of fact, of imagination, and mental quality. . . . this volume is worth reading."
—COMMERCIAL ADVERTISER.

LONGMANS, GREEN, & CO.,
15 East 16th Street, New York.

DARKNESS AND DAWN;

OR, SCENES IN THE DAYS OF NERO.

AN HISTORIC TALE.

By FREDERIC W. FARRAR, D.D.,
ARCHDEACON OF WESTMINSTER, AUTHOR OF "THE LIFE OF CHRIST," ETC., ETC.

Large Crown 8vo, 594 Pages, Cloth, Gilt Top, $2.00.

" A book which must unhesitatingly be classed as one of the most brilliant historical tales of the century. . . ."—BOSTON BEACON.

" No novel could be more fascinating, and few historical or theological works more accurate or more useful, than this ' historic tale.' Brilliant and truthful descriptions of the life in the Imperial palaces of Rome."—CHURCH TIMES.

" As a study of Ancient Roman life and character it is masterly, the events being historically authentic and the scenes startlingly real. The martyrdoms of Christians in the Amphi-theatre and the illumination of Rome by their burning are vividly portrayed, and the intention of the book commendable."—PHILADELPHIA PRESBYTERIAN.

"It is the ablest contribution to historical fiction that has been made in many years, and it deserves to rank with ' Ben Hur' as a vivid picture of the past."
—SAN FRANCISCO CHRONICLE.

" The work is done with notable breadth of stroke and uncommon vigor of coloring . . . it is all very real and engaging. . . ."—THE INDEPENDENT.

"The simple power and beauty of Christianity are rendered impressively real, and the heroism of even humble believers nerves and inspires to nobler living now. The story is sure of a wide reading and cannot but do good."—BOSTON CONGREGATIONALIST.

" This is a book of absorbing interest. It is not a novel, nor is it to be judged by such a standard. The story is based on the most reliable historic facts. The brilliant author takes his reader through the darkness of a decadent paganism into the dawn of Christianity."
—BUFFALO CHRISTIAN ADVOCATE.

" This book is in Archdeacon Farrar's best style, and the story, even in its driest historical portions, is told with that fascinating interest which his many readers are familiar with.

" We think that no one can read this historical tale without interest, and that every one who reads it will turn to the contemporary writings of the great apostle with an awakened understanding of the circumstances which called these writings forth."
—THE CHURCHMAN, N. Y.

" A picture not only of intense interest, but of the greatest historic value. . . . Its clear and vivid style, together with its delineation of character, make it a book not only of interest but importance. It is neatly bound and printed in large type."
—NASSAU LITERARY MAGAZINE.

" The work is characterized by learning, graphic skill, and a rare naturalness, and the historical elements may generally be depended upon."—N. Y. TRIBUNE.

" Written with accuracy of detail and great power of description. . . . A serious purpose inspired this book—an intention to show the secret of the triumph of Christianity."
—CHRISTIAN UNION.

" The book is quite voluminous, but apart from its literary excellence the story is one of the most thrilling interest, so that its length is a rare virtue rather than a detraction."
—N. Y. TIMES.

" A novel of considerable magnitude and decided interest . . . it has all the marks of Dr. Farrar's ripe historical culture."—THE BOOK BUYER.

" The reading of this noble volume will give any one new conceptions of life at the beginning of our era, and new reverence for religion that made its way, unaided by the sword or political influence, through the debris of a falling civilization."—PUBLIC OPINION.

"This book . . . has more than a novel's interest . . . and the treatment of all sacred subjects reverent."—N. Y. OBSERVER.

LONGMANS, GREEN, & CO., Publishers, 15 East 16th St., New York.

www.ingramcontent.com/pod-product-compliance
Lightning Source LLC
Chambersburg PA
CBHW030015240426
43672CB00007B/962